SPECIALTY SHOP RETAILING

HOW YOU CAN SUCCEED IN TODAY'S MARKET

4TH EDITION

Other books by Carol L. Schroeder:

Reflections
(poetry, under maiden name Carol Ehrlich)

A Bibliography of Danish Literature in English Translation
(published in Denmark by Det danske Selskab)

Stitches and Decorative Seams by Grete Petersen
(translator from Danish)

Embroidery Tips by Grete Petersen
(translator from Danish)

The Orange Tree Imports Cookbook
(editor)

Medical Terminology for Health Professions
(co-author with Ann Ehrlich)

Introduction to Medical Terminology
(co-author with Ann Ehrlich)

*Eat Smart in Denmark: How to Decipher the Menu,
Know the Market Foods &
Embark on a Tasting Adventure*
(co-author with Katrina A. Schroeder)

Specialty Shop Retailing: How to Run Your Own Store
(1st and Revised editions)

*Specialty Shop Retailing: Everything You Need to Know
to Run Your Own Store*
(3rd edition)

SPECIALTY SHOP RETAILING

HOW YOU CAN SUCCEED IN TODAY'S MARKET

4TH EDITION

CAROL L. SCHROEDER

HenschelHAUS Publishing
Milwaukee, Wisconsin

Published by HenschelHAUS Publishing, Inc.
www.henschelhausbooks.com

ISBN: 978159598-576-7
E-ISBN: 978159598-577-4

Publisher's Cataloging-In-Publication Data
(Prepared by The Donohue Group, Inc.)

Names: Schroeder, Carol L.
Title: Specialty shop retailing : how you can succeed in today's market / Carol L.
Schroeder.
Other Titles: How you can succeed in today's market
Description: 4th edition. | Milwaukee, Wisconsin : HenschelHAUS Publishing, [2018]
| Includes index. | Previously published: Hoboken, N.J. : John Wiley & Sons, c2007.
Identifiers: ISBN 9781595985767 | ISBN 9781595985774 (ebook)
Subjects: LCSH: Specialty stores--Management. | Retail trade--Management. | Success
in business.
Classification: LCC HF5429 .S35566 2018 (print) | LCC HF5429 (ebook) | DDC
658.8/7--dc23

Photo credits listed.

Printed in the United States of America.

In memory of my mother,
Ann Ehrlich,
whose life, work, and generous spirit
continue to inspire me

CONTENTS

PREFACE

I spent my junior year abroad studying Danish and English literature at the University of Copenhagen. During the long, dusky Danish winter days, the lights of Copenhagen's specialty shops cast an inviting glow out over the dim sidewalks. With idle hours to fill between university classes, I often succumbed to the lure of fine design and friendly European service, wandering from shop to shop along Copenhagen's winding pedestrian streets. As I browsed through displays of colorful handcrafts, candles, flowers, and furniture, I imagined someday creating a welcoming haven full of well-designed products back in America.

I never envisioned rivaling Macy's or Walmart. Their bottom-line oriented style of retailing held no appeal for me. Nor was it my dream to be at the helm of a fleet of 25 stores, with employees I'd never met and managers who reported to the home office via computer.

My vision was much simpler: to create a shop that would sell merchandise to enrich people's lives, through form, function, tradition, or amusement. I wanted to market this merchandise in an environment that would be pleasurable for customers and staff alike—a shop I would look forward to going to every morning at 10:00 a.m. (The fact that retailers don't have to report to work at 8:00 a.m. was a real plus, in my mind.) If I could create meaningful employment, give back to the community, and make a living at the same time, I would consider my shop a success.

After returning to the United States to get a master's degree in Scandinavian Studies at the University of Wisconsin, I found myself ready to think seriously about owning a store. Unfortunately, my work experience was limited to journalism and dental assisting, so I applied for a job at a Scandinavian furniture store here in Madison, Wisconsin. The store had no opening in sales, but the owner was willing to hire me to tutor her in Danish until a job came up. And the perfect one appeared just a few weeks later, managing her new campus branch store. To my surprise, I was offered the position, despite an appalling lack of experience.

We opened the campus branch of Bord & Stol (Danish for table and chair) in October of 1974. The store carried furniture, housewares, and gifts from Scandinavia. I thought our first day of business was a great success, but on the second day our first customer returned the expensive chair he bought the day before, resulting in a negative sales figure. Things could only get better!

Sales throughout the Christmas season were strong, but after the first of the year, this branch store began to compete with the main store for the limited cash available to fund its inventory. Suppliers stopped shipping to us, and it became clear that the branch would not survive for long. My husband Dean and I decided to buy the business, and on May 1, 1975, we renamed it Orange Tree Imports. My dream of owning a shop had come true.

Between the two of us, we brought to the business world undergraduate degrees in German, English, and Danish, and my MA in Scandinavian Studies. Neither of us had ever taken a business course, although at the time Dean was working for his father selling packaging machinery. He kept that job for the first year or two of Orange Tree Imports, quitting only when we knew that the store could support us both. Even before that time, he would walk over to the shop with a hot lunch of grilled cheese sandwiches and soup for us both and stay to help until he finally had to tear himself away to go back to his home office. Shopkeeping was a lot more fun than making sales calls.

Preface

Our store gradually grew from three employees to over two dozen, and tripled in size as we put on a new addition in 1980, then connected with the store next door in 1986. (We also added to our family, putting a little red crib in the upstairs office, first for Erik in 1981 and then for Katrina in 1984.) We expanded our merchandise mix from the basics of Scandinavian-influenced home accessories and kitchen supplies to include toys, jewelry, soap, stationery, seasonal decorations, candles, candy, cards, gift wrap, glassware, and garden gifts. We opened a cooking school to promote our cookware and kitchen gadgets, and not long after that accepted an award at the Plaza Hotel in New York for promoting sticker collecting. This diversity of product mix is, I think, one of the keys to our longevity.

When we started Orange Tree Imports in the mid-1970s, I was only 23 and didn't know a thing about return on investment or business ratios. But that didn't matter because profit did not interest us at all—until the year we didn't have one.

We had been lucky enough to start our store in prosperous times, and we grew steadily and had been profitable, in a modest way, almost from the start. But in the mid-1980s, things got tougher. There were too many retail stores in the Madison market, and our sales leveled off. Expenses, unfortunately, did not. Without a profit, the business could not continue to grow and eventually might cease to exist. We would no longer be able to sell wonderful products, please our customers, create a meaningful workplace for our staff, play an active part in our community, and make a living. Suddenly the bottom line became very important.

We were fortunate to have an excellent office of the Small Business Development Center (SBDC) in Madison. The people there helped us see that we really did know a lot about retailing—lessons learned through trial and error during our first years in business. They also taught us some things we didn't already know. We were able to survive the crisis and to turn Orange Tree Imports around.

SPECIALTY SHOP RETAILING

In honor of Orange Tree Imports' 20th anniversary in 1995, I decided to share some of the ideas we learned from the SBDC, from our own years of retailing, from our energetic and enthusiastic staff, and from many other shopkeepers, by writing *Specialty Shop Retailing*. It was my hope that those who were in the start-up stage would find the information in the book helpful in creating an innovative new specialty store, and that those who were already retailers would be inspired to try some fresh ideas. I've always believed that our participative democracy approach to management at Orange Tree Imports is one of the keys to our longevity, and this is one of the ideas I am most proud of being able to share with you.

The response to the first three editions of the book has been very gratifying, with letters and emails arriving from retailers all over the United States, and even Canada, Europe, and New Zealand. Several readers have made the trip to Madison to visit, including an entire busload of businesspeople from Japan (some of whom carried the book all that way to get it signed). A few years ago, *Specialty Shop Retailing* was translated into Russian, and I heard from a number of retailers thanking me for helping them take advantage of the new capitalistic opportunities. I am delighted to make a fourth edition available as both a trade paperback and e-book to reach as many retailers as possible with the latest innovations and ideas.

This edition includes many helpful forms—tools I wish I'd had available to me when I started my store—that are available to you to download for free at www.specialtyshopretailing.com. In addition, you'll find an extensive glossary of retailing terms there.

As much as I believe that there is a promising future for independent retailers who bring enthusiasm and creativity to their store, I acknowledge that we are dealing today with a "new normal" with extensive competition from both chain stores and aggressive online

Preface

retailers, especially Amazon. Sales levels for some shops may have peaked, but that doesn't mean that profits need to decline—or that we independent retailers have lost our reason to exist. I hope that this new edition will help both those setting up shop and those of us who have been in the field for some time to run a stronger, more sustainable business.

We all need to tend to our expenses diligently, and to schedule our staff carefully to try to make efficient use of our payroll dollars. We need to buy effectively, watching our inventory levels and taking early markdowns on slow-moving merchandise. My goal with the 4th edition of *Specialty Shop Retailing* is to give you the tools and encouragement you need to survive and thrive in this new retail environment.

If you find yourself in Madison, I do hope you'll visit our shop, which recently celebrated its 42nd anniversary. We still don't do everything perfectly, but we try every day to do things better than the day before. Let me know if you're coming, and I'll try to make time to share a cup of tea and talk with you about your store. If you can't come to Madison, I'd love to get an invitation to your grand opening or to hear about ideas you may have for future revisions of this book. Our address is 1721 Monroe Street, Madison, WI 53711, and you can find us online at www.OrangeTreeImports.com.

Carol "Orange" Schroeder

CHAPTER 1

THE JOY OF RETAILING: SALUTING SMALL STORE SUCCESS

Whether you are already in business and facing the challenges of maintaining and growing your market share, or just considering setting up a shop, I hope that this book will help you succeed. I love retailing: finding great new merchandise, creating effective displays, interacting with customers and employees. And I do believe that many of us will prevail as independent shopkeepers by doing what we do best—offering an extraordinary shopping experience that big box stores and the even bigger online giants can't replicate.

It's the customer's experience that makes a specialty shop unique. That sense of serendipity in discovering the perfect gift. The visual delights of a well-curated and displayed selection of merchandise. The warm feeling of being welcomed sincerely and given great service. The excitement of attending a special event, class, or demonstration. Clearly there is more to this type of shopping than just trading money for goods.

Our major competition today comes not just from our fellow retailers, be they big or small, but also from other places where consumers can spend money. Dining out, travel, outdoor adventures, exercise, pampering, arts performances and even grabbing a beer with friends all offer alternatives for the use of disposable income. We have to give customers a good reason to come into our stores, and to make them feel good about spending their hard-earned money on our merchandise.

The Importance of Independent Retailers

It is easy to see how local, independently owned businesses support the economy in ways that big box and online businesses do not. According to the Institute for Local Self-Reliance, just $14.00 of every $100.00 spent at chain stores stays in the local economy, compared to $48.00 spent at independent retailers. And despite its growth, Amazon destroys more jobs than it creates. For every $10 million in sales, Amazon employs just 19 people, compared to the 47 jobs provided by a brick-and mortar retailer.

COMMUNITY IDENTITY MATTERS

Locally-owned stores also help give a community its sense of place, differentiating your city or town from the "anywhere USA." And in addition to helping to provide our communities with a unique identity, we can create that important "third place"—defined by urban sociologist Ray Oldenburg as being somewhere between the private ("first place") environment of the home, and the public ("second place") of work. The third place is where people can interact with one another socially, and in the case of retail stores, also share an enjoyable shopping experience.

This desire for community works in favor of independent businesses. As Chris Churchill said in an article for the Albany, New York *Times Union*, "The malls and the big-box stores are in trouble, because they can't compete with the ease and convenience of online shopping and because shopping at those places isn't much fun. But the downtowns, the Main Streets, will be OK—and perhaps better than they have been since out-migration to suburbia began in the 1950s—because the successful ones are nice places to spend time. They offer community. They offer real connection and meaning."

The Joy of Retailing: Saluting Small Store Success

OUR VENDORS NEED US

Not only are locally owned businesses of importance to their communities, but independent retailers are also of growing importance to their suppliers. More and more of the big-box stores are going directly overseas for their merchandise, bypassing the sales representatives, manufacturers, and importers in the United States. While this is bad news for the suppliers, it can be good news to the retailers. We have seen minimums go down as suppliers reach out to smaller shops, and most new products are no longer offered first to the bigger stores.

Independent retailers are also much more likely to champion goods made in America, especially by local craftspeople, than any chain or Internet store. If we want to bring more jobs back to the US, it is the locally owned businesses that are most likely to offer consumers an alternative to the inexpensive imported merchandise that has flooded the American marketplace.

WE CREATE MEANINGFUL WORK

Americans spend more hours at work than in many other developed countries, often with a low level of satisfaction. Independent retail stores have the opportunity to provide jobs with a high level of social interaction in an aesthetically pleasing environment. We can allow our employees a flexible schedule that acknowledges the importance of the work-life balance. And applying the principles of management by participative democracy, discussed in Chapter 9, makes it possible for every employee to feel that his or her role in the store is valued.

Orange Tree Imports. (Photo courtesy of Peter Patau)

THE PRIDE OF OWNERSHIP

There are easier ways to make a living than being a shopkeeper, but after 42 years, I still feel proud to own Orange Tree Imports. The fact is that this business, created by combining my skills with those of my husband Dean and our talented staff, holds a unique place in the lives of our customers and our community. I love the role that we play in the success of our fellow businesses on Monroe Street, and that many visitors to Madison, Wisconsin make a point to visit our store. Every happy customer and employee interaction makes my heart sing.

The Joy of Retailing: Saluting Small Store Success

Why Customers Love "Local"

A 2015 Deloitte study published by MasterCard Advisors said that while supporting the local economy was the primary reason that shoppers supported small business, a close second was the ability "to find one-of-a-kind gifts." Rod Sides, leader of the retail and distribution practice at Deloitte, is quoted as saying, "I do think that uniqueness is what everybody's chasing. Whether it be a unique experience or whether it be a unique gift, those local boutiques kind of have that flair."

MAKE YOUR INVENTORY HELP YOU SUCCEED

Early discussions about how to survive the growth of retail competition recommended focusing on a niche not carried by big box stores. This advice still holds true, although it is harder to find goods that are not featured on at least one website. You certainly want to make sure that the majority of your merchandise is different than that being carried by other stores in your area, and to see whether there are some categories you can "own." If you have a very specialized business, such as a stamp and coin store, this won't be difficult. If you carry women's clothing, however, you will need to be more vigilant to find fashion lines and price points that are different than those already being offered—and ways to bring customers into your store instead of shopping online.

One advantage of being an independent retailer is having the ability to respond quickly to trends and to create value for your customer by always having the most current merchandise rather than rock-bottom prices. You also have the ability to surprise and delight with unexpected discoveries. Couple this with a dependable supply of your core merchandise, and you should be able to use your inventory to good competitive advantage.

GIVE GREAT CUSTOMER SERVICE

Even if you sell some of the same items as other stores in your area, you can offer what a bigger store cannot: a quality shopping experience and possibly also the prestige that can come from buying products at a store with a fine reputation, and status in the community as a locally owned business. A high level of service is key to all these factors.

It is a good idea to review your customer service standards periodically to be sure that you are making shopping a pleasant and efficient experience (time being a precious commodity to today's consumers). In addition, think of surprising ways you can delight your customers, such as the services listed in Chapter 8. You might also show your appreciation in unexpected ways:

- A coupon or gift card for a future visit
- Refreshments
- A birthday gift
- An anniversary card
- A thank-you chocolate in their package
- A follow-up phone call

Be sure that your staff knows how important customer service is to your store's success. Praise and reward service out of the ordinary, and provide tools and policies that encourage them to take the initiative to excel.

GO "OMNI-CHANNEL" —IF YOU WANT

An obvious option for expanding your retail market is to have a physical (brick-and-mortar) store and also to sell online, cleverly referred to as being "bricks and clicks." Some of us don't want to offer more than one "channel"—having an actual shop is the fulfilment of our dreams. But if you want to offer consumers as many ways of shopping with you as possible, by all means set up your business as an "omni-channel" or "multi-channel" retail operation. Chapter 13 covers some ideas for online sales, and there are many resources available that offer help in setting up a successful Internet business.

The Challenges We Face

When Walmart started to expand into small-town America, the repercussions for local retail were drastic. Big-box stores drained sales away from smaller shops in nearby communities, and many that were already in a fragile state did not survive. But this onslaught was minor in comparison to the threat posed today by online shopping—especially Amazon, with offerings that encompass almost every conceivable product and Amazon Prime's free and sometimes unbelievably speedy delivery. According to an article from *Slice Intelligence*, Amazon now accounts for 43% of all the revenue generated in the US online market, although it should be noted that some of those sales are from smaller retailers who sell through Amazon.

A particular worry for shopkeepers is the fact that some consumers are using their stores as a showroom, talking to the sales staff to get information, and then taking a photo of an item so they can order it online at a lower price. While it is a mistake to think that every shopper using her phone to take a photo in the store is "showrooming," it does happen.

A shift in spending habits that is of great concern to all retailers is the fact that instead of buying goods, consumers are spending money on dining out, and at "poured beverage" establishments, such as coffee shops and brew pubs. In fact, Americans now spend more money in restaurants and bars than in grocery stores. This means that many retail storefronts are being converted to eating and drinking establishments, which does not create a healthy tenant mix for downtowns, especially when it comes to daytime foot traffic. Some communities, including ours, are putting limits on new restaurant growth and are encouraging retailers by offering matching grants for "white box" improvements to their facades, interior walls and lighting. We are fortunate that a number of cities and towns recognize the need to invest in the type of community they want to be.

How to Survive—and Thrive

If your business is in a neighborhood that no longer has a viable mix of retail shops, or if your sales are declining precipitously due to online competition, you may find that you need to be open to change to go forward. That said, I do believe that while it is hard to predict what the future holds in terms of threats to independent retailers, there will always be opportunities for savvy shopkeepers when we play to our strengths. In fact, US News reported that a recent Pew Research Center survey showed that 65% of online shoppers indicated that they prefer buying from physical outlets if given the choice.

The closing of department and chain stores presents new opportunities for independent stores to attract their former customers looking for an in-person shopping experience. And one can hope that real estate options created by these vacancies may help stop rents from spiraling upwards once developers realize that national companies are no longer the most likely tenants.

The current emphasis on spending money on experiences is another source of potential market share. Many specialty shops are able to offer services beyond their displays of merchandise, and all can benefit from the fact that when tourism increases, so do tourist dollars.

There are countless ideas throughout this book to help you make the best of today's retail scene, either as an experienced shopkeeper or someone new to the field. Because what we do as independent shop owners means a great deal to the consumer and the community, and is worth fighting for!

CHAPTER 2

NEW TO RETAIL:
GETTING OFF TO A GREAT START

D espite my belief that retailing is one of the most exciting and creative fields of small business today, when budding entrepreneurs approach me for advice about starting a store, the first thing I do is try to talk them out of it. There are, of course, many good reasons *not* to open a store: the risk of losing everything you own; the fact that big-box stores and discounters often dominate the marketplace; competition from Amazon and other online retailers; the high percentage of new store failures. If no amount of arguing can deter a potential new retailer, I know that he or she has the determination and enthusiasm necessary to beat the odds and run a successful business.

We all start with a dream. Yours may be that you want to share merchandise you love with customers or that you've always wanted to be your own boss. Perhaps you've talked to friends about building a business together, or you've seen a wonderful storefront that inspires your creativity.

Turning your dream into reality starts with a marketing study and business plan to find out if your idea is economically feasible. Once you've opened the doors to your store, the challenge is to keep your vision alive while coping with the day-to-day duties of running a business. The better your preparation is before opening, the less likely you are to let your dream be overwhelmed by the challenges you face once your store is launched.

Finding Customers: Market Research

Retail chains spend thousands of research dollars before deciding on a new store location, yet many novice retailers determine the location and merchandise mix of their first store without paying much attention to whether there is an adequate demand for what they will be offering in the area the store will be serving.

Market research may sound complicated and expensive, but it is something you can do on your own simply by asking as many people as possible whether they think there is a ready market for your type of merchandise, at the prices you would need to charge. If the answer is yes, the next question to ask potential customers is where they think they would go to shop for this merchandise. Their answers will help you determine your best location.

If you haven't already decided what you'd like to sell but have a location or even a building in mind for a store, you will need to develop some ideas of what direction to take by finding out what shopping needs are currently going unmet in the area. Consider also what kind of merchandise will bring customers back often, because you'll be more successful if you're selling something that needs to be replenished regularly, such as foods, soap, candles and other consumables.

Start your market research informally, with family and friends. Tell everyone you know about your idea or your location and solicit their suggestions. Listen to what they say, and use this information to refine your concept before expanding the research to include your target customers. You might even start a Facebook page or Instagram feed with your idea to get feedback and start building some excitement on social media.

Two women once came to see me about an idea they'd had for an innovative way of marketing jewelry to rural Wisconsin women. When I asked if they had actually spoken to any rural Wisconsin women to see if they were interested in a new source for jewelry, one of the potential entrepreneurs exclaimed, "Wow, this is reality!" Reality is a good place to begin when you are considering investing your time and money in a new retail venture.

TALKING TO A FOCUS GROUP

Focus groups can be very helpful in determining the direction your business should take. Invite a group of 10 or 12 people with a potential interest in what you'll be selling to come together in a quiet setting and respond to a few simple questions. For example, for a yarn store, you might ask the following questions:

- Where do you currently buy yarn and other knitting supplies?
- Are there any types of yarn you can't find in this area?
- What price range do you look for in yarn?
- Where would you like to go to shop for knitting supplies?
- What special services would you expect a knitting store to offer?
- Do you think knitting is increasing or decreasing in popularity?

You might want to record the discussion so that you can review every detail later. Be sure to reward those who participate in your focus groups with a small gift. If you decide to go ahead with your business plan, send focus group members a special grand opening invitation and a gift card.

After your store has been open for some time, a focus group of customers can help you determine how well you are meeting your shoppers' needs. We have occasionally used a voluntary customer council, made up of a dozen or so of our best customers, to help us refine our customer services and merchandise selection.

SPECIALTY SHOP RETAILING

CHECKING OUT THE COMPETITION

Competition isn't always a reason to avoid going into business in a certain area; after all, McDonald's and Subway frequently build restaurants very near each other, though only after determining that there is enough business for them both. Customers like having choices, and certainly having several antique stores in one area will draw more customers than one antique store will, provided there is a large enough market in antiques to support them all.

How do you determine market size? Demographics, which are statistics relating to the population of an area, can be very useful. The larger the population or number of visitors, the more shops the area can support. The higher the per capita income, the higher the price of merchandise the shoppers can afford. Check to find out whether the area's population is growing or declining.

Sources for demographic information include the local chamber of commerce, the website of the US Census Bureau, and the site of the marketing research firm Claritas, which provides household income statistics by zip code at www.Claritas.com, under MyBestSegments ZIP Code Look-up. Real estate development companies usually have information about the customer base for the areas in which their properties are located, as do potential landlords.

In addition to studying the statistics, look at the existing shops. What type of merchandise do they sell? Are they prospering? Talk to the shopkeepers. Explain that you are thinking of opening a store in the area, and hopefully you'll get an honest answer when you ask, "How's business?"

Market size also determines how narrow your niche—that is, the shop's focus—can be. In a popular tourist area, such as Faneuil Hall Marketplace in Boston, shops can succeed featuring nothing but boxers, or brain teasers, or Boston team logos. With thousands of potential customers walking by each day, there is a good chance that an adequate number will be interested in a certain category of merchandise. In a small town, the only viable retailer may be the general store, with as broad a mix of merchandise as you can imagine.

Don't make the mistake of opening a highly specialized store in a small market. If only 5% of the population is interested in your merchandise, a town of 10,000 will yield a maximum of only 500 potential customers, fewer than two a day. Niche retailing is a viable way to compete with discount stores in prosperous areas with a large resident or tourist population, but diversity works best in more limited markets.

THE CONCEPT STORE OPTION

You may decide that opening a store focused on a traditional line of merchandise, such as yarn and knitting supplies, is not going to attract enough customers. A newer approach, and one that usually attracts a younger demographic, is the *concept store*.

Revival is a concept store in Rapid City, South Dakota, that describes itself as "an expert in lifestyle and home design, emulating the beauty of life in the Black Hills." (Photo courtesy of Debra Fletcher)

SPECIALTY SHOP RETAILING

Concept stores often include experiences in addition to shopping, with food, beverages, crafting, special events, and other attractions that help build community. They offer a changing selection of goods that evoke a certain lifestyle or aesthetic, carefully selected—"curated" is the buzzword often used—from across a range of brands, designers, and merchandise types. For example, a shop might offer some housewares along with clothing and beauty items that all fit with a rustic chic theme. Browsing in a concept store is entertaining because the product mix is unexpected, yet somehow fits together, thanks to the shopkeeper's vision and focus.

TARGETING WALMART AND OTHER DISCOUNT COMPETITORS

Give careful thought to opening a store that will attempt to compete head-to-head with a retail giant (often called a big-box store in reference to its exciting architecture). Some of these stores are category killers—Toys "R" Us, for example, is often considered to own the toy market in a community. If you want to compete with these big guys, you will need to do everything you can to make shopping in your store just as convenient for your potential customers—and more exciting and enjoyable.

In an area with a large customer base, you might succeed by focusing on a specific market segment not well served by these other stores. For example, you could stock exotic woods and special hand tools for the avid woodworker not available at the big-box building supply store down the street. Offer a wide selection of products in such categories, add classes and other services, and ensure your employees are extremely knowledgeable about your merchandise.

To offer services and merchandise that the big guys don't, you'll need to shop them constantly and be aware of what they are doing. Plan to cultivate a loyal customer base by stressing excellence in every aspect of your store's operation, and maintaining personal contact through social media.

New to Retail: Getting Off to a Great Start

Generalized big-box discounters and shops like Dollar General leave many gaps in their merchandise mix that a good specialty shop retailer can take advantage of. Shoppers often prefer the careful merchandise selection and personalized service of a smaller store, as long as the location and store hours are convenient. Try to find out what the shoppers in your area are looking for. Your chances of retail success are much greater if you provide something your customer base needs or wants and can't easily get anywhere else.

Ready for Retailing?

Once you have determined that you have a viable idea for a shop, it's time to determine whether you have the skills and capital necessary to take the plunge. Many potential shopkeepers have never worked in a store and have no idea how to set up a bookkeeping system or even calculate retail prices.

If at all possible, work in a small, established shop before you invest everything you own in your retail dream, but don't work for a competitor if you plan to open a store in the same area. Look for a part-time or seasonal job at a specialty shop while you continue to work at your current job. If you can't do that, you might offer to work in a store for free for a month or two so that you can learn as much as possible. Studies show, not surprisingly, that starting a business in a field you are familiar with dramatically increases your chances of success. Experience in a big corporate setting, or other past employment, may not be applicable to the challenges you'll face running a retail store.

> When Diane Witherall decided to open Cabin Crafts, she persuaded an art gallery owner to let her work for free in the evenings and on weekends to supplement her Yale MBA with practical retail experience.

SPECIALTY SHOP RETAILING

You don't need an MBA to be a shopkeeper, but a few courses in small business management will make it easier for you to get your store off to a successful start. These are often available through technical colleges or programs such as the Small Business Development Center (SBDC). Trade associations like the American Booksellers Association offer special seminars for potential new store owners, and trade shows often feature seminars on useful topics. You may be able to audit a college-level course, although most college retailing courses seem to focus on chain stores and fashion merchandising.

Use the months before you start your store to visit similar stores in other parts of the country. Subscribe to the trade magazines for the type of shop you'd like to open, and visit wholesale trade shows to get an idea of what merchandise is available to you and the overall range of whole-sale prices you can expect to pay. Talk to the sales representatives at the shows for information about market trends and other retailing advice. Check your local library or a bookstore for books on the various aspects of running a small business. The Specialty Shop Retailing Resource Guide on our website lists many excellent sources of information.

THE PERSONAL SIDE

Do you have the personality to run a retail store? The life of an entrepreneur is a busy one, dealing with daily challenges and long-term ups and downs. A high level of energy and optimism is required. Most shopkeepers hire employees, so you need to be ready to be an inspirational and even-handed boss. There will be the need to be fiscally responsible for your store, not only for your own sake, but also for the suppliers and staff who will be depending on you. Retailing also demands a high level of friendly personal engagement with customers. As the Chinese proverb states, "A man without a smiling face must not open a shop."

One way to find out whether you will enjoy the lifestyle of an entrepreneur is to chat casually with a number of store owners to find

New to Retail: Getting Off to a Great Start

out what their day-to-day work is like. This should give you a realistic image of what your life might be like as a retailer. You certainly won't be able to glean this information from the images of relaxed shopkeepers in movies or popular fiction.

The next question to ask is, "Am I emotionally and financially ready to open my own business?" Take an honest look at your life circumstances, and evaluate whether now is the right time for you to risk this new venture. Chances are good that you will put in long hours the first few years, and you may not have much take-home income. It's not uncommon for the owners of a new store to work 12-hour days, six or seven days a week, especially when the shop is young. There seems to be an endless amount of work to be done, and it takes some time to get staff trained well enough to delegate significant responsibilities. But if you are comfortable with the idea of putting in long hours, there is a special satisfaction that comes from working really hard for yourself rather than for someone else.

I recall a single mother with two preschool children who came to see me a few years ago about starting a store. She had a lucrative job that she hated, and she wanted to own a store similar to ours. She anticipated that she would be able to make as much from retailing as she currently earned at her state job and was disappointed to learn that such earnings would be highly unlikely for at least four or five years. I also pointed out that because her children were quite young, it would be hard for her to put in the evening hours that a new store often requires. The dream of having her own shop was reluctantly put on hold.

The support of family members is vital during the early years of a small business. There is a high degree of financial risk involved in starting your own store, and it is unfair to automatically expect that a spouse will want to share that risk. Talk over the pros and cons, and be realistic about the amount of time and money you plan to commit to the project. It will be a lot more fun to be in business if your spouse, siblings, or parents are supportive.

Don't risk more than you can afford to lose. This is a very important caveat. For some people, the idea of gambling most of their life savings or taking out a second mortgage on their home is not that threatening, but for others it is unbearable. It is not fair to burden your family by using up your retirement funds or by borrowing from your children's education funds.

We were in our early twenties when we launched our store, so we weren't afraid of having to start over again if the shop failed. Once we had taken on the responsibilities of having a family, we would have had to think carefully before pledging our home and savings to open a store. As with any other gamble, you should be comfortable with the idea that you may lose what you invest. If you are married and using joint funds, be sure your spouse also understands the risks.

One way to minimize the risks in the early days of a retail venture is to work a part-time job while you open the store, or have your spouse keep his or her full-time job. It can be very reassuring to have a steady income and benefits, such as health insurance, from some other source during the shop's risky start-up period.

BUSINESS PARTNERS

Should you go into business by yourself? A bad partner is worse than no partner at all, but a good partner can bring a wealth of additional experience and skills, as well as more capital, to the business. A partnership of two or more allows each owner some freedom from the day-to-day commitment of running the store. It can be a joy to have someone to share the ups and downs of a successful business.

A partnership is a lot like a marriage, however. You don't really know how compatible you will be with a partner until you have been in the relationship for some time, and unfortunately, a high percentage of partnerships don't last. A good *Partnership Agreement* or *LLC Operating Agreement*, like a prenup, can help smooth the way for a successful relationship. This form, which spells out details on expectations and authority, is discussed later in this chapter.

The division of ownership in a partnership may play an important role in solving disputes while running the business, and especially if the business is ever dissolved. More ownership, or stock, means more power, so a division of at least 49/51 gives one party slightly less say, however the minority owner should be aware of the potential "minority discount" for absence of control (i.e., 49% may not be worth 49%). My husband, Dean, and I are incorporated as 50/50 owners of our shop, and we alternate being president one year and vice president the next. Lawyers and accountants aren't fond of this arrangement because it means the business would be deadlocked if we ever had a major disagreement. Although it would have been impossible for us to set up our corporation any other way, we do understand the advantage to having one partner or stockholder have the majority vote.

WORKING WITH YOUR SPOUSE

Should you go into business with your husband or wife? The Mom-and-Pop shop is such a tradition in America that the term is actually found in most dictionaries. But not every couple can handle the stress of day-to-day contact in a small shop without its taking a toll on the marriage. Try to look realistically at your relationship, your communication style, and your individual strengths and weaknesses before deciding if you would make good business partners. If your spouse drives you crazy by leaving books and papers all over the house, you can imagine how you'll feel about him or her leaving catalogs and files all around the office. Starting a business together is not a good way to save a shaky marriage.

It took us some time to adjust to working with each other once Dean joined me in business about a year after Orange Tree Imports started. At first, I was so anxious to prove I knew how to do everything that I second -guessed all his decisions. We soon learned that for us, the secret to working together is to have separate areas of responsibility and to trust one another to make most decisions within those areas on our own.

At Orange Tree Imports, almost everything is divided into his and hers—even the office files. Dean is in charge of merchandise relating to food, cooking, and serving. He also handles insurance, advertising, and maintenance. My merchandise is broadly described as everything else, including seasonal goods, cards, stationery, soaps, candles, toys, jewelry, and general gifts. In addition, I'm responsible for personnel, community relations, and finances. Of course, we collaborate on all major decisions, and we don't always agree. We try to work out our disagreements in private, however, and present a united front to our staff and customers.

There is a temptation to take your work home when you work with your spouse, which means you may not get any break from the worries of the business. We established a rule that we wouldn't talk about personnel problems after 10:00 p.m. because we both found that topic stressful.

We have also found it helpful to take off one day a week alone, plus Sunday and Monday as our weekend together. This means that one of us is at the store all but those two days, yet we each work only four days a week—a very humane schedule, especially for families with children.

When our son and daughter were babies, we set up a little red crib in the office and brought them to work. We could do buying and perform other managerial functions with a baby on board, and our customers loved seeing the children in the store. But bringing a baby to work is a compromise. You can't devote your full attention to two things at once, and Erik and Katrina never napped for long. As soon as they started crawling, we found a home daycare in the neighborhood for the three days a week when we both were at work.

One of the advantages of working with your spouse is the time you get to spend with each other, working toward a common goal. There are long hours to be put in when a store is new, but we didn't mind because we were doing it together. We especially enjoyed going back to the store in the evening and working in the quiet, closed shop until the deep voice of the jazz announcer on Milwaukee's WFMR announced that it was midnight, time for us to go home.

Franchise Opportunities

There is a higher success rate for businesses that are part of a franchise operation than for independents. When you buy into a franchise such as Learning Express Toys or Wild Birds Unlimited, you gain the right to open a store with that name and concept. Franchise rights usually grant you exclusivity within a certain geographic area. You pay an initial fee for the franchise privilege and an annual fee or a percentage of sales, or both, for as long as you own the business.

Franchisers offer a wide arrangement of proprietary support, such as store design systems, standardized fixtures, advertising programs, personnel procedures, signage, in-store packaging, staff uniforms, and specially selected merchandise. Many franchisers supply merchandise manufactured exclusively for them; others provide buying guidelines so that the franchisee can buy from a variety of suppliers, sometimes at special pricing.

One reason for the high success rate for franchise operations is that a franchise store is a market-tested, proven retail concept. You are buying the experience and success of the franchiser instead of starting from scratch. Another reason, one less frequently mentioned, is that buying a franchise requires a large amount of capital—for example, an average of $126,000 to $199,000 for a Wild Birds Unlimited franchise, according to *Entrepreneur* magazine. Few retailers starting a store on their own invest or borrow that much capital. If they did, their chances of success would be closer to those of a franchise store, provided they also had some business experience and savvy.

Some entrepreneurs are attracted to retailing because they love the idea of owning a store—but they don't have a passion for any particular type of merchandise. If this is true of you, it is worth looking into a franchise. You don't need to have extensive prior knowledge about the products you will be selling, and the market studies and initial merchandising decisions will already be in place.

The field of fast-food restaurants is dominated by franchise operations, but this is not true of specialty shop retailing. Only two of the top 40 *Entrepreneur* magazine franchises for 2017 are not service and restaurant businesses: Ace Hardware and 7-Eleven.

Name recognition, one of the primary reasons for purchasing a franchise, is not as important in specialty shop retailing as it is in the food industry, and many retail stores don't offer a concept unusual enough to make the franchise rights salable. Independent shops wishing to expand frequently do so by opening company-owned branch stores rather than by selling franchise rights.

Listings of the specialty shop stores available by franchise can be found in business magazines, including the annual Franchise 500 in *Entrepreneur,* and also at special events, called franchise fairs, aimed at potential new owners. For more information about a franchise store you have visited, ask the owner to put you in touch with the home office.

> It doesn't hurt to thoroughly research franchises, even if you have no intention of opening one. My initial estimates and figures came from studying what a franchised similar business required. Hallmark posted lots of figures online for everyone to see! All the information is there and based on a great deal of experience.
> —Lisa Gustafson,
> Periwinkle, Glendora, CA

If you decide to buy into a franchise, do your homework and read all the fine print before signing the contract. Research the viability of the store's concept for your area. Determine exactly what the franchise fee will cover and what other expenses are not included, and make sure to understand the financial strength and viability of the franchisor. Ask how much freedom you will have to make your own decisions and select your own merchandise.

Consider whether you'll be happy paying the franchise fee every year for the life of the business. Talk to other franchise holders to see if they feel this is a worthwhile expense and whether they are pleased with the level of support and communication they receive from the home office. Ask whether their franchise is profitable. Ideally you will find an experienced franchise operation with strong name recognition, a unique marketing concept, and enthusiastic franchisees in other geographic areas. Be sure to have your banker and a lawyer experienced in franchise work scrutinize all contracts and agreements before you sign.

Buying an Existing Business

Many of the difficulties of a new store start-up can be avoided by purchasing an existing shop. The store's owners may be ready to retire, or perhaps their interests have changed. It never hurts to ask if a favorite store's owners would be interested in entertaining a purchase offer.

You may find a business that includes seller financing, with the current owner continuing in the business for a transitional period of time. This can be particularly effective if you don't have direct and related experience. Keep in mind, however, that establishing and agreeing on an asking price can be a long, drawn-out process. You might want to consult a business broker who, much like a real estate agent, can tell you which businesses are already for sale and their listed selling prices.

What do you get when you buy a business? Few retail stores own their locations, so real estate is not usually included in the deal. You therefore need to be certain the landlord will allow you to assume the seller's lease or negotiate a new one with you if you wish to stay in the same location.

As with a franchise, you pay a price for the name and the reputation of the business. This part of the package is a nebulous item called *goodwill*. More concretely, you usually buy the merchandise in stock, devaluing any goods that are older or shopworn; supplies on hand; and the furniture and fixtures that are part of the store's operation.

Do a credit check on the business (your bank can help arrange for this) to see if there are any liens against it and whether bills have been paid in a timely manner. Find out if there are outstanding debts or receivables that you will assume with the ownership of the store.

You'll also want to know whether key employees are interested in staying. If at all possible, speak directly to the staff members, because the current owner may not know their plans. Experienced personnel can make for a smooth transition.

The following factors will help you determine whether it is wiser to start on your own or to buy an existing business:

- Is the existing business profitable? Ask to see at least three to five years of financial statements and tax records to determine whether the store is doing well.

- If the business is not profitable, do you have the expertise, capital, and experience to turn it around?

- Why does the owner want to sell?

- Is the business in a location you would like for your store?

- Does the business have a good reputation? (If not, it may help to change the name or announce that it is under new management after the purchase.)

- Does the current owner have a positive relationship with major suppliers? Orders from a business that has had financial problems may not be welcome, even with new owners at the helm.

- Is the merchandise in the store top-quality, salable goods?

- Are the fixtures and other supplies worth the asking price?

New to Retail: Getting Off to a Great Start

As with buying a home, the purchase of a business involves some negotiation. You may make an offer that does not include some items you don't want, such as older fixtures. The seller may counter with an offer increasing the amount being asked for the **covenant not to compete**, a promise that for a certain number of years, the seller will not open a competing store in the same area.

The valuing of an existing business is a complex and sometimes unscientific computation, taking into account the reputation of the business, the age of various segments of the inventory, the desirability of the store's location, and of course, how eager the buyer and the seller are to have the transaction take place. You will need the advice of your lawyer, banker, and perhaps also a business broker who specializes in this type of transaction.

We have purchased two existing businesses. Over forty years ago, we bought the six-month-old campus branch of Bord & Stol, a Scandinavian furniture store I had managed in the six months it had been open, and thirty years ago, we expanded by purchasing Cabrini Gifts, the store next door to ours. In both cases, we wanted the locations more than the names (which we did not keep) or the merchandise selection (which we modified to suit our needs). We paid for goodwill and a covenant not to compete, although neither business was profitable at the time of purchase. It could be argued that we paid more than we should have, but we were eager to purchase these businesses and think that the extra expenditure turned out to be worthwhile.

Starting Small —or Staying Small

Opening a traditional retail store isn't always the best way to test the market for your store concept. Consider getting some feedback from the buying public by first leasing a freestanding kiosk or pushcart at a mall or tourist destination. These small retail ventures, also called RMUs (retail merchandising units), often receive special support and encouragement from mall management because they add color and variety to the shopping center, and sometimes they grow up to be full-size, permanent tenants. Many of these kiosks are seasonal or temporary, a type of retailing that may end up being a better option for you than full-time store ownership. If you like this idea, check out the magazine and website *Specialty Retail Report*, which includes sources for turnkey packages for those who want to start a kiosk or cart business with merchandise provided by a single vendor.

You may want to start your adventure in retailing on the Internet, testing the market for your products nationally. It is not difficult to start a small storefront on Amazon, Etsy, or eBay (see Chapter 13), although driving traffic to a new site can be a challenge. If you are successful online, you can base your inventory on the best sellers from your website

Bull Market is an innovative pushcart program located in Faneuil Hall Marketplace in Boston. Started over 30 years ago, it offers local artisans, designers, retailers, and entrepreneurs a chance to test new products, concepts, and trends. (Photo courtesy of Faneuil Hall Marketplace)

and continue to do business online after you open your store. And using both platforms offers you two different potential sources of income.

Another way to test your retail idea is by renting a table at a weekend flea market. Or if you plan to sell crafts that you make, start by selling at an art or maker fair. See if there is a indoor crafters showcase or art gallery near you that provides a year-round setting for craft sales. Some of these ventures are cooperatives in which you share the commitment of staffing the store with others, and some are retail stores in which your products are sold on consignment, or for a fee. You may find that you prefer concentrating on your art and letting others do the selling, or decide to develop a wholesale business instead of getting into retail.

In addition to discovering whether there is a market in your area for the type of merchandise you plan to sell, a small venture will allow you to decide whether you like retailing. The experience of owning your own shop is, of course, quite different from having a booth at a weekend craft fair, but both experiences do involve selling and dealing with the public. It's important that you enjoy both these activities if you are to last long as a shopkeeper.

Writing a Successful Business Plan

A business plan is a good way to give shape to your dream of opening your own store or to map out your plan to invest in a franchise or purchase an existing store. The purpose of writing a business plan is to create the successful business you envision. It's also an important tool in arranging necessary financing. Your plan should include the following:

- ◆ Your business goal: a brief description of the shop as you see it, plus any plans for supplemental omnichannel income (for example online or wholesale sales)

- ◆ Your qualifications for running this business

- ◆ Your plans to promote the store

- ◆ The target customers for your shop, supported by market research
- ◆ A proposed budget and cash flow plan
- ◆ Financing needs and potential sources of funds
- ◆ Long-range goals (five to ten years)

Be sure to start with a description of your vision: what the store will look like, what type of merchandise it will feature, what customers you hope it will appeal to. When you describe how you plan to market your business, describe the ways in which your store will differ from the competition. If you already have a location, include details of your lease or purchase arrangement and perhaps photographs or sketches showing the store's exterior and interior. Give information about your background and experience, as well as the qualifications of any other owners or managers involved in the operation.

Once you have done the market study for your business plan, you can map out a budget, which is crucial for securing financing and for your own awareness of the many different expenses involved in running a store. The problem with the early stages of budget planning is that you must use imaginary sales figures. You can research industry standards at the library or on the Internet to help estimate expenditures, such as rent, utilities, payroll, and advertising, but until you've been open a few months, you won't really know what your income will be. Balancing the budget hinges on this key fact.

Do your best to be realistic in your income and expense figures. You can then use your business plan budget as a starting point, but don't believe the figures until you've actually been in business for some time. And in projecting your sales, keep in mind that most specialty stores don't have an even distribution of sales throughout the year. Our shop, for example, brings in 40% of its annual income in November and December.

New to Retail: Getting Off to a Great Start

In creating a budget for your new business, or analyzing the results of an existing store, you may find it helpful to refer to benchmark, or average, statistics for a specific type of store. The Risk Management Association (RMA) compiles composite numbers based on hundreds of reporting stores within each retail segment. Although they charge for their reports, your bank may be able to get them for you at a reduced cost. The Retail Owners Institute offers *Retail Benchmark Trend Charts* showing the median value of stores in various sectors as reported by the Risk Management Association's Annual Statement Studies.

These studies will help you get an idea of the median inventory turns, which are discussed in Chapter 5, gross profit, return on investment, and other statistics. As with all averages, you may find your results vary widely from those reported to the RMA. However, it is sometimes helpful to have some data to go by when making your case to lenders.

The goal in writing a business plan budget is to show how your business will be profitable. But you might consider adding a worst-case budget showing you have thought about what you would do if sales don't live up to your hopeful projections. This type of planning shows bankers and other potential investors that you have a realistic grasp of the challenges you face.

Experienced business banker Barbara Conley agrees. "Project what would happen to your business's earnings, cash flow, and working capital needs if your worst-case scenario for sales becomes a reality. Rarely have I seen start-up forecasts for years 1 and 2 come in as projected. It may be helpful to work backwards, starting with the cash you have available to fund losses and then identifying the level of sales, expenses, and gross margin required to reach breakeven from a cash perspective. In other words, how much can your business lose in its first two years before you deplete your cash reserves?"

The business plan should show how you intend to finance the business, including the amount you hope to borrow, how and when you will repay any loans, and what you plan to use as loan collateral. Be sure to include regular payments of the interest on all business loans in your budget.

When describing the long-range plan for your business, discuss whether your goal is to have one store or to eventually have branches or franchise your concept. Maxine Clark, founder of the successful Build-A-Bear Workshop stores, knew all along that she wanted to build a major brand that would be publicly traded, and her planning and financing from the very start reflected this goal.

There are numerous books available describing how to write a business plan; several are listed in the Resource Guide. Another option is to use a computer program, such as *LivePlan*, *BizPlan Builder*, or *Business Plan Pro*, which will save you from having to make manual calculations. You could also set up your budget using an Excel spreadsheet and do the text part of the plan in Word.

Selecting a Legal Format

The format of a business is its legal structure. Your store can be set up as a sole proprietorship, partnership, corporation, cooperative, or limited liability company (LLC). There are advantages and disadvantages to each format, primarily having to do with tax cost and personal liability. Look into which one is best for you at this stage of your business development, and remember that you can always change the format later. We began as a sole proprietorship and incorporated a few years later when our growth, and profits, made that move advantageous from a tax planning standpoint.

THE SOLE PROPRIETORSHIP

Most small businesses start as sole proprietorships, and in fact, no formal action is required to form a sole proprietorship. If you are the only owner (or in some states, a married couple), this status automatically comes from your business activities. You will pay taxes on your business income as if it were a personal salary, assuming full liability for anything that goes wrong. As a sole proprietor, you must pay self-employment tax for Social Security and Medicare coverage.

There is little paperwork involved in setting up a sole proprietorship, except obtaining the necessary selling permits and other licenses, and notifying city, county, or state authorities of your intention to "do business as" (DBA) an assumed name. A sole proprietorship can be changed into a corporation as the business and its profits grow.

BECOMING A CORPORATION

Corporations have two major advantages: a lower tax rate on profits above a certain level and the limitation of liability. In many cases, the limited fiscal and legal liability is considered the more important benefit because it prevents creditors from going after your personal assets if the business fails or if you are sued. Many business loans, however, require borrowers to pledge personal assets such as homes, cars, and savings as collateral, in which case incorporating will not protect these assets if the lender forecloses on the loan.

Another advantage of incorporating is that it allows you to apply to have a fiscal year that is not the same as the calendar year. The fiscal year is the accounting period used for reporting taxable income to the government. An actual count of everything in the store, called a physical inventory, must be taken at the end of the fiscal year. This is because the IRS requires a business to state its inventory value on its annual tax return.

Corporations are separate legal entities, owned by one or more shareholders. States require corporations to file an application giving a business name, usually ending in company or incorporated, and stating how many shares have been issued. You may need the assistance of a lawyer to incorporate, unless you feel confident filing the paperwork yourself using a kit of forms available from an office supply store or a book on self-incorporating, such as Judith McQuown's *Inc. Yourself*.

Plan to set up and maintain a separate checking account and financial records for your corporation. Some states also require corporations to hold annual meetings of a board of directors elected by the shareholders and to keep records of these meetings, along with a set of bylaws, in a corporate record book.

There are several types of corporations, and your accountant or attorney can advise you as to whether you should file as a regular C corporation, which means both your salary and the profit of the corporation are subject to taxation, or a special subchapter S corporation, which allows you to claim the income of the corporation on your personal tax return.

The S corporation may work well if you have other income and plan to use a loss from your business occasionally to offset other taxes due, but if your store does very well, your tax bill may be higher than it would have been with a C corporation.

The limited liability company (LLC) is another type of corporation that is now predominant for small businesses in many states. An LLC functions much like an S corporation, but it does not have the same restrictions on the number and types of shareholders.

Corporations can be used as a way of generating cash for a new business. Those investing funds or expertise in your store can be rewarded with interest on their loan or by dividend-paying stock. The amount of the dividend, determined each year by a board of directors elected by the shareholders, is based on the company's profits. Your corporation can issue stock even though it is a privately held (or closed) corporation. The shares are not offered to the public on the stock exchange but can be sold to family or other investors. You can also be your corporation's only stockholder if you like. That certainly makes it easy to arrange for a meeting of the board.

New to Retail: Getting Off to a Great Start

SETTING UP A PARTNERSHIP

If you have one or more partners in your business, you can set up a corporation with each of you as a shareholder, or you can use a partnership agreement. A partnership is like a sole proprietorship in that the income of the company is taxed to the partners as if it were personal income, and the partners are all personally liable for any debts incurred by the business. It is assumed unless otherwise stated that the partners share the profits, assets, and liabilities equally.

Note: An unincorporated business jointly owned by a married couple is generally classified as a partnership for federal tax purposes. However, a business whose only members are a married couple filing a joint return can elect to be treated as a "qualified joint venture" instead of a partnership.

Although not required by law, a carefully thought-out partnership contract, called the *Articles of Partnership*, can ease many misunderstandings that may occur at a later date. This will spell out details on expectations and authority, and in some cases, buy/sell provisions. These provisions are a legally binding buyout agreement between co-owners of a business that governs the situation if a co-owner dies or is otherwise forced to leave the business, or chooses to leave the business. If buy/sell provisions aren't in the LLC Operating Agreement, Partnership Agreement, or Corporate Bylaws, a separate buy/sell agreement is advisable.

The partnership agreement should include provisions for one partner leaving the business by choice or due to death, illness, or bankruptcy without the store having to be sold to buy out that partner's portion of the business. A clear understanding of how many hours each partner will work, how much compensation each person will receive, and how much money each partner will invest can also help avoid later problems. Consult an attorney experienced in the area of partnerships for assistance in drawing up Articles of Partnership early in the planning stages of your business.

A limited partnership is an investment vehicle rather than a true partnership. It allows one (or more) partners to be liable only for debts equal to the amount of equity the individual has invested. In a limited partnership, there must also be at least one party whose liability is not restricted in this manner. Limited (or silent) partners are basically investors. They don't participate in the management of the business.

ANOTHER ALTERNATIVE: COOPERATIVES

Although cooperatives are not common in the field of specialty shop retailing, they are a viable business structure for certain types of stores. There are hundreds of independent local cooperative grocery stores, owned and controlled by the customers who use them, rather than by outside investors, private owners, or partners.

Members buy stock in the cooperative, which is a corporation structured with limited liability, somewhat like an LLC. Members democratically elect a board of directors, which hires staff and makes management decisions. "Cooperatives are not in business to give a return on investment to shareholders, but instead serve their owners," explains Anne Reynolds, Executive Director of the University of Wisconsin Center for Cooperatives.

The cooperative structure is a good alternative for groups of artists or craftspeople wishing to set up a shop to market their wares. In many cases, the members contribute a set number of work hours in addition to making a financial investment. There may be some paid staff or a paid manager, but often all the work is done by co-op members in exchange for having a viable way to sell their arts or crafts.

There's also increasing interest in converting small businesses from private ownership to employee-owned cooperatives. With careful financial and strategic planning, workers can buy out an owner and preserve the viability of a locally-owned business.

Regulations governing the establishment of cooperatives vary by state and are usually part of the state's corporate code. For more information on setting up a cooperative, check out the University of Wisconsin Center for Cooperatives' website: www.uwcc.wisc.edu.

Financing Your Business

A trade magazine editor once told me that when potential retailers called to ask her thoughts about opening a store with a small amount of capital, she advised them to use the money to go on a luxury cruise instead. They'd have more fun, she said, and it would save themselves the pain of going out of business.

There is no amount of money that is a magical formula for retail success—many stores have started with plenty and still failed—but the fact remains that a well-financed business has a much better chance of surviving the difficult first years.

How much money do you need to start a store? The budget you drew up for your business plan will give you some idea how much inventory you would like to start with and what the operating expenses may be during the first year. In addition, you'll need to pay for signage, lighting, supplies, down-payments on utilities and your lease, computer and office equipment, furniture, and display fixtures before you open. Renovations to your new space may be costly, especially if you are paying rent for several months while the work takes place. You should have some money to put aside for unexpected emergencies, such as repairs to equipment. And if you have quit your other job to pursue this dream, you will need money to live on. The worst-case forecast you did in your business plan will show you some of your potential cash flow needs. One rule of thumb is to start with the cash you think you'll need, and then double it.

SPECIALTY SHOP RETAILING

Where is all this money to come from? Hopefully you've been saving for this moment and have some funds built up in cash, securities, a retirement fund, or equity in real estate you own. You might also be able to borrow against a life insurance policy. The more funds you can bring to the table, the better—because it's a cold, hard fact that borrowing money without having money is difficult. Lenders want some collateral—an asset of yours that goes to the lender if you default on your loan—as well as proof of your commitment to the project and your financial reliability. Most lenders require you to provide something other than the store's inventory as collateral in case the business fails. Let's face it: a bank wouldn't know what to do with $20,000 worth of women's shoes.

When we first looked into financing our business, we were advised to use part of our savings as collateral rather than putting it all into the store. This proved to be excellent advice because we were able to pledge

The biggest surprise for me in opening my store was how much money I laid out before I even opened the doors for business. Permits, signage, insurance, fixtures, inventory, advertising, POS system and equipment, phone, cable, WiFi, and 2 months' rent while I got everything up and ready.

In fact, my very first sale was to the building inspector—we weren't open for business yet, but I was unpacking some matching mother/daughter aprons when he came in to do our inspection. He said it was his daughter's birthday and she would love one of the aprons, so he bought one for his daughter and one for her mother, too!
—Stephany East, The Squirrels Nest, Frederick, Maryland

it temporarily as collateral and know it would eventually be available to us as cash funds. When we needed money to expand our business later, we had funds waiting for us so that we didn't have to try to turn $5,000 worth of toys and gifts into cash in a hurry.

BORROWING FROM A BANK

Banks are a traditional source of small business loans, and for years, the Small Business Administration (SBA) has encouraged banks to make loans to entrepreneurs by assuming some of the risk. You apply for an SBA-guaranteed loan through your local bank, allowing you to develop a personal relationship with a banker who may serve as one of your store's advisers.

For a new business, the SBA generally requires that a minimum of 33% of the start-up funds come from the applicant. You must also show that you have the knowledge and experience needed to operate a successful business. For an SBA loan information kit, visit their website, www.sba.gov, or call your local SBA office or the SBA Small Business Answer Desk.

The government sponsors a number of loan programs targeted at encouraging new businesses owned by women and minorities. Other special loans may be available if your store will aid in the economic revitalization of a depressed area or the renovation of a run-down building in an old neighborhood. Most of these programs do still require you to provide some collateral. Check with your community's economic development office or the SBA for details.

Even if you don't turn to a bank for an initial loan, you will need a bank to handle your deposits and other transactions. Working closely with the bank will help if you need to turn to it for financing in the future as your business grows. Many stores use short-term loans for specific financing needs. For example, for many years we maintained a line of credit loan that we draw on each year to build up our inventory for the holiday season, paying it off on Christmas Eve. The line of credit arrangement, which is approved for a fixed amount and must be repaid within a short time, saved us from having to apply for a new loan each year. It also meant that we were using a short-term loan to finance short-term, variable needs, such as buying additional merchandise for the holiday season. Longer-term loans are used to finance capital improvements, daily basic inventory, and other needs.

PRIVATE MONEY FOR YOUR SHOP

What about private sources of capital? Many businesses begin with loans from friends and relatives, funds sometimes referred to as "love money." If you do borrow money from individuals, make sure they are aware of the risk they are taking. Set up any loans in a professional manner as promissory notes with a fixed interest rate and repayment schedule.

Like any other loan, a privately held note should be secured by some collateral, such as real estate. The Internal Revenue Service may consider a private loan to be a gift if it is not properly documented. A relative or friend with good credit standing can also help you get started by cosigning your bank loan, which means that person agrees to be liable if you default.

You may find someone who is interested in investing in your business rather than in making you a loan to be paid back at a fixed rate and by a certain date. An investor owns a part of your business and gets a return based on the store's profitability. He or she may feel justified in having some say in how you run the business, especially when it comes to decisions such as how much salary you pay yourself. With a loan, you know that when you pay it off, you'll have full control of the business. With equity investors, this may not be the case.

Venture capitalists are professional investment groups that look for promising entrepreneurs in need of loans, although these companies are not usually interested in investments of less than $500,000. Unfortunately, some venture capitalists have earned the nickname "vulture capitalists"

New to Retail: Getting Off to a Great Start

by withdrawing their funds swiftly from young companies that don't look as if they are going to earn the investors a sizable return on their money quickly enough. Retailing rarely shows a profit the first year or two, so impatient venture capitalists are not likely to be attracted to the field. If you work with a venture capitalist, be realistic about the time it may take to be profitable.

Crowdsourcing (discussed in Chapter 16) may work if you are already known in your community. But be aware that some of these platforms, such as Kickstarter, only collect on pledges and give you the funds raised if you reach your full goal within a set period of time.

Occasionally a new business owner is lucky enough to attract an angel investor who wants to help a new venture get started by investing in it. This is especially true if your business appeals to someone with money who has a special interest in your field, such as an art collector if you are opening a gallery. You may also find a businessperson who has had a successful career in your field and is willing to help you get a good start by lending you funds. But the fact is that angel investment is a rare thing in retailing.

New retail store owners sometimes get into a cash crunch right from the start and yield to the temptation to pay for merchandise by credit card. More and more suppliers are willing to take credit cards to avoid the expense and credit risk of setting up an open account, which allows the store to pay for the merchandise after receiving it. Some store owners end up using a credit card as a line of credit, paying a high interest rate to the credit card company. If you are going to use a credit card for merchandise payments, pay the balance off each month, and look for a card that gives you added features, such as frequent flyer miles. Find a credit card with a competitive, fixed interest rate (not an introductory rate that can be raised soon after you sign up) in case you are unable to pay off the balance.

No matter where you borrow your funds, be sure to include the interest on loans in your budgeted business expenses. If you borrow a large amount of money at a high interest rate, this expense could ruin an otherwise successful retail operation. Several large department store chains have fallen victim to this problem. Look for the lowest possible interest rate, and don't borrow more than you need. Too much debt can be a crushing burden to the business and a constant worry to the business owner. At the same time, you should be realistic about the amount of money necessary to get your business to the point at which it will be profitable. Lending institutions are notoriously reluctant to make emergency loans to businesses in crisis.

Getting the Necessary Permits and Licenses

A seller's permit (or resale number) is required by all states with a sales tax. This permit allows you to buy merchandise at wholesale without paying sales tax, but commits you to paying the state sales tax on taxable merchandise when sold at retail. Normally, the consumer pays the sales tax at the time of purchase, and POS (point of sale) systems and cash registers automatically calculate and add state and local sales tax onto taxable items. Because states differ as to which categories of merchandise, such as food and clothing, are exempt from sales tax, you will need to program your system accordingly.

In addition to a state seller's permit, the IRS requires you to obtain an employer identification number (EIN) if you will be hiring employees or if you have incorporated with yourself as an employee. The EIN is used to identify your business records relating to withholding income tax and paying Medicare and the Federal Insurance Contributions Act (FICA), which covers the collection of Social Security funds. The IRS offers lists of guidelines for new businesses that can be obtained by calling 800-829-4933 or by visiting their informative website, www.irs.gov. States with income tax may require a separate identification number for the withholding of state taxes from payroll. This information may be obtained by calling your state's department of revenue.

Finding the Perfect Location

No book on retailing worth its salt can resist repeating the old adage that the three most important keys to retail success are location, location, and location. Although a great location may not guarantee success, a bad location will almost always guarantee failure. You must locate your business, at least initially, where there is a base of customers. Even if your shop is what is called a *destination store*, which means shoppers will make a special trip to buy from you, it is easier to start out in a place shoppers already frequent.

Look for a location with a reasonable degree of security, access to public transportation (for your customers and your employees), good visibility, and adequate parking. Observe the traffic patterns in the area at various times of day to see how easy it will be for customers to get to your location, especially when driving home from work. Keep in mind that you'll also need a way for large trucks and other vehicles to reach you with deliveries, adequate storage space for your back stock of merchandise, and room for an office.

Most stores are located in one of four types of shopping areas: an enclosed shopping center, a strip mall (a shopping center with outside entrances for each store), a neighborhood shopping street, or an area of freestanding buildings with their own parking lots.

Your own shopping habits, and those of your potential customers, can help you decide what type of location is best for your new business. Where do shoppers in your area like to shop? Is there a need for a store like yours in a certain area? What type of store building will allow you to create the shop you envision? You want a location that already has good foot (pedestrian) or motor traffic and the potential for future growth.

SPECIALTY SHOP RETAILING

The size of the merchandise you'll be carrying will have a major effect on the size of the shop you'll need. Furniture obviously requires more room than jewelry. Because you'll be paying by the square foot, don't rent a space larger than you need for the merchandise you plan to stock. Too small a space may also be a problem. Some experts feel that a store with less than 1,000 square feet is too small to stock a wide enough selection to be viable.

Keep in mind also that the store's location will determine the hours you need to keep. Most mall stores are open seven days a week and at least five evenings until 9:00 p.m. Malls require all stores to keep the same hours. In neighborhood shopping areas, stores often try to standardize their hours as a convenience to customers. The number of hours your store will be open will have an important impact on your work week and your payroll needs.

The mix of other shops is an important factor in selecting a location. In a shopping mall, examine the current tenant mix to see if you will fit well. On a shopping street, look for a variety of stores that appeal to the type of shopper you want to attract. For example, if you sell high-end home accessories, you'll want to be near other businesses that attract that demographic—not a bar or a dollar store. Statistics show that a lower-middle-class consumer will go into a high-income neighborhood to shop, but that the opposite is not true.

In a mall, one or two large department stores have traditionally served as magnets to attract customers and are therefore referred to as "anchors." An anchor store today might be a discounter or even a large grocery store, but an enclosed mall without any anchor store may not be a viable location. If the leasing agent promises that an important anchor is going to locate in the mall in the future, ask for lower rent until the big store opens and an escape clause in your lease should the anchor back out. You will also want some protection should the anchor's space become vacant in the future or if a significant number of other store-fronts are empty.

Another consideration in selecting your first location is where you plan to live. There are many advantages to living close to your store, especially when you get that dreaded middle-of-the-night burglar alarm call. It is helpful to play an active role in the community where you plan to do business, and, certainly, living there makes this easier.

You may have to wait some time for the right location to become available. Once you feel the timing is right for you personally and for the market you hope to serve, start approaching landlords, rental agents, and area businesspeople to let them know you are looking. Hopefully, you will be the first to hear when the right space opens up.

TO RENT OR TO BUY

Most new retailers lease space rather than purchase a building; of course, in a shopping center or mall, leasing is the only option. Cash flow is a consideration in deciding whether to lease or buy, as is the amount of experience you have with the type of business you'll be running. If you are a novice shopkeeper, my advice is to concentrate your energy and funds on building your business rather than buying a building. If your store doesn't succeed, you can usually sublet a leased space. If it succeeds beyond your wildest dreams, you can move to a larger location.

We were able to buy our 95-year-old freestanding building a few years after we started Orange Tree Imports, and 30 years ago, we also purchased the 110-year-old store next door and connected it to ours. Both buildings have been good investments, despite the headaches involved in being our own landlord (we own the buildings as individuals and lease the space back to our corporation).

If you decide to purchase a building for your store, check with local authorities about any zoning restrictions. Retail stores require commercial zoning, so you cannot open a store in most residential areas. Because cities also have building codes for commercial buildings that must be followed carefully, be certain you have the necessary building permits before beginning any construction or major remodeling. In buying or building real estate for your store, remember that should your business fail, you will have to sell or lease the property. When making changes to the building, try to keep the space flexible in case you need to sell or rent it to someone else someday.

LOOKING FOR A BUSINESS COMMUNITY

Shopping centers and malls usually provide joint advertising and special events, and all tenants are required to participate. The mall's management organizes promotions, such as special crafts and antique shows, charity fundraisers, or a visit-with-Santa booth, to bring more traffic to the center. When considering a mall location, find out what types of promotions the center usually features and whether tenant input is encouraged. Ask how much you should allow in your budget for merchant participation fees in your business plan.

If you are considering a neighborhood location, look for an area with an active merchants' association or chamber of commerce. Cooperation among retailers makes the promotion of a shopping area more efficient and helps ease the isolation new business owners sometimes feel. A well-established merchants' group is the sign of a retail neighborhood that cares about its future. If there is no organization in the area you choose, consider starting one once you've gotten your business off the ground.

NEGOTIATING A LEASE

If you have ever rented an apartment, you are familiar with some of the basic concepts of leases: a lease covers a specific period of time, with a penalty for breaking the lease, and a security deposit is usually required. But commercial leases often have added features, adding up to a total referred to as the "occupancy cost."

New to Retail: Getting Off to a Great Start

In addition to monthly base rent, your lease may specify that you pay percentage rent, a share of all your sales, or possibly profits, above a certain level. Or you might be offered a net lease, which states that you are responsible for expenses such as utilities, maintenance, and insurance in addition to rent. There are even net-net-net leases, which require the tenant to pay all expenses, including structural repairs to the building. The landlord may offer to pay for carpeting, painting, or some of the other preparation of the space, but often these leasehold improvements are the responsibility of the tenant, even though they will remain behind when you leave.

If your shop is successful, a long-term lease will allow you to stay in that location as long as you want. A commercial lease is usually written for several years, with an option to renew at the end of the lease period, albeit often at a higher rate. But you also need to limit your liability should your shop fail. Ask for a provision allowing you to surrender the lease after giving a certain amount of notice and perhaps paying a penalty or to sublet the space to someone else.

You may be able to find a location for your store by subletting a space from a store that is moving or going out of business. Find out whether the location, or the landlord, had anything to do with the previous shop not wanting to stay. Meet with the property owner or leasing agent yourself before taking on the remainder of someone else's lease.

Retail space is usually priced by the square foot, per year. A 2,000-square-foot store renting for $25.00 per square foot would cost $50,000 per year, or $4,166 per month. In theory, the higher the cost per square foot, the more desirable the space. This presents a real dilemma for the new retailer: should you commit to a high rent in an area with more potential customers or try to save money by renting in a less popular area? How do you know if the rental rate is fair?

The chamber of commerce or library should be able to provide you with a chart showing comparative rental rates for different retail locations in your community. In trying to determine the level of rent you should pay, check to see what types of businesses are prospering in each area. Because shopping center management sets the rent for all the spaces in a mall, you can talk to current mall retailers about how their businesses are faring at their rental rate. On a shopping street with many different landlords, ask around to find out whether the rate you are being charged is comparable to other rents in the area and whether the merchants feel there is an adequate level of customer traffic.

Commercial leases are usually subject to negotiation. You can always ask for concessions from the landlord, such as a lower rate, a few months' free rent, or a set-up allowance, if you feel these requests can be justified. Go over all the details carefully with the assistance of a lawyer or accountant experienced with this type of transaction before agreeing to a lease. There are also real estate companies with expertise in site selection and lease negotiations, and you may wish to engage the services of one of these site-selection consultants to help you choose the best possible location.

Choosing a Name

Naming a store is rather like naming a baby. You come up with lots of ideas and reject most of them for one reason or another. There are many poor choices of names for babies, and for shops. The store we bought when we went into business was called Bord & Stol, which an insignificant percentage of the Madison population knew was Danish for table and chair—and even fewer people knew how to say it.

Try for a store name that is easy to pronounce, spell, and remember. If you are going to run a niche store, committed to carrying basically one category of merchandise, look for a name that readily identifies what the store sells. If you want to be able to carry a wider range of merchandise, you'll need a name that doesn't limit you to one category. Even the name Orange Tree Imports, based on my nickname, Orange, and the fact that we sell mostly imported merchandise ("tree" was thrown in to give the name some consonants) occasionally causes customers to ask whether we actually import orange trees.

You might consider using your first or last name as part of the business name or, perhaps, an imaginary name that appeals to you. You might choose a name that reflects the style of merchandise you plan to carry, such as art deco or country, or perhaps an attitude, such as whimsical or traditional. Some stores are named after a location, although this can limit your options if you decide to relocate.

When you have narrowed your list of name choices, check with your library reference desk to be certain the name, or one very much like it, is not already in use in your area. You can find out if the name is in use anywhere in the country by doing an Internet search. You'll also want to see if there is a website with a similar name, and avoid that if it will cause confusion. As soon as you've chosen your store's name, make sure you own your online presence by registering for the closest domain name (URL) available.

> In *Ellen*, a popular TV show in the 1990s, the main character ran a shop called "Buy the Book." The name is memorable for its cleverness and instantly conveys the fact that the store sells books.

It is advisable also to search the US Patent and Trademark Office to make sure the name has not been trademarked; you can conduct a free search at www.USPTO.gov. Most states (through the secretary of state) and some cities allow you to register a trade name and logo. This registration does not provide name protection beyond that of common law, but it does serve as official notice to anyone who inquires whether the name is already taken and how long it has been in use.

Obtaining national trademark registration is a more expensive and time-consuming process, but it is the only way to stake out legal rights to a name or logo. Avoid choosing a name similar to one that is already trademark protected by a large corporation, such as Disney. No matter how small your operation, Mickey's lawyers will find you and force you to change your name.

Developing a Logo and Brand Identity

Once you have selected a name for your business, you'll want to determine a typestyle, or font, in which to print it. Look for a legible typestyle in keeping with the image you have of your store and its merchandise. There are now thousands of distinctive fonts available to download, and it is easy to design your own ads and graphics if you select one of these.

In addition to a logo font, you will probably want to develop a symbol to represent your store. This logo can be used on store packaging and signage and in print advertising. A good logo should be easily recognized and should be in some way representative of your store and what it sells.

How do you begin to design a logo? If you want to create your own, look into public domain art, or purchase access to images through a paid service such as iClipart. There are also "build-a-logo" apps that offer instant and inexpensive results, but the resulting image may not be exclusive to your shop. Local art students are also a good source of logo designs. You might be fortunate enough to have a commercial art program design your logo as a class project, providing you with a number of options to choose from. Be sure to provide fair compensation for the student whose art you select.

There are many commercial artists talented at designing logos, but you may find that you cannot afford a professional. Check with several advertising or design agencies to get an idea of their fees before authorizing proposals for a logo. Large corporations spend thousands of dollars on logo design, but a fledgling retail shop should probably not spend more than $1,000. Remember that you can always start out with a typestyle logo of your business name and get a symbol logo later, when you are successful enough to have money to spare.

You can add a short slogan or tag line to your store's name to help define more specifically what your store sells. For example, Kit Kat's Korner might use the tag line "Gifts for Cats and Cat Lovers." This concept, which is discussed in Chapter 11, will help consumers know what you specialize in.

STATING YOUR MISSION AND VISION

A mission statement can help you bring your goals into focus, and writing one provides an opportunity to refine your retailing philosophy—and perhaps also your views on social responsibility. This statement should answer the question, "What do you do?" You may also want to have a vision statement, which is more about how things will look if you succeed.

Many businesses post these statements where the public can see them, and all should share them with their staff. The mission statements of Poopsie's in Galena, Illinois, and the mission statement and vision of international Scandinavian home furnishings retailer IKEA are shown below. Even if you were not already familiar with these companies, you would know about their focus from these statements.

"Poopsie's is a fun, funky shop located at the beginning of Main Street in downtown Galena, Illinois. With a focus on impeccable customer service, we strive for a "Beyond the Ordinary" experience for everyone who walks through our doors."

IKEA's vision is "To create a better everyday life for the many people impacted by our business." They add that their business idea is "to offer a wide range of well-designed, functional home furnishing products at prices so low that as many people as possible will be able to afford them."

SPECIALTY SHOP RETAILING

Where to Get Help

There is an oft-quoted African proverb: "If you want to go fast, go alone. If you want to go far, go with others." As you begin to plan your new venture, look for mentors who can help you establish a business that will be around for a long time to come. Other retailers are often a great source of information, provided your store will not be a direct competitor. Come prepared with a short list of specific questions. To avoid the constant interruptions of customers and telephone calls, you might treat the retailer to lunch.

The start-up period is a good time to form an advisory team for your business. You will need the services of an accountant and a lawyer experienced in retail. Once you have established which bank you'll be dealing with, bring your banker onto the advisory team. Be sure these individuals know and respect each other because they will all be working to help you create a successful business.

You should also establish a comfortable relationship with an insurance agent who can help you with the variety of insurance needs you will have (see Chapter 16). In addition to these paid professional advisers, invite a few customers and experienced businesspeople to serve on a voluntary advisory team. Most people are pleased to be asked to share their opinions and expertise.

The US Small Business Administration (SBA) can provide you with general information, as well as individual counseling. The SBA maintains an extensive website at www.sba.gov and a national toll-free answer desk at 1-800-U-ASK-SBA. If you live in an urban area, there is probably also a local SBA office. Contact them for help with specific questions or for some of their informative materials.

A resource partner of the SBA, the Service Corps of Retired Executives (SCORE), maintains its own website at www.score.org. Retired businesspersons volunteer through SCORE to counsel novice businesses, and you may be lucky to find someone with expertise in your retail field. You can contact your local SCORE program to be assigned a volunteer or arrange for email counseling through their website.

The Small Business Development Center (SBDC), a collaborative effort between local colleges and universities and the SBA, provides excellent seminars and counseling services for retail businesses. Find out if there is one in your area by visiting www.sba.gov/sbdc, and call to find out how they can assist you. Your local chamber of commerce may also have a specialist whose job it is to encourage new businesses. Why try to go it alone when so much help and expertise is available?

Ready, Set, GO!

If you're convinced that you're ready to take the plunge into retailing, you may find the following checklist a helpful guideline for your activities over the next few months. Try to find a few friends or family members to share your ideas with as you go. Many writers—and dieters—find it helpful to get together regularly with others for feedback and encouragement. Ask your support team to hold you accountable for some progress every week as you work toward opening day.

This timetable is just a guideline, intended to help you plan your tasks as you get ready to open your store. Some items may take much longer than the time listed (custom fixtures, for instance, might take six to nine months to produce and are difficult to design before you have a space leased). But because money in use costs you interest, you should try not to pay for rent, utilities, merchandise, fixtures, equipment, or anything else earlier than necessary.

Three or more months before you open:

- ❑ Write business plan
- ❑ Choose store name, register it
- ❑ Get financing and store credit card
- ❑ Open checking account in store name
- ❑ Hire accountant
- ❑ Meet with lawyer, if necessary
- ❑ Visit first trade show(s)
- ❑ Apply for state sales permit, federal EIN (Employer Identification number)
- ❑ Begin site selection process
- ❑ Plan store layout, start to order fixtures, lighting

New to Retail: Getting Off to a Great Start

Two months or more before you open (site should be set):

- ❑ Order phone line(s), get phone and fax numbers
- ❑ Check about phone book's annual deadline
- ❑ Design logo, make business cards, letterhead
- ❑ Begin ordering merchandise
- ❑ Apply for insurance
- ❑ Set up basic website, register domain name
- ❑ Get price guns, labels
- ❑ Order gift boxes and bags with logo
- ❑ Select and order store signage
- ❑ Set up store computer, bookkeeping system
- ❑ Sign up with credit card processing company

When you take possession of your space:

- ❑ Put up signage, including opening date
- ❑ Paint, wallpaper, or carpet area as needed
- ❑ Set up displays, lighting, and checkout counter
- ❑ Set up stockroom storage for merchandise
- ❑ Set up office with vendor files, computer
- ❑ Install phone lines and WiFi

One month before you open:

- ❑ Buy cash registers or point-of-sale (POS) equipment
- ❑ Plan advertising for first few months
- ❑ Create return policies, other procedures
- ❑ Develop personnel forms, payroll system
- ❑ Hire employees one to two weeks before opening

One week before you open:

- ❑ Train employees
- ❑ Create in-store and window displays
- ❑ Get start-up cash (till, petty cash) from the bank
- ❑ Invite friends in for a "dry run"

CHAPTER 3
BOOKKEEPING 101: MANAGING STORE FINANCES

Many store owners start a business without a clear understanding of record keeping and finances, so you'll want to read this chapter no matter where you are on your store's journey. Even with a computer system to do the actual record keeping, or a part-time bookkeeper, you need to understand the basic principles. One of the goals of a good bookkeeping system is to produce figures that can help guide your business decisions, but these figures are useless if you don't understand where they come from and how to interpret them. I know because it took me years to be able to make sense out of a balance sheet and income statement. They just don't teach those skills in Scandinavian Studies.

You may well want to do your own bookkeeping if you have a good understanding of this field, but even so it is a good idea to have an accountant to make sure you are filing taxes correctly and to give you business advice. One of the factors involved in store failures is the inability of the owner to make good decisions based on financial data. Other owners fail because of inadequate cash flow planning, making it impossible to pay bills in a timely fashion, even if the business is showing a profit. A hands-on approach to money management may prevent these problems, and also help prevent the misappropriation of funds by a dishonest employee.

Bookkeeping 101: Managing Store Finances

Bookkeeping Basics

The goal of bookkeeping is, in a nutshell, to keep a record of income and expenses to track assets and liabilities. If the expenses outweigh the sales income, you are in the red, or losing money. This is a natural situation the first year, or even two, but if you don't make money in five years, the Internal Revenue Service (IRS) could consider your business a hobby, which could lead to serious tax consequences. When your sales outweigh your expenses, you are in the black and making a profit.

The salary you pay yourself has an enormous effect on whether there is any profit left. The IRS will consider any profit on a sole proprietorship or partnership to be your income, whether or not you have taken it home as a salary. But if your business is going well, there should be money left as a profit even after you've been paid a reasonable salary. Taking an excessively large salary, however, may drain the store's cash reserves, hindering its ability to invest in inventory and prosper. You should leave some of the store's profits in the business each year as seed money to help it grow.

Most businesses use a form of double-entry bookkeeping, a system of checks and balances that must have been designed by Alice after stepping through the looking glass. Everything that should·be a positive number, such as sales, is negative, and everything that should be a negative number, such as expenses, is positive. The reason the system is called "double entry" is that every item is posted twice.

Even before you open, you should have a system in place with a sales and cash receipts journal that tracks money coming in and another for disbursements, or money going out. The expenses you begin to track will hopefully soon be joined by sales income, and if all goes well, the income eventually will outweigh the expenditures.

Sales income is posted to both the cash/checking account and to total sales. A check to a vendor for merchandise is posted to cash/checking and to inventory purchases, usually by product category. For every debit,

*It seems like everything that should be positive is negative,
and everything that should be negative is positive. . . .*

there must be a corresponding credit entry. The goal is to have all the accounts come out balanced when a trial balance of debits and credits is done at the end of each month. The accounts must balance before the income statement and balance sheet can be considered accurate.

Setting up a Software Program

It would be wise to set up a computer for your store's bookkeeping program right away. You'll also find it useful for all sorts of word processing, sign making, mailing list management, and much more. A fairly basic system with good WiFi and a color inkjet printer should serve your needs. It is important to have at least one means for backing up your data and to do it regularly, ideally with both an external hard drive and a cloud-based storage program.

Bookkeeping 101: Managing Store Finances

Ask your accountant or other retailers for recommendations for bookkeeping software programs—you are most likely to end up with QuickBooks, which at the moment is used by some 80% of all small businesses. Whatever you decide on, it is important to select a software program that your CPA is familiar with, as you will be handing over the reports and data the program generates to him or her for review. It is also probably a good idea to get professional help in setting up your categories for expenditures, income, and vendor ledgers. Once you have created these categories, called the "Chart of Accounts," it is difficult to make changes without disrupting your bookkeeping history trail.

Every time your business spends money, by cash or check, it should be recorded in a disbursement account. Setting up these accounts is one of the first tasks when you start your bookkeeping system. Some of the category titles will be obvious, such as rent, advertising, and payroll. Others may be specific to your store, such as mall participation fees.

You can make as many categories as you like, and the more categories, the better, for making these records useful tools. For example, you may wish to have telephone expense as a separate category rather than including it with heating and lighting under utilities. Merchandise purchases can be a single category or separate categories for each department of the store. Separate merchandise categories will be helpful as you track inventory purchases and budget future buying.

It will be worthwhile to seek the guidance of an accountant in setting up your disbursement categories because you should try not to change them once you have gotten the system underway. The data you have collected become difficult to track if you make changes in the categories.

Money should never be taken out of the register to pay for even a small purchase, because then the till will not balance with the sales report at the end of the day. Set up a petty cash fund for such purchases with a fixed amount of money, perhaps $50.00. Keep receipts for any purchases made from this fund. When petty cash is depleted, write a check to bring the balance back up to $50.00, posting the disbursements to the various accounts listed on the receipts or petty cash slips.

A business credit card can be an effective way to track incidental purchases for the store, as well as for buying trip travel expenses. Keep all receipts, and when the credit card invoice is paid, disburse each expense to the appropriate account.

In addition to disbursement categories, you will want to create vendor ledgers or accounts to track the purchases you make from each supplier. We buy from hundreds of companies (undoubtedly more than we should) and need to be able to tell at a glance what our standing is with each one.

Understanding Financial Reports

The system you use to record the money coming into your business and going out of your business should provide a monthly or quarterly summary of this information called an *income statement,* or *profit and loss statement* (P&L). The wholesale cost of the merchandise is subtracted from the total (or net) sales figure to produce the gross margin. Operating costs and other expenses, such as depreciation, are subtracted from the gross margin, resulting in a net profit or loss.

The wholesale cost of the merchandise is also referred to as the *cost of goods sold* (COGS). It is calculated by taking the beginning inventory, adding merchandise purchases (including freight costs), and subtracting the ending inventory. Most stores do a physical count of the inventory only once a year, so the COGS is usually determined at that time and applied as a percentage the rest of the year. Our current COGS, for example, is 59%. A slightly lower percentage would be better.

The COGS figure reflects not only the cost of the goods sold, but also any goods stolen, disposed of, purchased at an employee discount, or given to charity. Even if your margin on every item is 50%, your COGS

Bookkeeping 101: Managing Store Finances

will be a higher percentage due to these factors, as well as markdowns taken on slow-moving merchandise.

The other standard accounting report you will need to produce is a *balance sheet*. Unlike the income statement, which changes every day as money comes in and out of the business, the balance sheet is a big picture report, showing a comparison of the business assets and short- and long-term liabilities. Any increase in the value of the inventory or cash in the bank adds to the assets. A new loan, or taxes owed but not yet paid, increases the liabilities. A healthy business has more assets than liabilities.

The balance sheet also shows the capital invested in the business, such as the owner's equity, plus retained profits and less any money (dividends) taken out by the owners. For a sole proprietorship or partnership, the capital is attributed to the proprietor(s). In a corporation, the value of the business is the sum of its capital stock and retained earnings. Funds paid out to stockholders are listed as dividends.

RATIOS AND COMPARISONS

Financial statements allow you to analyze how the store is doing by comparing the figures. These comparisons, called financial and operating ratios, are one way to take the pulse of the business.

The *current ratio*, for example, is the current assets divided by the current liabilities. A ratio of two or higher is considered healthy.

The *ratio of net sales to net profit* shows the percentage of profit your business is earning and is useful in comparing one year with the next as the business grows. If this percentage gets too low, consider what action to take to increase sales or decrease expenses.

Return on investment (ROI) is calculated by dividing the net profit by the amount of money invested in the business. This ratio can be a painful one for small retailers because it often shows that one would earn a higher rate of return on the investment by putting it in a mutual fund instead of the business.

But ROI doesn't reflect the satisfaction of creating an imaginative, well-run specialty shop. Nor does it take into account the fact that before the profit is calculated, you and all your employees (or if you are a sole proprietorship, just the employees) have been paid a good wage. The money generated for your own salary is a benefit of the business you've created, and the money you pay your staff is a positive contribution to the local economy.

WORKING WITH AN ACCOUNTANT

You may be able to produce balance sheets and income statements with the store's computer software, but you still should have the work checked by an accountant. You will want to have an accountant help you get set up for all the tax filings required of a small business, most of which can now be done online using a method called e-filing. The penalties for missing a tax deadline can be severe, and as with other areas of the law, ignorance is no defense. A CPA who works with other retailers can also advise you about some of the difficult financial decisions you will need to make as a business owner.

The bank or other investors helping to finance your business will want to see periodic financial statements, and these documents carry

---

Know your numbers. Know ALL your numbers. It's easy to get caught up in the "fun" part of owning a store but from day one you absolutely must know everything from inventory and price points to your balance sheet, to how much money it costs to open every day, to how much money you have in the bank. To understand how your business is working (and if it is working) you have to understand your numbers. No one likes to talk about the money, but if you don't you'll be finished before you start.
—Linda O'Boyle, Metro Home Style, Syracuse, New York

more weight if they have been prepared or reviewed by an accountant. Keep a binder of your statements where you can find them easily to compare past and present performance.

Creating Budgets and Future Planning

The business plan provides a road map for the first year or two of a business; many retailers find it useful to continue to set financial goals and plans as the business matures. The store's monthly financial statements can be very useful in setting realistic financial goals for the future. You can do a budget projection for all aspects of your operation, including sales and operating expenses, or you can use a budget specifically for planning the best way to spend the dollars in a certain category such as advertising or payroll. Open-to-buy budgeting, discussed in Chapter 5, helps you plan inventory purchases by month and by category, maximizing the effectiveness of the money invested in merchandise.

One important budget planning process, especially for new businesses, is cash-flow forecasting. Never spend money you don't have. To order merchandise, hire carpenters to do remodeling, or commit to an advertising campaign without having any idea how you are going to pay the bills could be seen as unethical, or at least a bad business practice. Estimate what your income will be each month, and know what your cash reserves are in advance. Then budget your expenditures based on these two factors. If there won't be enough cash to cover your needs, you will have to choose between cutting back on purchases and expenses, or finding additional outside funding and increasing the store's debt.

Your bookkeeping software should allow you to enter budget figures, as well as any previous years' figures, and print out variance reports comparing actual results with previous and budgeted amounts. These reports can help you see where you need to make adjustments throughout the year to bring you closer to reaching your goals.

SPECIALTY SHOP RETAILING

Choosing or Updating Your Sales System

Most of your income will come through a cash register or POS (point-of-sale) system, so it is important to select the best one for your store. There are many options today, from traditional cash registers (which we still use) to sophisticated systems that generate an array of reports that will help with inventory management and provide information about your customers and their shopping habits. Deciding what works best for you can be challenging, and may be something that you want to revisit if you've been in business for some time.

POS, SaaS and Other Options

A *point-of-sale system (POS)* is a computerized cash register system, usually using the Universal Product Code (UPC), or barcode, on each product to match it to the price or price look up (PLU) assigned to the item. A POS system is normally used with a barcode scanner, however numeric codes from price tags can be entered into the system manually.

A traditional or legacy POS system feeds information about each sale directly into the computer's database on the premises, for example, downloading daily sales totals directly into your bookkeeping software (make sure they are compatible). They will sometimes also integrate with Excel, creating spreadsheets of reports. The sophisticated terminals used with these systems come with a fairly high hardware cost, and there is sometimes a charge for updates.

Square is an example of a cloud-based POS system, also called *Software-as-a-Service*, or *SaaS*, that can be accessed via the Internet using a mobile device, such as an iPad or even a smartphone. You can equip this system with a Bluetooth barcode scanner, as well as a cash drawer and a receipt printer. Not all customers want a printed receipt, although they are very useful when processing returns—so they may wish to have their receipt emailed to them. There may be some data security issues to consider with a SaaS system, along with the fact that performance is dependent on good Internet access.

In addition to processing sales, cloud-based POS systems have optional apps available such as Shopventory, which adds inventory management and sales reporting. This program can be used by a single shop, or by multiple locations needing to compare and compile data.

The up-front costs for these systems is generally lower than for a hardwired POS system. However, there may be monthly charges to factor in. The programs often include credit card processing, which is one way providers earn income from their system.

A POS system can track customers and their purchases, building a detailed database and mailing list for the store. Some systems will automatically generate email marketing or suggest targeted promotions based on a customer's purchase patterns. When a POS system is used to track purchases for a customer loyalty program (discussed in Chapter 14), it saves buying a separate data terminal just for this purpose.

If you are selling online, you may want a POS system that can integrate your in-store and web sales automatically. Another option is to use a cloud-based POS system that allows you to log on using your office computer to enter online sales data into your system.

Shops with more than one location can easily combine data from their POS systems for centralized reordering. A POS system can be set up to generate a reorder automatically when stock on an item falls below a certain level—especially useful if much of your stock remains the same from one order to the next and if multiple locations make it difficult to keep an eye on inventory levels.

There is also a personnel component to many POS systems, with a time clock and a code for tracking individual employees' sales efforts. Attendance data can sometimes be fed directly into your payroll system, which is an added convenience. Sales tax reporting is another service provided by most POS systems, along with the processing of gift cards.

SPECIALTY SHOP RETAILING

A POS system will often allow you to change the message on the register tape and even add a coupon valid on a future visit, or gift receipt. You might want to periodically feature an online customer satisfaction survey on the receipt, with a prize drawing for all those who take the time to participate.

As with any computer program, a POS system is only useful if the data that is put into it is accurate and if you make use of the reports that it generates. You will need to budget the resources to have someone enter inventory arrivals into the system on a regular basis. However, this system does have the potential to increase your profitability by lowering inventory costs, improving customer service, and allocating personnel time more efficiently.

POS systems tend to be expensive, and the expense may be hard to justify in small, single-location stores unless you own the type of shop for which proprietary software is already available, for example, an independent bookstore. If you do decide to purchase one, start by visiting other retailers to talk to them about the system they use. Compile a list of the features that are important to you, and research which companies offer a software system that would serve your needs now—and also in the future, especially if you are planning multiple locations. Ask the salesperson from each company to give you a live demonstration.

Be sure to select a software company with a good track record for customer service, because you will be dependent upon the system functioning smoothly to process sales. (You might want to have a paper receipt book on hand to use if the system goes down, or if your WiFi fails—make sure that you'll be able to enter the sales manually when you're back online.) It is also important that there is adequate training provided for you in setting up the system, and that you train your staff thoroughly on its use.

Barcode labeling is becoming increasingly common, even on imported goods, and it is possible to print barcode labels for those items that don't have them using the store computer. This brings up the question as to whether price tags are really necessary. For grocery and discount stores that no longer use price tags, having the merchandise arrive already barcoded results in a huge savings in stock handling costs. The majority of specialty stores, however, continue to price each piece of merchandise for the convenience of the customer.

CASH REGISTERS FOR SMALLER SHOPS

We have still not made the leap to a POS system, in part because we only have one store—and a conversion after this many years would be costly. I don't always recommend an expensive POS system for a single-location shop that does not plan to have branches or an extensive ecommerce business, although a cloud-based system may be a viable option.

Our cash registers do track sales by category, just like a POS would. We use the 26 letters of the alphabet to code merchandise by category on our price tags and ring each item up on one of the 26 letter keys on the register. The keys for our only nontaxable category, food, and for nontaxable services, such as gift wrapping, are programmed not to add sales tax. We use separate terminals to swipe credit cards and to input data into our customer rewards program.

CREDIT AND DEBIT CARD PROCESSING

Cash is still a universally accepted method of paying for any purchase. Nevertheless, the ease of using a debit card and the free grace period on many credit cards make plastic a more convenient and cost-effective way for customers to pay for a purchase. The debit or credit card service charge and other fees paid by the merchant, however, can be as high as 4%. It pays to shop around for the best rate on these charges, although it is confusing to try to compare them.

Most banks offer credit card services for MasterCard, Visa, American Express, and other credit cards, as do several national processing companies. If you don't want to deal with an out-of-state service, you might ask your local bank if it can match the competitor's rate. Credit card service charges are based to some extent on volume, so you may be able to negotiate a better rate as your business grows.

The speed with which funds are transferred from the service into your checking account is also an important factor to consider, and this varies from one company to the next. Be sure to take this into account when setting up your card processing.

Unless you are using a cash register, you won't need to buy a separate electronic data-capture terminal to allow you to scan a credit card and automatically transfer the sales information to the company that will service the transaction. Whether you are using a terminal or your POS system, you should note that some credit card processors deduct their service charge from the daily deposit; others debit your checking account for their fee once a month.

The data-capture system automatically authorizes the transaction and collects payment data. If a card has been reported lost or stolen, or if the customer is over his or her credit limit, authorization will be denied. When this happens, you can try to run the card one more time, or request another form of payment.

Speedy feedback on each transaction is made possible through a direct connection to the Internet via an ethernet cable connected to your broadband router or network switch. WiFi should only be considered if it is installed by a professional who understands wireless data security using current encryption standards and strong passwords, and who knows how to configure it not to transmit its name (for example). It should also be completely separate from any guest WiFi, if you provide this for customers, for security reasons.

Customers are now paying for as much as 40% of all purchases with debit cards, which deduct the amount of the purchase from the customer's bank account. Although most retail stores only take signature debits for the amount of purchase, customers may wish to withdraw additional cash from their account at the time of purchase. If you choose to allow this, you will need a data-capture system with a personal identification number (PIN) pad that shoppers can use to input their code. Because the PIN code is confidential, store staff should not be able to see the numbers the customer types.

A data-capture terminal allowing the consumer to enter a PIN is technically required when accepting a credit card with an EMV chip (EMV stands for Europay, MasterCard, and Visa). The concept is that chip cards are almost impossible to counterfeit because of the one-time code generated at the time of a sale. However, the prevalence of the traditional magnetic card swipe terminals has made American implementation of this new technology slow.

MOBILE PAYMENTS

Yet another payment option is the use of information stored in a smartphone to make a purchase without the use of cash or a card. Customers just tap their phone on the credit card reader to use a program such as ApplePay, AndroidPay, or GoogleWallet to transmit their credit or debit account data. There is a prediction that these digital wallets, which can store many different mobile payment options and also preferred customer card data, will eventually replace the use of traditional credit and debit cards. Accepting contactless payments does require a card reader equipped with Near Field Communication (NFC).

Before You Start Selling

Sales are usually broken down as taxable and nontaxable. You will need to program your system to reflect the rules for taxable goods in your state to produce the data needed for sales tax reporting. There are other nontaxable transactions as well, such as sales to nonprofit organizations and merchandise to be shipped out of state. A tax shift key is used to remove the sales tax from taxable items when the purchase is nontaxable, and we record the nonprofit organization's tax-exempt number in a special log.

Any type of sale system can be set up to include a record of which sales assistant rings up a sale, essential data for stores paying commissions. This information can also be useful if you are concerned about employee accuracy and efficiency or suspect an employee of dishonesty.

Don't forget to order extra rolls of paper receipt tape and ink when you order your system. When it arrives, hold several practice sessions for staff members to get them comfortable with ringing up sales and returns and changing the paper, and let them know where to call if they need technical assistance.

FILLING THE TILL

The register fund (or till) needs some coins and bills to start each day. Decide on an even amount, such as $100.00, to have on hand when you open, and put aside that amount in a variety of small bills and coins when you close every night.

We also keep a stock of rolls of coins near the checkout counter, and "buy" a roll of quarters or pennies from this fund with bills from the register. As part of our daily cash reconciliation, we count the money in the change fund to be sure it totals the correct amount. For special events, very busy weekends, and holidays when the banks are closed, we plan ahead to have extra change on hand.

POS systems calculate the amount of change owed to a customer, but sales staff should still acknowledge the amount received and count out the money as they give change. This is a courtesy that also prevents disagreements about how much was tendered and how much change the customer received.

Bookkeeping 101: Managing Store Finances

At the end of the day, the sales system will provide the day's sales figures broken down into cash, check, and credit card sales. If an employee mistakenly hits the wrong key for a transaction, he or she should leave a note so the figures can be adjusted. We have made up a customized reconciliation form to use each day to assure that the amount deposited into the store's bank account matches the register's figures for the day.

The cash, check, and credit card figures from the register's daily report are listed across the top of the form. These figures are matched up with the total amount of cash in the till, minus the daily start-up fund of $100.00; a calculator total of the checks, and the data capture units total of credit card transactions. Any discrepancies in the totals are noted on the reconciliation form for the bookkeeper to investigate before making the deposit the next day.

The bookkeeper compiles the sales data from the cash registers into the sales record section of the bookkeeping program on the store's computer. (Most POS systems will transmit this data directly.) In addition to bank reconciliation, accurate sales records are essential for sales tax reporting. Sales tax forms will often ask for a description of all nontaxable sales, such as shipments out of state, sales to nonprofits, or the sale of food items, so taxable and nontaxable sales need to be recorded separately by category.

ACCEPTING CHECKS

Bounced checks used to be a real headache for retailers, however, the use of personal checks is declining. When a check is returned by the bank marked NSF (non-sufficient funds), you have the option of waiting a few days and redepositing it. In many cases, the check will clear the second time because the customer has made an innocent error. But if the check bounces a second time, it usually cannot be redeposited. Your only choice then is to call and ask the customer to bring in the cash. Failing this, you can call the police or hire a collection agency.

Some stores discourage bad checks by posting a policy of fining customers as much as $35.00 for each returned check. This fine helps cover the fee that banks assess for handling an NSF check, but is helpful only if you are able to collect for the check and the charge.

An alternate form of check acceptance is electronic check conversion. When a customer presents a check, it is processed through an electronic system that captures the bank account information and the amount of the check. Once the check has been processed, it is returned to the customer. The information from the check is transmitted electronically, and the funds are transferred into the store's account. This eliminates the risk of the check bouncing later. However, it also eliminates the float period that some customers may count on to make sure the check is covered.

Stores need to have a policy regarding checks written for more than the amount of purchase, cashing third-party checks made out to someone other than your store, and accepting out-of-state checks. Help your staff treat all customers fairly by spelling out your check acceptance policies in writing.

Paying Your Vendors

Making accurate and timely payments is an essential function of your bookkeeping system. Keeping good records will be easier if you are set up with a checking account from the start. Allow time to order preprinted checks in your store's name.

ESTABLISHING YOUR STORE'S FINANCIAL CREDIBILITY

When you start ordering merchandise (Chapter 5), you'll need to show suppliers that your business is reputable. You will be asking these companies to believe that your business is creditworthy enough to receive valuable merchandise on account and that you will pay for it when the invoice is due. A credit sheet, or list of *credit references*, is a financial resume for your store. When you apply for open credit terms from a supplier, you want to make a good impression. The credit reference sheet should clearly present all the pertinent details about your business:

- Logo
- Name
- Address
- Phone and fax numbers
- Website and email address
- Date the store opened
- The store's legal entity (corporation, partnership, or sole proprietorship)
- The name of the store's owner(s)
- Resale number
- Name and address of the store's bank
- Name, address, phone number and email of at least 6 current suppliers

Be sure to give the contact information for the suppliers you list as references along with the account number assigned to your business by those companies. Some vendors are not willing to serve as a credit reference and will not give out information if asked; check with potential references to avoid listing those that will not be helpful in establishing credit terms. It is a good idea to give a mix of companies in different parts of the country and various types of vendors if you can. A sample form is shown in below.

Once you have been in business for some time, you will be approached by the credit reporting firm of Dun & Bradstreet. Dun & Bradstreet compiles credit rating information from you and from the suppliers you buy from, and it assigns your business a code number (your D&B number) and a rating. If you are punctual in paying all your bills and have a healthy balance sheet, your positive D&B rating should help

CREDIT REFERENCES

– LOGO –

STORE NAME
Mailing Address
Phone • Fax
Email Address • Website

Owner Name(s)
Established in _____
Bank, including phone and mailing address

D & B # • State Sellers Permit # • Fed. ID #

VENDOR #1	VENDOR #4
Street Address	Street Address
City, State, Zip	City, State, Zip
Phone • Email	Phone • Email
Account #	Account #
VENDOR #2	VENDOR #5
Street Address	Street Address
City, State, Zip	City, State, Zip
Phone • Email	Phone • Email
Account #	Account #
VENDOR #3	VENDOR #6
Street Address	Street Address
City, State, Zip	City, State, Zip
Phone • Email	Phone • Email
Account #	Account #

All parties listed about are hereby authorized to provide
credit information upon request.

Please note that it is our policy not to pay freight on backorders
of under $50 without prior authorization.

Awards
Buying Groups Membership(s)
Additional Information
date last updated

Sample credit reference sheet.

you get open credit terms quickly with new accounts. Be sure to list your D&B number on your credit reference sheet.

We also use this form as an opportunity to mention our policy of not accepting backorders (small shipments of items that had been out of stock) of under $50.00 unless the supplier pays the freight. Other shops may give their preferences for certain freight companies or other details that will affect their orders. You can make your credit references more impressive by including a photograph of the store or listing any awards you have received.

If you are new in business, you won't have much information to put on a credit sheet. Nevertheless, put it together with whatever data is available, even if your only references are local businesses, such as a printer, that have extended you credit. You may find that most new vendors will still insist on payment by credit card, but at least you have established yourself as a legitimate business.

Even a well-established store will often be asked to provide a credit card for payment of the first or even second order from a new vendor. Checking references can take time, delaying the order by several weeks, and can be a somewhat costly process for the vendor. By stating that no first orders will be on open account, companies avoid setting up accounts for what may turn out to be one-time buyers.

Business Office Essentials

Your store's office, which should be handicapped accessible, if possible, needs electrical and phone lines for computers and telephones, as well as space for vendor files, financial records, desks, and storage of office supplies. It is helpful to have a table for meetings with sales representatives, who often need room to spread out their bulky catalogs and product samples. We have a multipurpose office that our bookkeepers share with the gift wrapping counter. Both bookkeepers have been known to pitch in with the wrapping when we get busy.

The computer and its printer will probably be the central feature of your store's office. As you are setting up the office, have it wired for high speed Internet. Even if you don't plan to sell online, you'll find that most of your suppliers have merchandise information available on their websites, so you'll want to have dependable access. You may want a fax machine—we still use ours to send out orders, although we now send just as many via email.

While you are arranging for phone lines, inquire about the cost of establishing a toll-free number for customers outside your area code. This service is not very expensive and may be a real plus if you are interested in selling online. Shop around for the best package of rates as your monthly phone bill can really add up.

RECORDS AND FILES

There is a lot of paperwork involved in running a retail store. We file vendor catalogs and paid invoices from the previous 12 months in alphabetical file folders in the store office. Paid invoices, stapled to their purchase orders and packing lists, are filed in chronological order in the front of these files, with catalogs and price lists in the back. Periodically, we weed our files of duplicate and outdated product literature. One of my pet peeves is that vendors often don't clearly date their price lists and catalogs, making it difficult to know which ones to discard. Before filing product literature, jot down the date received in an upper corner.

Invoices yet to be paid are in alphabetical order in the bookkeeper's file, together with the purchase order and any other paperwork relating to the pending invoice. The invoice data is entered in a vendor ledger in the bookkeeping system on the computer.

We also maintain a file of sales representatives' business cards and a spreadsheet of all our vendors listing the names of the current sales representatives. In the gift industry, companies seem to change their minds capriciously about who is representing their line in an area. I note all sales rep changes in our files in an attempt to make sure the current rep gets credit for every order.

One filing cabinet in our office contains employee records, and this is the only cabinet that is kept locked. Employees have access to their own file but not to the personnel files of others. We also have files for the various types of taxes we pay and for non-vendor expenditures, such as insurance, store supplies, trade shows, and advertising.

The government requires that businesses retain many documents for years in case of an audit, but these do not need to be kept close at hand in the business office. Payroll records, invoices, tax forms, financial statements, and canceled checks all need a place to be stored. Check with your CPA or the IRS for the current regulations about how long each record should be kept. We store past records in inexpensive cardboard files, called bankers' boxes, available at office supply stores. They are clearly dated on the outside, and when we put in the current year's documents, the expired year's papers go into the recycling bin or get shredded.

You may also want to use an inexpensive, wastepaper-basket-sized shredder for sensitive financial documents, customer credit card information, and any personnel documents you are discarding. Consider the added bonus of using it as a stress reducer when times get tough: You can write out a long list of all your frustrations and watch the shredder quickly render them into meaningless little strips.

Tax Requirement: Taking Inventory

Once a year, you are required by the IRS to take a complete physical inventory of all the merchandise on hand for tax purposes. This is usually done on the last day of your fiscal year, although you may wish to select the closest Sunday or another slow day of the week, if you need to be closed to do the count. You will then need to adjust for the sales on the days between the year end and inventory day.

Stores with a barcode scanning system can use hand-held scanners to read the shelves of merchandise, but many still take inventory manually. We have our entire staff of 20 on hand to count inventory and get it done in one day. If you don't have enough employees, invite family and friends to help. Some stores even use members of a nonprofit group for inventory assistance, making a donation to the cause in exchange for a few hours of work. No advance training is required if your inventory system is well planned.

Divide the store into sections based on product categories. Assign a pair of inventory counters to each section, armed with a clipboard and a calculator. One person counts the items while the other records the figures. You can use the memory function of a small printing calculator to multiply as you go, or enter the number of items at each price point and extend the totals later. For those who choose to record the number of items at each price, instead of just totals, OTB Retail Systems creator Mort Haaz suggests making copies of a list of your most common price points ($1.00, $1.25, $1.50, $1.75, $2.00, etc.) and putting hash marks next to each price for every item you count at that price.

We get a head start on inventory day by counting merchandise in back stock during the week before. Once an area has been counted, a note is posted by it so that anyone removing merchandise will record what is taken, and the inventory will be adjusted. We also count seasonal merchandise as we pack it away at the end of the season and keep those figures on file for inventory day.

All of our inventory is counted at its retail price. We then go back through the figures and try to calculate the wholesale value, based on what we know of the markup taken on each merchandise category.

The physical inventory figure is an important tool in calculating the store's financial status. Inventory taking is also a good opportunity to

Bookkeeping 101: Managing Store Finances

account for every piece of merchandise in stock and to make sure that each item is on display or stored where it is easily accessible. We try to neaten and dust shelves as we count, and when we are done, the store looks ready for the new year.

The Bottom Line

One book on small shop retailing suggests that readers think of their stores as cash machines, but the vast majority of us would be very unhappy with our shops if we viewed them that way. It has been said that most retailers would enjoy a greater return on investment from a well-managed investment portfolio than they do from their stores. Many shopkeepers are satisfied with the accomplishments of their business despite the absence of a large profit. They enjoy the freedom of owning their own business, the challenge of creative retailing, and the opportunity to provide a steady, but modest, income to themselves and their staff.

Of course, profit is a good thing to have. Being profitable provides a sense of security, and when you don't have to worry constantly about your business, you have more freedom to experiment with new ideas, products, and services. Being profitable also allows you to do more for your community and your employees, and it allows your store to grow. But profitability is only one measure of a successful business. Keep the bottom line at the bottom, where it belongs.

CHAPTER 4
STORE DESIGN:
MAKING THE MOST OF YOUR SPACE

The late Apple CEO Steve Jobs said in a conversation with Disney CEO Bob Iger that retailers should always ask themselves one question: "If a store could talk, what would it say to the people entering it?" Think of a customer walking through the front door of your shop for the very first time. What do you want that person to see, hear, and sense?

Creating an exciting retail environment for your customers involves much more than putting up shelves to display the merchandise. A good specialty shop integrates such diverse elements as lighting, flooring, displays, windows, signage, music, and even aroma to create the perfect setting for its product selection.

The Rainforest Café's gift shop at the Mall of America stops traffic with an animatronic snake in the entryway and Tracy Tree greeting shoppers once they enter the store. In this era of imaginative retailing, many customers are looking for shopping experiences that are entertaining, aesthetically pleasing, or relaxing. You may not want a talking tree, or a wall of TV screens, in your shop, but you need to let your imagination roam beyond the traditional rows of shelves and hooks. Your shop design should make your merchandise look special and your customers feel special.

Shop Design: Making the Most of Your Space

Establishing a Design Budget

The size of your store and the amount of remodeling required to convert the space you've leased into the store of your dreams will dictate whether you need to hire an architect, store designer, or other professionals to assist you. If the shop is small and you have good design sense, along with some basic construction skills, you may be able to do much of the work yourself.

In planning, it is important to include key factors specific to store design: traffic flow, lighting, security, product display, storage, and checkout functions. A design professional with retail experience should be able to help you incorporate these elements into the store design while still maintaining your vision of what the store should be. If you cannot afford a store designer, check to see if any of the suppliers of store fixtures offer knowledgeable design assistance.

Keep in mind that there are requirements that must be met regarding handicapped access (both state codes and the national standards set by the Americans with Disabilities Act), fire regulations, building codes, zoning regulations, and possibly also Occupational Safety and Health Administration standards. The

> Select a designer who is adept at translating your personal store concept into reality. According to Frank Lloyd Wright expert Richard Cleary, when Wright designed the V. C. Morris Gift Shop in San Francisco in 1949, he took such a proprietary interest in the project that he would visit the shop after its completion and correct any displays or arrangements of furnishings that conflicted with his vision of the store.

requirements often vary depending on whether you are taking over an existing store without making changes, doing extensive remodeling to an existing space, or building a new structure. It is best to find out about all the requirements that will apply to your store when you are still in the design stage. Contact your local planning department immediately, unless you will be working with an architect or store designer who is already knowledgeable about applicable regulations in your area.

Be realistic about what you decide to spend on store renovations, including design services. It is a mistake to cut corners so much that the store looks amateurish or unfinished, but many new retailers err in the opposite direction. In an attempt to look successful and well established from the start, novice retailers sometimes spend so much on fixtures and other furnishings that there is not enough money left for merchandise and the first year's operating expenses.

Many professional store designers are used to working with chain stores with deep pockets, so you should establish a realistic budget early in the design process, and assume you will go over it by 10 or 20%. You might be able to stretch your budget by purchasing some fixtures used from a store going out of business or remodeling. You may also be able to get some displays at no charge from your suppliers.

Companies sometimes create special shelving units, wire spinners, or racks for their products and offer these fixtures to stores for free or at a price offset by free merchandise. Old furniture and storage containers can be refurbished and transformed into displays. Crate & Barrel, which now has many sophisticated retail stores, started out as a small shop displaying merchandise in the crates and barrels it arrived in.

Flexibility should be a key element in the design of a new store. If you have never owned a shop before, chances are good that your store will go through several major changes in the first year or two. You will refine your merchandise selection as you learn what customers want. The checkout and storage areas, and perhaps even the store layout, will change as you see what works best for you and your staff. Look for shelves that are adjustable, fixtures that are movable, lighting that is flexible, and flooring that allows you to make layout changes easily.

Shop Design: Making the Most of Your Space

UPDATING YOUR LOOK

Few store designs are timeless. Even when your store is well established, you will need to redesign sections of it every few years to keep up with the times and to upgrade areas with a dated design concept. A stale, out-of-date store has a difficult time contending with newer competitors. Your merchandise mix will probably change over the years, you may need to bring in new technology, and perhaps you will need to expand. Remodeling can be done as a total makeover, which may require being closed for some time, or piecemeal during off-hours.

Be sure to involve your staff in remodeling plans, asking them what they think could be improved. Check sales by department to see if some product categories deserve more floor space. Look for display fixtures and ideas that you like as you attend trade shows and visit stores in other areas. Your increasing experience in retailing should make design decisions easier each time you make a change.

The Perfect Design Concept

The store's merchandise focus will largely dictate the design direction you will choose to follow. Expensive jewelry, for example, requires a more subdued and elegant setting than art supplies. Traditionally, the more luxurious the merchandise, the more spacious the open areas of the store. A narrow doorway, subtle lighting, and soft carpeting also create a feeling of exclusivity. Expensive items are usually featured in displays that highlight individual pieces rather than being massed on a shelf.

The color range of the merchandise to be featured may inspire a store design concept. I remember my first visit to the natural soaps and cosmetics shop Origins in New York. The simple packaging and ingredients of Origins products inspired a store with a modern, environmental look, incorporating blonde wood fixtures accented by a green wall. Floor-to-ceiling windows on two sides brought in lots of natural light during the day, and miniature halogen fixtures fell like stars from the ceiling to illuminate the store by night.

At the time, Crabtree & Evelyn's stores were also selling bath and body products, but their approach to store design was completely different. Inspired by the English origin of much of the company's merchandise, Crabtree & Evelyn stores had a traditional Victorian feeling, with dark wood fixtures and floral wallpaper. (Crabtree has since revised their stores to have a more contemporary look, because like all good retailers, they realize the need to keep up with changing shopper demographics.)

Some types of merchandise require special facilities, such as fitting rooms, mirrors, seating, or easy access to back stock. You may want to design a space that is flexible enough to be used for occasional classes and lectures as well as merchandise, or a display fixture that can also work as a counter for demonstrations and samplings.

Visiting other stores selling the same types of goods can give you a sense of what works best for them. Make a list of special layout needs before you begin the design process. Keep in mind that fitting rooms and other special facilities need to be handicapped accessible. The regulations for the height of the fitting room mirror, the size of the door, and other factors essential to the comfort of customers in wheelchairs are very precise.

In addition to the merchandise mix, it is important to base your store design on the types of customers you hope the store will attract. A toy store with a colorful and playful design will appeal to children and their parents. A shop selling clothes for teens might want to go with a high-tech look, with TV screens showing fashion videos.

The store design concept should encompass a color scheme and a look that can be carried through in all the elements of the store: the storefront, signage, fixtures, lighting, and merchandising. The design concept will also influence the store's advertising, product selection, and in some cases, even the way employees dress. The more clearly defined the design concept is, the stronger the shop's brand identity will be.

Shop Design: Making the Most of Your Space

Welcome: The Storefront and Entrance

Your storefront should be as engaging and attractive as possible in whatever way is appropriate to your retailing vision. The location and architecture of your store are key elements in determining the type of storefront you can consider. Stores located on shopping streets need to keep the nature of the streetscape in mind, and those in malls must conform to management's standards for storefront design. Within these parameters, it is important to create a distinctive and attractive look for your shop because the storefront is the first impression you make on passersby and will often determine whether they come through the door.

Few stores can survive without display windows, and for many, the window display is their most successful advertising. To create dynamic window displays, you need storefront windows with adequate space, easy access, several electrical outlets, a ceiling grid for suspending things, and flexible lighting. The back of these show windows can be open, with a view of the store, or closed off with a curtain, sliding glass, or a wood panel. A closed back allows more creative use of backdrops and prevents customers from reaching into the display, but an open-backed window is considered better for security purposes because it allows those walking by to see what is happening in the store.

Stores selling small items, such as jewelry, will find it easier to showcase their merchandise to passersby in smaller windows—either independent shadowbox windows, allowing for separate themed displays, or one long, narrow window at a good viewing level for pedestrians. If valuables will need to be removed from the window at night for security purposes, the backs of the displays should provide easy access for staff, but not for customers. For ideas about in-store merchandise display, see Chapter 7.

The location and accessibility of the door may influence whether people decide to enter the store. Some mall stores have wide, open entrances that span almost the entire storefront, in contrast to the locked and guarded doors of exclusive jewelry or antique stores. The nature of the doorway can communicate a great deal about the store's range of merchandise and prices. In an area without a large base of wealthy shoppers, creating a store entrance that intimidates the average customer would be a mistake. Most people judge a store's level of exclusivity from its exterior and might not go inside to see whether the shop's merchandise actually happens to be within their price range.

Stores with parking lots or even sidewalk space have an added opportunity to create a pleasing first impression. Build a low fence around your parking area, and landscape it with flowers and bushes. Place pots of flowering plants by the store entrance or flower boxes under the display windows. In the winter, hang small white string- or net-lights in any trees and bushes near your store. Be sure to allow for enough electrical outlets for seasonal lighting when planning your landscaping.

SIGNS AND AWNINGS

Good signage is an essential part of any store's advertising program, communicating a quick message about the store to all those who drive or walk by. An effective sign, well lit, is an important part of the store image, especially for stores that are not in a mall. The store's signage or awnings and the design of the logo and graphics should complement the overall design concept to make a clear statement of the store's brand identity.

Determine whether your community has specific codes about what types of signs and awnings are permissible before commissioning this work or any other exterior changes. At our store, we were surprised to learn that technically, we are not even allowed to take down our sign to clean it without getting a permit from the city.

A free-hanging "blade" sign, hung perpendicular to the store, can be an effective way to catch the attention of pedestrians. Most stores also need a sign across the front of the store, or by the entrance, that gives the name of the store and perhaps a brief tagline describing what it sells.

The material and type style (font) used for the main sign should be in keeping with the image you are trying to develop for the shop. You might paint the name on wood or purchase an illuminated box sign with the name or logo applied to a sheet of opaque plastic that is lit from behind.

Another way of writing the store name is to use individual letters, like the gold ones we found for our storefront. These sturdy letters look as if they are made of painted wood, but are actually durable plastic. Other signs use separate letters that are illuminated from behind, giving good visibility at night and an attractive appearance during the day.

One popular trend is to feature the name of the store on an awning, either a retractable one intended for rain and sun protection or a permanent architectural feature used to add character to a storefront. Permanent awnings can be quite effective as a facelift for an older building and can be lit from inside or above. Awnings do detract somewhat from the visibility of the store windows, which should be taken into account when deciding whether to use them.

Neon logo and name signs can be an effective design element on a storefront or in a window if the bright look of neon is in keeping with your store image. Neon is visible from some distance and comes in a wide variety of colors that can echo the color scheme used in the store. Neon in the window should be hung high enough that it will not interfere with window displays, because it is not easy to move once it is in place. Some store design specialists claim that a neon open sign can be one of the most important features in a store's window. Certainly freestanding stores open evening and weekend hours may want to promote this fact with a lit "open" sign. Be sure to keep all sections of any neon sign functioning at all times; a burned-out letter or two makes a poor first impression.

Can your store be seen from the side, as well as the front? This presents an added opportunity for signage or, perhaps, an attractive mural that incorporates the store name. Although the store has moved to suburban Edina, many people remember Schmitt Music Center's Minneapolis location for its huge painting of sheet music by Maurice Ravel on the side of its building.

If your shop is located on a neighborhood street, check sign ordinances to see if you are allowed to place a sandwich-board sign between the sidewalk and the curb. This sign can state the name of the shop and the fact that you are open, or it can include a chalkboard area to announce daily specials. Stores set back from the street or on an upper level may be able to arrange for a signpost near the sidewalk with information about the store.

Stores not in malls need to feature their street number in large letters on the storefront or on or above the door. Customers often have difficulty finding a certain address because many stores don't use numbers large enough to be seen from a car. There should also be a sign on the door saying "Welcome" and giving the store hours. Make your own hours sign if those that are commercially available are not in keeping with the image you are trying to create.

THE ENTRANCEWAY

Paco Underhill, in his important work on the science of shopping entitled *Why We Buy: The Science of Shopping*, emphasizes the importance of the transition zone when customers first enter the store and have not yet adjusted to the lighting level, aroma, scale, and temperature of the shop. "Whatever is in the zone they cross before making the transition from outside to inside is pretty much lost on them," according to Underhill.

He feels particularly strongly that shopping baskets should not be placed in this entryway, but rather should be accessible to shoppers once they have their hands full. "Put a stack of shopping baskets just inside the door. Shoppers will barely see them, and will almost never pick them

Shop Design: Making the Most of Your Space

A spacious, inviting entryway welcomes customers into Sweet Twist, Greenwich, Rhode Island. (Photo courtesy of Sheila Vinacco)

up. Move them 10 feet in and the baskets will disappear." It also helps to offer a shopping basket to any customers holding three or more items, and Underhill's studies show that customers will almost always accept this offer and buy more.

After reading *Why We Buy* (a book I highly recommend to all retailers), we purchased larger shopping baskets for our customers, having noticed shoppers tend to stop shopping when the basket is full. This did indeed lead to an increase in sales. Having small shopping carts, if you have room, will encourage even larger purchases. Some stores have had great success with nylon shopping totes that can be carried over the shoulder. Have your sales associates carry a supply of the totes as they move through the store, offering them as needed.

SPECIALTY SHOP RETAILING

Efficient Layout Plans

Once the customer walks through the entranceway, the layout of the displays and other fixtures will influence the path he or she takes through the store. Although shoppers today value an efficient and convenient shopping experience, it is not in your best interest to create a layout that customers can scan too quickly. Instead, you want to lead them from one fascinating area to another on a pleasurable voyage of discovery. Paco Underhill notes, "Our studies prove that the longer a shopper remains in a store, the more he or she will buy. And the amount of time a shopper spends in a store depends on how comfortable and enjoyable the experience is."

If your retail space is rectangular, you may be tempted to line up displays parallel to the walls, forming orderly, straight aisles. This grid layout is fine for grocery or convenience stores, but it is too boring for specialty shops concerned with creating an interesting atmosphere. Try putting up partial partitions perpendicular to the walls, forming small display alcoves, or setting up new walls extending out from the existing walls in a zigzag pattern. Freestanding displays can be used to break up a rectangle into smaller spaces that invite shoppers to explore.

Although you don't want to create totally hidden nooks and crannies that are tempting to shoplifters, you do want to give the impression that the store has more to it than can be seen at a quick glance. In a mall, it is especially important to create an eye-catching display against the back wall to draw shoppers all the way into your store.

Traditional wisdom has it that most customers turn to the right when they enter a store, at least in countries where cars drive on the right. This can be helpful in deciding what merchandise to feature in that key area. Large stores sometimes use an oval racetrack of vinyl flooring to lead customers through the store, counterclockwise, with merchandise displays off to the right and left of the oval in carpeted areas.

Shop Design: Making the Most of Your Space

When laying out the floor plan, keep in mind that customers in wheelchairs or pushing strollers need to be able to negotiate the aisles and the spaces between displays. Apparel stores especially tend to pack too many fixtures into a small space, making it difficult for anyone to get through, let alone browse comfortably.

Paco Underhill relates his theory of the "butt-brush effect" in *Why We Buy*, claiming that evidence proves shoppers will not linger in any aisle so narrow that someone might bump or brush into them when they lean over to examine merchandise. He also makes the valid observation that products intended for less agile shoppers (senior citizens, for example) should be placed higher up on displays, rather than at floor level. Plan for 36 inches of clearance on all sides of your displays, keeping in mind that clothing hangers and merchandise often extend out from the display unit itself. Good store design shows respect for customers' comfort and highlights the merchandise to its best advantage.

The location of amenities, such as the checkout counter, should be determined early in the layout process. There are many factors to take into account in deciding what shape to make this counter and where to put it. Some security-minded stores build central, elevated round "checkout fortresses." These allow staff to view shoppers throughout the store but are a barrier to staff interaction with customers.

Ideally, sales associates should be able to get out from behind the counter easily to assist customers. A checkout counter placed in the back of a small store allows staff to see customers entering the store but may allow shoplifters to make a quick retreat with merchandise stolen from displays near the entrance. A checkout counter located too close to the entrance, on the other hand, does not invite shoppers to come in and browse. For most stores, the best solution is to locate one or more checkouts part way into the store, but not so far back that the sales associates at the counter cannot greet customers soon after they enter.

WELL-GROUNDED: FLOORING MATERIALS

The path the customer takes through the store can be influenced by the flooring you choose. Vinyl, rubber, wood, or linoleum is often used in entranceways and checkout areas. When used to highlight heavily trafficked paths through the store, this hard flooring delineates the route the shopper is expected to take. These types of flooring are easier to maintain than carpeting and can be covered with rented mats in inclement weather. Rental mat service costs more than owning your own floor mats, but we love having our service pick up our wet and muddy mats on Friday and replace them with clean, dry ones—almost like diaper delivery service, and every bit as welcome.

Carpeting creates a feeling of luxury and may be used throughout the store or just in display areas. Nylon carpets with a low pile are durable and will last many years if cleaned regularly. Be sure to buy high-quality, commercial-grade carpeting, and select a shade and blend or pattern (not a solid color) that will not readily show dirt. You want something that will last a long time, since installing new carpeting requires dismantling most of the fixtures in the store unless you have planned ahead with moveable units.

Keep handicapped and low-vision customers in mind when selecting your flooring. Dense, short-pile carpeting is easier than other types of carpeting for those in wheelchairs. And changes in surface texture help signal a step up or a ramp for those with vision problems.

THE BACKDROP: WALL TREATMENTS

The walls of a shop usually are used to form a neutral backdrop for the merchandise and fixtures. Some merchandise, however, needs a bright background to liven it up. Dramatic wall treatments, including murals, can also be used to draw attention to displays of small items such as shoes. Walls of different colors can be used to distinguish one area of the store from another, but, of course, these colors must be well coordinated.

Shop Design: Making the Most of Your Space

Most recently built or remodeled stores start out with walls of plain drywall, a surface that takes well to paint or wallpaper. Some stores paint their walls in a strong color, others leave the walls a light, neutral color that does not overpower the merchandise. A compromise is to have one accent wall or areas around the top of the walls painted in a distinctive color, while the rest of the walls are neutral. These accent areas can be repainted or wallpapered periodically to reflect changes in the seasons or in color trends of merchandise, giving the store a fresh look.

Brick or block walls, usually found in older buildings, add warmth and character to a store but are difficult to drill into. Freestanding display fixtures work best in this situation, along with a rail along the top of the wall that allows you to attach wires for hanging pictures, posters, and banners.

The hanging shelves at Pod in Cambridge, Massachusetts make great use of the shop's vintage brickwork as a background. (Photo courtesy of Julie Baine)

Wood paneling is a warm, comfortable wall surface but does not allow for easy change and can overpower rather than complement some merchandise. Fabric panels that can be taken down and recovered are more versatile and can give the store a whole new look each time the color scheme is changed.

Lighting for Effect and Energy Efficiency

The correct choice of lighting is essential to setting the store's mood and displaying merchandise to its best advantage. Visiting a variety of stores to see what type of lighting is used can be very helpful, because most of us don't normally pay conscious attention to this detail. You will notice that most grocery and discount stores use economical, bright fluorescent or high-intensity discharge (HID) lighting. Specialty shops are more likely to use compact fluorescent bulbs (CFLs), halogen lights, and light-emitting diode (LED) lamps.

Keep in mind energy costs and the environment when selecting your lighting: CFLs are significantly more efficient than halogen lighting. Halogen lights emit more heat than LEDs and last a considerably shorter time, but the color of the light may be more pleasing.

You will most likely have a variety of lighting needs in your store:

- General or ambient lighting
- Accent lighting
- Task lighting

Fluorescent lights, especially full-spectrum bulbs designed to resemble daylight, work well in areas needing general or ambient lighting. Fluorescents are energy efficient and require less maintenance than other types of bulbs. Some stores use compact fluorescents or tubes in a valance around the perimeter walls and also overhead to give general lighting, with spotlights to highlight merchandise and show the true color of the goods.

Many smaller shops avoid fluorescents altogether, except in storage and work areas, finding that subdued lighting is one factor that helps distinguish a specialty shop from the glaring, impersonal feeling of a big-box discounter. A few, however, go too far in trying to appear intimate or exclusive and create a dark, uninviting space. A store needs to look as if it is open for business. Excessively dim lighting is intimidating and makes it difficult for customers to see the merchandise.

Accent lighting needs to be adjustable to focus on your merchandise displays. Track lighting is a versatile option that can be attached to fixed rails on the ceiling or wall, or on hanging parallel wires. In our store, we use CFL reflector floodlights or spotlights in inexpensive clamp-on fixtures attached to the ceiling grids throughout the store. For certain merchandise, such as glassware and silver, we use special low-voltage halogen MR (multifaceted reflector) bulbs that enhance the sparkle of these items. Another advantage of these full-spectrum halogen bulbs is that they are excellent for true color rendering, with a CRI (color rendering index) of 85+. When focusing lighting on a display, be sure to provide enough light for the customer to see details, such as the price and description, and avoid shadows and glare.

In addition to ambient and merchandise illumination, lighting is needed for specialized task areas, such as the checkout counter. Suspended pendants, for example small halogens or LEDs, are an attractive way to demarcate and illuminate these areas. Be sure that lights in work areas do not shine in anyone's eyes or force a standing customer or seated employee to look at an exposed bulb.

Ideally, natural light should be used some of the time, saving energy and showing merchandise exactly as it will look outside the store. But natural light can be a challenge to work with unless you live in a dependably sunny climate, and even then, you will need operable window shades to prevent sun that is too strong. Natural light requires that you have supplementary lighting available for rainy days and for after sunset. We use a timer on the lights in our display windows so they are only illuminated from dusk to early morning, but we have not yet managed to adjust our interior lighting to the ever-changing Wisconsin weather.

Emergency lighting should be set up at the same time that your lighting system is installed. Exit lights are available with battery backups so that they will remain illuminated during a power outage. You may also want to install self-charging, battery-operated lights that will maintain at least a minimal amount of lighting in an emergency. All shops should have a few working flashlights on hand, along with a battery-operated radio.

Store designers are usually very knowledgeable about the special lighting needs of a retail environment. Other sources of information include display fixture companies, wholesale suppliers of light bulbs, and your local electric utility. Home improvement stores selling light fixtures for homes may have many types of lighting that you can use, but you cannot count on the sales staff knowing much about retail lighting. You will also find it helpful to work with an electrician experienced in commercial, not just residential, installation.

Some localities require commercial users to submit calculations of their proposed energy usage, which will affect your lighting options. Be sure to check with your local energy agency before purchasing light fixtures. You may be pleased to discover that you can reduce your energy costs by carefully selecting the types of bulbs you use.

A Different Kind of Overhead: Ceilings

The type of lighting you choose will strongly influence the ceiling treatment that works best in your store. We painted our ceilings black, with a wooden grid hanging a few feet below to hold our metal reflector clamp lights. Track lighting tends to look best attached to a solid ceiling painted a neutral color. Acoustic tile with built-in fluorescent fixtures is not particularly exciting, but may work well in areas where it is not necessary to focus lighting on merchandise displays.

Older buildings with high ceilings pose a special challenge. If the ceiling is attractive—for example, an antique tin ceiling—consider leaving it exposed, but focus customers' attention on merchandise at eye level by using lots of small droplights, a wooden grid, or a wire system with track lighting. Pipes, wiring, and other exposed utilities on the ceiling can be painted black so they disappear, or they can become part of the store decor. Very high ceilings may create the feeling of an impersonal, unfriendly space, so it is important to keep lighting and displays at a height that is comfortable for the average shopper.

Selling on Several Levels

Stores with a balcony, mezzanine, or upper level face a special challenge. Customers are much more likely to browse on the main floor on impulse, but to get anyone to go up a flight of stairs, there must be special motivation. Upper levels are best used for merchandise that customers have specifically come in for and for which they are willing to make an extra effort.

Good signage is essential to draw customers to an upper level, and it is important that sales assistance be available once the customer has climbed the stairs. We have a workstation on the second floor so we can make good use of the time between customers, but shoppers are sometimes reluctant to ask us for help if we are working there, despite the large "customer assistance" sign above the desk.

Using a second floor as retail space poses two main drawbacks. The first is that customers who are physically challenged find it difficult or impossible to come upstairs unless there is an elevator, so of course, that level is not ADA compliant. And shoplifting is a greater problem upstairs because there are usually fewer customers and sales associates present. We now have a motion detector (designed for homes with a non-hearing resident) that subtly flashes to alert us when someone goes up the stairs.

Fixtures for Maximal Merchandising

Some retailers view store layout as an exact science, with the location and number of square feet allotted to each merchandise department determined by the dollar volume and profitability of that area. Others like store design to be a bit more spontaneous. You don't know from the outset which merchandise categories will be the most popular anyway, and customers often enjoy an element of serendipity. The store that develops somewhat organically can easily adapt to trends in merchandising and decide at any time to allot more space to a department showing a major increase in sales.

A good store layout and exciting displays will lead customers through the entire shop, so the only really key decision is what to place in the front of the store to draw shoppers in. Front displays should make a statement about the store and what it has to offer. Never put clearance merchandise in the front part of the store, unless you are promoting price above selection or quality.

HIGHLIGHTING SPECIAL ITEMS

There are two basic approaches to displaying merchandise: showcasing a few examples of each item, with more in back stock, or massing the items out for self-service. We live in an era of mass merchandising, and most retail stores put as much merchandise as possible on the selling floor. This cuts down on storage costs and customer service expense, but it is not the best way for all stores to show all merchandise. In general, the more expensive the item, the fewer you should have on display. Highlighting a single sample of an item makes it seem special. This exclusivity is a positive selling point for jewelry, art, craft items, designer clothing, antiques, and other high-end merchandise.

The types of fixtures used for single-item display are different from those designed to hold as much as possible. Locked showcases are necessary for the security of very expensive items. Keep the keys to these showcases in a place accessible only to staff, and be sure to have a second set in case the keys are misplaced. A large, unusual object used as the key ring may help keep a thief from pocketing the showcase keys—and prevent staff members from inadvertently leaving them where they don't belong.

For unique products that do not need to be under lock and key, glass shelving may work best. It allows light to focus on the item from all four sides and can be attached to the wall or built-in shelf units or used in freestanding standards made of wood or metal. Display systems made up of glass cubes are generally adjustable and versatile in their display uses. The

> Søstrene Grene, an innovative Copenhagen shop selling an eclectic mix of inexpensive gifts, foods, art supplies and home decor, makes humorous use of locked glass display cases by playfully spotlighting a single sample of two or three $1.00 items as if they were precious gems.

one disadvantage to using glass is that it shows dust and fingerprints easily and needs constant attention to prevent customers from seeing telltale outlines when they pick up items to examine them.

Many stores use furniture to display their products, creating settings that help customers imagine how the merchandise might look in their own homes. The warm color of wooden furniture makes an excellent background for many items, and tables and bookshelves can be accessorized with runners, tablecloths, or other fabric to change their look throughout the year. The main drawbacks to using furniture are that most étagères and hutches lack the adjustability one looks for in a display fixture, and large tables can take up a lot of floor space without allowing for merchandise to be displayed above or below the tabletop level. Some stores offer the furniture they display merchandise on for sale, getting double duty out of their display space (though you may face a display crisis if a customer decides to buy a key fixture).

If you are trying to outfit your store as economically as possible, be sure to check used and unfinished furniture stores, as well as fixture sales by stores that are closing or remodeling. One of our favorite sources of shelving for the store is IKEA. They have some fixtures specifically

Mabel's on 4th in Tucscon, Arizona uses antique appliances, like this vintage stove, to create a fun ambiance in their kitchen boutique. (Photo courtesy of Nicole Carrillo)

designed for small retail shops in their product mix, as well as many home products that will work.

Mass Merchandising

Mass merchandising need not be unattractive. The repetition of one item many times over can create a pleasing pattern, especially if attention is paid to color placement and to making sure the display is always full and neat. The customer looking at a massed display gets the impression that the store believes strongly in an item (otherwise why would there be so many of them?) and that the item is probably not very expensive. Many customers appreciate the fact that a massed display allows them to help themselves rather than looking for a sales associate for help.

Glass fixtures and wood furniture can, of course, also be used to put out large quantities of each item. Mass merchandising traditionally uses fixtures such as wall systems, wire grid cubes, rounders (circular clothing racks), bins, and the omnipresent gondola, a freestanding display with adjustable shelving along the two long sides and merchandise on the end caps as well.

Creative alternatives to traditional shelves and racks can give your store a unique look. We have used terra-cotta pipes and clay flower pots to show merchandise, as well as heavy plastic buckets and tubs. We use lots of baskets in our displays, most of which are also for sale.

Many stores use pedestals of various heights to display merchandise and find that these units are also useful in window displays. Small, round display tables can be found in inexpensive versions made of particleboard, or even cardboard and plastic, and covered in a wardrobe of tablecloths to match the season or the merchandise. Basic platforms, raised a few inches off the floor, help highlight big stacks of packaged merchandise being massed on display, a technique colorfully referred to as tonnage.

In displaying clothing, the use of varied heights also effectively highlights fashionable merchandise. Instead of rounders, which display everything in a circle, all at the same level, consider waterfalls, t-stands, and wall units with hooks at various heights.

WALL UNITS

There are several systems for using walls and the back panels of gondolas to hold hooks and shelves. Slatwall, a grooved panel system available in many wood, laminate, mirror, or paintable finishes, is a current favorite for specialty shop retailers. A wide variety of hooks, clothing merchandisers, acrylic shelves, and bins are available to hook into slatwall.

Slatwall allows displays to be changed quickly and easily, although the surface color of the slatwall itself may be more difficult to alter if it is made of one of the durable laminated materials. Slatwall can be put around a column to take advantage of space that might otherwise go to waste. There are also slatwall spinners that can be used with shallow shelves or short hooks to create compact but effective displayers for small items.

One drawback to slatwall is that its horizontal pattern can be monotonous if overused. Areas of slatwall need to be broken up by occasional flat surfaces or other textures or patterns. Another drawback is that slatwall is so ubiquitous that it doesn't look fresh and original. Take a look at some of the alternatives now available, including strips that take slatwall hooks and brackets but don't cover the wall's entire surface.

Wire grid systems can be used to hang merchandise on hooks or hangers, either as a free-hanging display panel or up against a wall. A hardware store, for instance, could hang a wire grid panel with work gloves and gardening gloves clipped onto both sides. We have grids hanging from the ceiling to show our line of stainless ladles, tongs, and spatulas, and keep a few extra on hand for customers who want to use the same idea to store the utensils in their own kitchen.

Remember that whatever fixtures you choose, the merchandise should remain the primary focus. Display fixtures should allow the goods to be displayed attractively and help keep them neat. Traditionally, shelving for massed merchandise is adjusted so there is a standard two-inch space between the items and the shelf above. This is not practical when a shelf is used for an assortment of merchandise of varying heights, but it can be used to create an efficient and attractive display of uniform items.

Interior Signage that Sells

A thorough design plan should include interior graphics that reinforce the store's name and logo and point customers toward the restroom and various merchandise departments. If you carry brand-name merchandise, each vendor's familiar logo may be a positive selling point when featured in your signage, and companies sometimes help pay for this type of sign. Signs can be painted on hanging panels or directly on the walls. Fabric banners are an effective way to highlight seasonal merchandise. They add color to the store and can easily be changed.

Consider painting the store name or logo on the wall behind the cash register and using your logo and logo typestyle for signs throughout the store. We discovered that the hand-painted pub-style sign we had made for us in England couldn't survive outside in the harsh midwestern winters, so we display it over a fireplace mantle inside the store. It is surprising how many customers, even with a visual cue like this, still aren't sure what store they are in. Word-of-mouth advertising is the best kind, so it's important that customers know and remember your store name so they can mention it to their friends.

SHELF TALKERS

Many shops show great care in selecting coordinated display fixtures but forget to pay attention to the need for a well-designed program of product information signs throughout the store. The official retailing term for these signs is *shelf talkers*, because they communicate prices, sizes, and the benefits of the products to shoppers. You can never have enough sales staff to explain every item to every customer. Signs that are beautifully made and thoughtfully worded can give the impression that you are speaking directly to the shoppers, telling them what you'd like them to know.

A visit to a dozen specialty shops in New York's SoHo district reveals that almost every shop has a distinctive look for its shelf talkers. Each store uses a recognizable background paper, typestyle, and frame for its signs. Careful thought has obviously been given to selecting a look consistent with that shop's decor. A garden accessories store uses natural kraft paper signs with its logo at the top, whereas a bed linen shop prints display signs on a paper with a subtle floral pattern.

Display signs can be strictly factual, giving the sizes and prices for each item, announcing new arrivals, or highlighting a sale. But some of the best point of purchase (POP) signs are almost conversational in tone, pointing out the virtues of a product and telling the customer something about where the item was made or about the craftsperson or tradition behind the product. Think of what you would say about the item if you were enthusiastically describing it to a customer or writing about it in a catalog.

For handmade and imported items, consider having copies of some of your signage in a file at the checkout counter to include when the item is being given as a gift. That way, you can tell the product's background story to the recipient as well. Don't forget to put your store name and logo at the bottom.

Shop Design: Making the Most of Your Space

WorldFinds Fair Trade provides shelf talkers at no charge to its retail accounts to help convey the story of their fair trade items, such as Kantha cloth jewelry and accessories. (Courtesy of Kelly Weinberger)

What is **Kantha?**

- Quilts handmade in India using cotton sari scraps
- One-of-a-kind fabrics
- Distinctive allover running stitch
- Repurposed into modern accessories
- Fair trade made
- Supports artisans and communities

Our artisans repurpose these traditional quilts and hand-sew them into unique, modern accessories.

WorldFinds is a proud member of the Fair Trade Federation

Bookshops often use shelf talkers to tell customers which selections are their staff's favorites, and we've recently started doing this in our store. Shoppers especially appreciate this service when it includes a few lines by the employees expanding on their recommendations.

We have developed standard signs with our logo on them that we keep in a file on our computer. We add the text and print them on white card stock, inserting them into inexpensive acrylic frames or laminating them using self-adhesive sheets or our small laminating machine. It's an easy way to have all the signs in the store present the same look.

You might also want to purchase a Brother P-Touch labeler, which allows you to print out strips of words in neat black or colored type on self-adhesive tape that is either clear or white. We use our P-Touch machine to label shelves and to put descriptions or prices on display samples of products.

Checking Out the Cash Wrap Area

Every detail in the planning of the customer's side of the checkout area (also called the cash wrap counter) should contribute to making the experience of buying something from your store simple and pleasant. Sales associates will spend much of their time on the other side of the counter, so careful attention to planning the behind-the-counter area will pay off in a more efficient and contented staff.

The height of the check-writing area of the counter is usually 42 inches; however, this is too high for customers in wheelchairs. Providing one counter 29 to 36 inches high or a pullout shelf at wheelchair level is a courtesy to disabled customers; in addition, it may be required by local building codes and is specified in the Americans with Disabilities Act. Find out about these regulations before finalizing your design.

For the comfort of employees, some stores have the customers' side of the counter at standard height and the sales associates' work area behind it somewhat lower so the employee can either be seated on a stool or standing while ringing up purchases, bagging, and wrapping.

You should also take into account whether the design of the counter and the area behind it would allow an employee in a wheelchair to wait on customers. The Americans with Disabilities Act, together with local and state building codes, requires that efforts be made to create equal access to jobs for all potential employees.

The length of the counter is determined by how many POS systems/ cash registers will be on the counter, as well as any additional equipment such as scanners and credit card data capture units. Because there is no way to predict the future of retail technology, it is wise to allow extra space and electrical outlets for changes. Also be sure to allow ample room on the counter for the customers' merchandise, especially if you intend to have small displays of impulse items by the register. The front of the checkout counter can be used for shallow shelves or even recessed slatwall with short pegs holding small items.

BEHIND THE COUNTER

Comfort and safety are primary concerns for the employee side of the counter. Flooring should be easy on the feet, and stools should be provided for occasional rest breaks. To discourage money theft, the area directly adjacent to the cash register drawer should be accessible only to staff. A telephone or intercom for easy communication with other parts of the store should be within easy reach.

The back side of the checkout counter is often used to store sheets of tissue, a bin of shredded tissue for cushioning items being boxed, flat merchandise bags, and gift boxes. The more shelves you have, the better for separating gift box sizes so that each size has its own compartment. Staff members can then put their hands on the right size box or lid in a hurry, and restocking these supplies every day is easy. Shopping bags can also be stored under the counter or hung nearby.

If there are two checkout stations at the same counter, the most commonly used supplies should be duplicated on each side so sales personnel don't have to reach across each other to access them. It is also useful to keep pens, paper clips, staplers, additional register tape, scissors, tape, notepaper, tissues, customer request forms, and business cards under the counter, along with a waste basket and recycling bin.

Additional supplies for boxing and wrapping are often located in an adjacent counter area or behind the checkout counter. Stores that sell many items that need to be wrapped in tissue paper may wish to have a slightly lower well in the wrap counter to fill to counter level with a stack of ready-to-use tissue sheets. Spools of ribbons and rolls of paper for gift wrapping can be hung on the wall behind the register, together with gift wrap samples for customers to choose from. Remember that any area that is visible to customers must be kept neat and attractive.

We put merchandise in boxes behind the checkout counter but have our gift wrapping department located elsewhere in the store. We try to make the best use of limited space in our small building, and there just isn't room for rolls of wrap behind the counter. Customers don't seem to mind having to go to another part of the store to have packages wrapped, and this does cut down on the congestion around the checkout counter when we are really busy. Some stores that normally do gift wrap behind the counter set up a second wrapping area during the hectic holiday season.

A filing cabinet behind the checkout counter is useful for storing frequently consulted product information files, as well as wedding registries and forms for services such as shipping, customer reward programs, gift cards, and special orders. We also keep a folder for each employee in the cabinet behind the counter (mostly for payroll receipts, notes, and newsletters) and a file for concert tickets we have agreed to sell for local arts groups.

We keep a change box with rolls of coins in a cabinet behind the checkout counter. When a register needs change, a sales associate "buys" a roll from this change box with money from the till.

During the slower months, our sales staff occasionally checks in merchandise behind the counter. This lightens the workload of the stock staff and also makes the time go by faster when there are not many customers to wait on. We try to keep a work surface clear for this activity and have all the supplies for pricing nearby. A large shipment can make quite a mess behind the counter, so ideally only small orders are brought up to be worked on. It is a challenge to be ready to help customers at any moment while also unpacking merchandise, but we emphasize to the staff that no matter what else they are doing, customer service is always their top priority.

Shop Design: Making the Most of Your Space

Signage near the checkout counter should promote gift cards, gift wrapping, and any other special services. There should be a sign explaining the store's return policy and indicating which credit cards you accept. Have a supply of business cards on hand and lots of pens for customers to use when writing checks or signing charge card receipts. We keep a self-inking endorsement stamp by the register to stamp the back of each check as we receive it, saving us time at the end of the day and preventing anyone from being able to steal and cash our checks.

Store Security Concerns

In addition to making sure that your checkout counter is well located for the security and comfort of your staff, you may want to take measures to protect your store from shoplifting, a crime that is unfortunately a fact of life for all retailers. If you plan to carry very expensive (or easily resold) items, you'll want to install shoplifting sensors in your entranceway, which will limit its width. Products being protected by the system will need to have reusable hard tags attached to them to be removed upon purchase or some other encoding that will set off the sensor if not deactivated.

You might also want to have a video security system scanning the store at all times with these images viewable in a back office and stored on videotape in case of a crime. (These cameras are also now being used by some corporate retailers to check up on their sales staff's activities.) Video security systems and exit sensors are both available in an inexpensive dummy form that may deter some shoplifters, as do convex and domed mirrors that help you see into blind areas.

Don't forget to look into smoke alarms, sprinklers, and emergency exit lights in case of fire and an alarm system for after-hours protection. You may also want to build in a safe or other locked location for storing cash. Many of these issues are discussed in Chapter 15.

SPECIALTY SHOP RETAILING

Background Music for Shopping Pleasure

Stores should not be silent. Customers feel self-conscious walking into a quiet space, intimidated by the fact that the sales staff can hear every word they say. Background music not only helps customers relax but also can help create a memorable atmosphere that reinforces your store image. The music you choose should be pleasing to the majority of your customers and agreeable to your staff. Because staff members listen to the background music for hours and hours, it is important to have a large selection of management-approved music to help prevent audio boredom. Music choice and volume level should not be left up to chance or the staff's whim.

What type of music is best for your shop? Some specialty shops will be able to find music that carries out the store's theme, such as seasonal music for a Christmas shop or soothing music with nature sounds for a New Age store. Others will need to look at what type of music creates the best mood for their customers. Studies have shown that instrumental music is in general less distracting than vocals, although customers might be drawn into a shop selling retro clothing by the sound of Billie Holiday singing the blues.

The volume level is a crucial factor in creating a pleasing audio atmosphere. Music should not distract customers from their shopping or intrude on conversation. Nor should it be so quiet that it can barely be heard.

You won't want to play a commercial radio station in the background, with ads, news, weather, and announcer chitchat. If you have WiFi in your store there are various paid online services that will provide a variety of music all day long based on the genre you prefer. Note that consumer subscription services, such as Pandora, are not licensed for commercial settings (or for bowling, skating or organized dancing, it turns out), but in some cases, they have a separate arrangement with additional fees that include the necessary permissions.

Shop Design: Making the Most of Your Space

We have uploaded hundreds of musical tracks from CDs that we own that include a wide range of piano music, light jazz, instrumental classics, and folk tunes. These are played using the shuffle feature of an iPad so that we hear a random sampling from the whole collection throughout the week.

But playing this music in the store brings up the thorny issue of paying for the rights to use the recordings commercially. Technically, a store playing the radio or a computer playlist is required to pay an annual licensing fee to either ASCAP or BMI or both. These fees, which go to the artists whose music you are playing, are based on the number of speakers used in the store. The only legal way to avoid paying for licensing is to sign up for a subscription music service that will procure these rights for you.

Creating an Aromatic Environment

The effect of fragrance on the mind is not widely acknowledged, and few stores use fragrance to create atmosphere unless the scent is from a product being sold. We all know that customers can be turned off by too strong a fragrance, such as burning incense, either because they are allergic, dislike the aroma, or because they don't wish to have it clinging to their clothes when they leave the store.

> Anita Roddick of The Body Shop sprayed strawberry essence on the sidewalk leading up to her first shop to attract the public's attention.

A pleasant, light aroma is known to have a pleasing effect on most people. The scent of pine can help create the right atmosphere in a Christmas shop, even if the weather outside says summer. A shop promoting bathing suits in the winter could use a sea-scented spray to help set the mood. Potpourri, room spray, and diffusers are all options for establishing a subtle aroma in a store.

Storage and Shipping Space

The high cost per square foot of many retail locations makes it tempting to devote almost every inch to the sales floor to maximize display space. Certainly the area devoted to merchandise is the most important part of a shop, but few stores could survive without an unloading area, storage space, and an office.

A shop can never have enough storage space. It is not a luxury; rather, storage space is often a key to good customer service. Customers find it frustrating when a store is out of an item they want. Adequate storage space allows the store to carry enough depth of stock in key items to prevent outages that result in lost sales. Of course, too much storage space can encourage costly stockpiling of merchandise, but few retailers feel that they have enough storage room, especially on site.

Many stores with multiple locations take advantage of less expensive storage in a nonretail area and supply each store's needs from a central warehouse. Individual stores also sometimes find space in another location, such as commercial rental storage units, to store merchandise, displays, and supplies. Be sure to check your insurance coverage for any items stored off premises, even if the storage is in your own garage or basement.

Keep storage areas clean and neat, with aisles clear for employees carrying boxes of merchandise. A messy stockroom can be a fire hazard, as well as an inefficient way of keeping merchandise accessible and in perfect, salable condition.

Stock arriving by truck should not come in through the front of the store, and there should be a place for unpacking merchandise without making a mess on the sales floor. Ideally, the space for unpacking merchandise should be located near the freight entrance and should be roomy enough to accommodate new arrivals, as well as merchandise not yet checked in. Supplies such as price guns, tags, pens, box-cutters, and forms for checking in and routing merchandise should be close at hand, with bins for sorting trash and recyclables nearby.

A store also needs a place to keep supplies, such as brooms, vacuum cleaners, and (in our climate) snow shovels. Cleaning supplies that may contain harmful chemicals should not be stored unlocked in a bathroom available for customer use. Trash and recycling awaiting removal needs a place to be stored. Shops sometimes find that trash left outside is gone through by people looking for discarded merchandise, and occasionally dishonest employees stash merchandise in a dumpster to be picked up by an accomplice after the store has closed. A locked bin for general trash and a dumpster for recyclable paper and cardboard may be the solution.

If you are planning to do much business on the Internet or to regularly ship customers' purchases, you will need a shipping area with cartons, packing materials, and a method of labeling packages. For frequent shippers, it is most efficient to integrate your computer program with the shipping function so that address labels, packing lists, and shipping information are all generated through the same system. Check with the US Postal Service, FedEx, and UPS to see what they have to offer.

Restrooms, Offices, and Other Backstage Needs

Customers and staff alike appreciate access to a clean restroom. In most states, stores are required to provide a restroom easily accessible to customers and large enough for use by someone in a wheelchair. The restroom should have a safety bar and other features specified by the Americans with Disabilities Act.

A comfortable and efficient office, stock area, and employee break room make for a happy bookkeeping, buying, and stockperson staff. But few stores, including ours, have enough room to make these areas as spacious as they should be. Remodeling money tends to get put first into the parts of the store where customers can see it.

In designing behind-the-scenes spaces, remember that staff members need a place to eat lunch and to keep their coats and other personal items. We keep a small refrigerator stocked with cans of soda for our staff and a microwave for heating up lunches. If you have room, it is a good idea to provide individual lockers (with locks) for employees' purses and other personal possessions.

QUIET TIMES

You will probably spend as much time at your store as you do at home, at least during the first few years, so include a few amenities to make your life more comfortable. A small kitchen area with a refrigerator, microwave, and sink will be appreciated by your staff as well. Make sure there is a place to relax, with comfortable seating and good reading light.

During the day, the store belongs to the public, but in the early morning or late evening, it's all yours. Enjoy the calm and solitude and the opportunity to get some work done without the distractions of customers and staff. There's no reason not to have a pair of bunny slippers tucked under your desk and a collection of favorite music to listen to when you're working late.

CHAPTER 5
MERCHANDISE BUYING:
GATHERING THE GOODS

A local discount appliance store used to boast, "How do we do it? We buy right!" The key to keeping retail prices down and profit margins up is indeed to buy right. Good customer service also hinges on good buying because you need to have what customers want, when they want it. Even an experienced buyer can never get complacent, because this task requires that you are constantly aware of changes in the marketplace.

How do you know what to order, especially when you are just beginning to plan your shop? Mel Ziegler, co-founder of Banana Republic, once said "I would not think of starting a business unless I was its first customer." You should know and love the type of merchandise you plan to sell and be familiar with the strengths and weaknesses of the products available in the field.

Start with what you know you want your store to offer, and through focus groups and other discussions try to learn what else your potential customers would be interested in buying. Visiting stores similar to yours in other areas will show you the types of products they feature. If a successful store stocks an item in depth, it's probably because it is selling well.

The main types of merchandise you decide to carry will dictate the related products that customers will find interesting, and which will help make your shop more visually attractive. A store selling dresses, for instance, can create interesting displays by also carrying a variety of jewelry, scarves, hats, and other accessories. These less expensive add-on items will help attract repeat visits from customers and may even produce more sales than the basic stock.

A new store's first orders should be **broad and shallow**, which means you will be buying a sampling of a wide variety of merchandise without stocking a large quantity of each item. You do need to order enough merchandise to do an inviting display of each line, but not so much that you will have a deep back stock if it doesn't sell well. You can always place a reorder once you see which items sell best. It is important that your merchandise assortment features a variety of price points. Once your store is open, sales will show you what price range your customers are most comfortable with.

Concentrating on one price level will help you target your best customers; however, to attract as many shoppers as possible, you might consider having some variation in your price range. Department stores traditionally feature three levels of quality: good, better, and best. This allows them to appeal to different consumers, but it also gives their shoppers choices. The same customer might be willing to spend a lot on a dress for a special occasion, but only a moderate amount on casual summer clothes. Higher priced items often make less expensive ones seem like a good buy.

Buyers need to be attuned to what items customers expect to find in the store by listening to what they ask for. Have a notebook behind the register to keep track of these requests, watching for any trends that emerge. You cannot be all things to all people, but you should carefully consider customer requests that are within the focus of your shop. The ability to find out what customers want and get it for them quickly is one of the strengths that sets a good specialty shop apart from its mass market competitors.

Merchandise Buying: Gathering the Goods

Targeting Your Typical Customer

When you did your initial market research, you started to think about the customers you hoped your store will appeal to. It is worth revisiting this exercise from time to time as you continuously work to focus your buying on your primary market.

When you imagine a customer walking through your door, who do you see? What can you can tell about that person? Male or female? Age? Any idea about income or education level? Interests? A model train shop, for example, might assume its target customer will be a middle-aged male with disposable income who is interested in trains as a hobby. This shop's buying decisions will be different from those of the train buyer for a toy store whose typical customer is the parent of a young child. Keeping your target customer in mind can help guide your buying. It can also be helpful to get the input of staff members and the members of any focus groups you have established.

When thinking about your typical customer, it is important to balance the picture by realizing that although the average shopper in your store may be a 43-year-old white female with a family income of $75,000, you will undoubtedly also attract many customers who do not fit this profile at all. Selling to a wide range of customers is one of the delights and challenges of retailing. At Orange Tree Imports, our shoppers range from five-year-olds spending their allowance on stickers to Buddhist monks buying rice bowls, so we need to be prepared to serve this diverse customer base.

Determining Your Buying Budget

For new retailers, the amount you spend on your initial inventory will be determined in part by how much money you have available. You need to keep funds free to pay overhead expenses and to buy additional merchandise once you see what sells well. It is useful to know that there will be a direct correlation between how much merchandise you have on hand and the sales you can expect to generate when you are trying to predict your first year's sales. After that time, maintaining the correct amount of inventory will help you manage your cash flow.

CALCULATING INVENTORY TURNS

Ideally, the amount of merchandise you have at retail should result in at least two or four times that amount in annual sales, a figure referred to as the number of times you are turning your inventory. The more *inventory turns* the better, up to a point (if your inventory is turning six or more times a year, you are probably often sold out of items customers might buy), but few shops actually achieve more than four turns a year. Most are probably closer to two, which means that maintaining an average inventory of $100,000 at retail will produce $200,000 in sales if your merchandise selection and location attract sufficient customer traffic. Here is the formula for calculating turns:

Your annual sales at retail
Your average inventory at retail

The total amount spent on inventory is a key figure, but it is also important to allocate these dollars wisely. Think of your inventory purchases as investments. By setting up merchandise categories in your POS system, you will be able to see which types of merchandise sell best and plan to put more money into those areas in the future.

Divide your inventory dollars carefully into the categories you establish for your store, and track these wholesale purchases by category as you pay the invoices. By comparing retail sales and wholesale inventory purchases by category, you can see whether your inventory dollars are correctly distributed based on the ratio of sales to stock. Merchandise categories that sell best should get a higher percentage of the buying budget.

Merchandise Buying: Gathering the Goods

You may also wish to use a similar system to check whether the amount of space in the store allotted to a category reflects the percentage of sales and profits generated by that category. Keep in mind, however, that a category that starts out with more shelf space and more merchandise is bound to outperform one with less of each.

OPEN-TO-BUY BUDGETING

Once you have established your merchandise categories and collected some sales data over the first few months your store has been open, you may choose to set up a formal system of budgeting merchandise dollars by category. Large stores often use this method, called *open-to-buy budgeting*. An open-to-buy allowance simply refers to the amount of money available for receiving orders of new merchandise for a particular merchandise category during a monthly or quarterly time period.

This figure is determined by looking at the starting inventory and the seasonal sales history for that category. Cookware, for example, usually sells well in January. By determining the anticipated sales of cookware in January and knowing the amount likely to be left at the end of December, we can set a budget for how much cookware we want to have arrive in January. This system prevents a slow category from taking up too many inventory dollars and also ensures adequate stock on hand for busy sales months.

Do most specialty shops use open-to-buy budgets? Not in the strictest sense of the word. Many stores have a general idea of what categories are strongest for them and order accordingly. Space on the sales floor is also allocated informally along these lines in many shops. But real open-to-buy budgeting requires making good use of the extensive data generated by a POS system.

Despite the fact that we realize budgeting would make our inventory dollars work more efficiently, most of us just aren't that disciplined. We also realize that the ability to spot a hot trend and order accordingly, no matter what sales history tells us, is one of the strengths that allows specialty shops to compete with bigger, budget-encumbered stores.

Where to Look for Great Merchandise

There are countless ways to find goods for your store, from reading trade magazines in bed at night to traveling to meet with native suppliers on the floor of the rain forest like the late Anita Roddick of The Body Shop. Trade shows, usually held once or twice a year and open only to qualified wholesale buyers, have traditionally been a primary source of new lines. In addition to temporary trade show exhibits, some market centers feature permanent showrooms. These showrooms are usually open certain days outside of trade show weeks, which is convenient if you need to place orders right away. To find information about wholesale shows, check the websites of trade magazines in your field.

Trade magazines target a specific line of retailing, and these are great for finding out who the wholesalers are for your type of merchandise. Samples of the latest issues of magazines are often given out at trade shows, or you could ask for recommendations from other retailers.

The Internet is now a key resource for finding product lines, and going online is especially productive when you have seen an item you like and need more information. Some companies will send you a catalog if you request it, but their websites allow you to peruse their full range of goods immediately. Pricing to the trade, however, is usually not given, and often access to the wholesale part of a site requires registration showing a seller's permit number. You may also find sites specifically aimed at businesses (called B2B or business-to-business sites) that feature closeouts or special buys from a number of different vendors and provide centralized billing and shipping if you choose to place an order.

Merchandise Buying: Gathering the Goods

The Benefit of Working with Reps

One of our favorite ways of discovering new merchandise is by meeting with sales reps, which is industry shorthand for sales representatives. A good sales rep can be a real asset to buyers, conveying information about best-sellers, giving display ideas, arranging for help with promotions and advertising, and assisting with any problems that may arise. A rep may know where else the merchandise is being sold, a concern if the competitor is nearby. Some reps even set up displays, restock them, and take inventory counts for reorders. These services are often provided to chain stores and other large accounts; small retailers may have to ask for them.

We see sales reps by appointment only. If a new rep calls without any lines we already buy (this is tough for reps to do; it's called **cold calling**, probably referring to the chilly reception they receive from most buyers), we ask a few questions before deciding whether to give an appointment. Obviously, this is an easy decision to make if the rep is selling jewelry and your shop doesn't carry jewelry, but often, you really can't say yes or no to new lines without seeing them. However, once a rep is in your store, it's hard to say no to him or her.

Ever since we saw *Death of a Salesman*, we've had great sympathy for the trials of the sales rep, and we rarely turn anyone away without some sort of an order. If we think we may have to, we grant the appointment with the qualification that we may just be taking a look this time. That way the rep can decide if it's worth coming to see us. We both know that if we don't order anything, the rep won't get paid for the sales call.

I use a system of seeing reps at 11:00, 1:00, and 3:00, three days a week. This gives some structure to my workday and lets the reps know that each appointment must take no longer than two hours. Other stores have a policy of seeing reps only one day a week, which can be a hardship for reps trying to plan their travel schedule.

It is useful for buyers to be aware of how the sales rep system works in order to form a mutually beneficial relationship. A company rep works for only one vendor, usually receiving a base salary plus a commission on products sold. Other sales reps are self-employed or work for a sales organization and represent a number of different lines. Their income is usually based entirely on commissions from the variety of products they sell. Commissions vary depending on the type of product, but generally fall into the 15 to 20% range of wholesale.

Travel expenses, which can be quite high depending on the price of gas, are usually paid out of pocket by the rep. Sales agencies negotiate with vendors for the lines to be carried, assign them to reps throughout a certain territory, and often maintain a permanent or temporary show-room at wholesale trade shows.

In most cases, it will be clear which rep covers the territory in which your shop is located, and this is the person you will work with. Unfortunately, some companies have been known to assign more than one rep to a territory in the hopes of opening more accounts. In this situation, the buyer is in the awkward position of not knowing to whom to give the order, and this can be especially difficult if the two reps both call on the store regularly.

Most sales reps are not paid their commission until the vendor's invoice is paid, and they may not receive any commission at all if your payment is delinquent—another reason that it is important to stay current with your bills. A rep may also not get a commission on an order placed online or at a trade show. Keep in mind that sales reps' time is valuable. If it looks as if you won't be placing an order or will place only a very small one, try to take up as little of their time as possible. Reps are usually understanding of the fact that you may be interrupted to wait on customers or to attend to problems that come up.

A good sales rep will help you make wise buying decisions and will not encourage you to order too much, in the hopes that you will want to reorder. I knew one buyer who asserted his independence by refusing to buy anything a rep recommended—so he missed out on all the items that

Merchandise Buying: Gathering the Goods

were selling well in other shops. Sales reps call on many different businesses in their territory and can spot trends in customer buying that may be very useful to you.

A wise buyer remains open to ideas from all sources and will give thoughtful consideration to any new merchandise. I am always surprised that some buyers refuse to see sales reps or to go to trade shows to look for new lines. You should always be on the lookout for new items that fit with your merchandise mix. Shopkeepers without the time and energy to find new lines need to delegate some of their other duties.

Knowing What to Order

An exciting, eclectic selection of merchandise is one of the key components to a successful specialty shop. Customers have the option of spending their dollars many different places, and to a great extent, the same goods are available in most stores. The specialty store distinguishes itself by presenting shoppers with products carefully chosen and enticingly displayed.

Stanley Marcus, who served as chairman emeritus of Neiman Marcus until his death at age 96, gave a great definition of today's buzzword "curated inventory" when he pointed out that customers want the specialty shop buyer to edit the options for them and present those they think are the very best or the best value at a good price.

Specialty shop buyers need to be risk-takers, constantly looking for products unique in their market. As soon as an item turns up in a discount store, the time has come for the small retailer to consider dropping it. Whenever possible, the specialty shop buyer should look for items not available to mass marketers. This helps eliminate price competition, which is a game that's hard to win when you don't have the buying clout of a big chain.

Are there still products that are not being sold to the big stores? One way to find out is to shop these stores regularly, paying attention to new merchandise. Ask your customers where else they shop, and look for weaknesses in the merchandise and services being offered by those stores. Make sure you offer something different—perhaps by doing some direct importing or by commissioning products from craftspeople or small manufacturers that will be unique to your store. Buying goods made under *fair trade* conditions (discussed in Chapter 15) allows you to support excluded and disadvantaged artisans through your merchandise selection. It is also a good idea to favor lines whose marketing is focused solely on the independent retailer.

Although specialty shop customers do not tend to make choices exclusively based on price, price is an important factor in most buying decisions. When I consider a product, I need to determine right away whether it is in a price range appropriate for my store. Because it is very difficult to run a store profitably at only *keystone*, which is a markup of 100% on top of the wholesale price, I need to consider whether the item would be likely to sell at a slightly higher markup.

One way to maintain a good margin while still offering attractive prices is to get the lowest possible wholesale price. We are constantly looking for good prices, special discounts, and extended terms from suppliers. We try to buy directly from the source rather than through a distributor or middleman. Whenever possible, we buy in case packs, which often offer a lower price per piece than broken, or partial, packs. Some companies offer step discounting, a higher level of discount or better terms, depending on the size of the order. It never hurts to ask "Is this the best price I can get?"

Some stores band together to form buying groups, or co-ops, combining the buying power of many independent small shops into larger orders to get better terms and lower prices. Other buying groups such as Purchasing Power Plus/Retail Advantage Group and HTI (we belong to both) negotiate discounts for their members with a variety of vendors.

Merchandise Buying: Gathering the Goods

Many buyers choose items only on the basis of whether they like them, but, of course, they are not going to be the retail customers buying the merchandise. One exasperated vendor said, "I'd like to banish the words 'I don't like it' from buyers' vocabulary! It doesn't matter if they like it or not if it fits well in their shop, and if it is selling well, they should try it."

Another salesperson reported that a buyer wouldn't carry cat items in her shop because she didn't like cats. If her customers like cats, and some of them undoubtedly do, she should consider carrying cat items unless, of course, her shop is called The Dog House. This is not to say that you need to carry merchandise that you find to be in poor taste or offensive. We draw the line at war toys, for example, and we won't carry Halloween decorations that make irritating electronic noises, no matter how well they might sell.

When considering new merchandise, try to imagine where the line will go in your store and how you will display it. What category will it fit into? Do you need more merchandise in that category? If you use an open -to-buy budget, are there dollars available in that department for the time period in which the order will arrive? Don't rush your buying decisions. You may wish to wait until after you have compared several lines before deciding which one to buy. Try to test new lines in your off-season so you can reorder heavily if they sell well.

Determining the Quantity

It can be very difficult to determine how many of each item to buy. When my husband, Dean, came into business with me, I was shocked by the size of the orders he wrote, and 40 years later, he still sometimes orders by the gross (144 items), while I order by the dozen. He is often right, which means he will have enough of a good seller on hand to break sales records. But when testing a new item or line, I feel safer ordering conservatively. Still, you must order enough of a line to "make a statement" and to present it fairly. If a line has several different items, styles, colors, or price points, consider ordering a variety of products to make a display. As a rule, order at least two of each item ("one to show and one to go"). Otherwise, you will never know if more than one customer is interested in the product.

It stands to reason that the more merchandise you order, the less frequently you will need to reorder, saving time and effort. Ordering in large quantities will usually also get you better prices and sometimes special invoice terms. Consolidating orders into a few big shipments instead of many small ones helps keep freight costs down.

The flip side of ordering in depth, of course, is that you will have to store the additional merchandise until you can sell it, and your money will be tied up in the stock. The fact that the money used to purchase certain inventory is not available to use for some other purpose is referred to as the *opportunity cost*—although *lost* opportunity cost might be more accurate.

There is also the risk, especially early in your retailing career, that you will purchase a large quantity of an item that bombs. Reserve quantity purchases for items you have tested already or merchandise that is basic to your stock. Avoid buying in quantity just to get a bargain. It's not a bargain unless you can sell the entire shipment in a reasonable amount of time.

Stretching Your Budget by Consignment

One way to stretch your inventory dollar is to purchase on consignment, which means you don't pay unless the product sells. The risk of stocking the merchandise is thus placed on the vendor, not the store. Problems may arise, however, if merchandise on consignment is damaged or stolen. And you need to take into account that your shelf space is valuable, so consignment merchandise still carries some overhead cost, despite the fact that these items don't tie up inventory dollars.

Merchandise Buying: Gathering the Goods

Goods sold on consignment also usually have a lower markup than merchandise purchased outright, so your profit margin will often be 40% or less. A consignment arrangement makes it less risky to try unusual merchandise you are not sure will sell but would like to try. It is a method best used for art, crafts, or expensive items such as antiques.

Keep careful track of consignment goods so that at the end of the predetermined period, you remember to return the remaining portion of the order and to pay for what you have sold. A price tag with a tear-off stub that can be removed at the time of purchase is one way to track consignment merchandise. Another way is to assign a code for each consignment vendor and to have that as a category in your POS system.

> Innovative Appalachian gift shop owner Ginger Hill uses the front area of her store for a changing display highlighting the work of one local artist or craftsperson. Although most of the store's merchandise is not consignment goods, the items brought in for these special exhibits are paid for only if sold.

Developing Original, Exclusive Products

Another way to ensure a unique selection of merchandise in your shop is to arrange to have merchandise produced exclusively for you. If you sell gifts for pet owners, for example, you could contact a local potter to make cat bowls for your shop or a jeweler to create earrings featuring popular breeds of dogs. It is fun to help develop new products, and you (or the craftsperson) might be able to wholesale them to other stores outside your trading area. We carried a line of silkscreened cards by local artist (and scientist) Vaughn James, and one night, I had a dream that Vaughn turned his card designs into t-shirts. Vaughn was happy to follow up on my idea and sold thousands of silkscreened t-shirts—the only product I've literally dreamed up.

SPECIALTY SHOP RETAILING

A good way to find craftspeople willing to create exclusive goods for you is to visit an arts or crafts fair, or websites such as Etsy that provide an online marketplace for independent artisans. (Etsy also has a wholesale division which makes it easy to find out which craftspeople are interested in selling to stores.) The Maker's Faire movement adds the element of small manufacturing and 3D printing to traditional handmade merchandise, providing small-scale producers, known as "makers," as yet another potential source of unique goods for your shop.

Some manufacturers will put your store name and logo on their products, a process called *private labeling*. Private-label merchandise reinforces your store name and image and gives the consumer the impression that your operation is large enough to include manufacturing. Customers who love your shop like the idea of owning something exclusive from it, such as the bath and body and food lines we carried for a time with our logo on them.

It is hard for consumers to compare prices on private-label products, so extra markup can usually be taken on these items. Chain stores often feature one or more private-label brands of clothing and other merchandise, and the profit on these products is considerably greater than on competitive name brands.

Private-label manufacturing usually requires placing large orders, if for no other reason than the expense of printing full-color labels. Look for products that can share the same label, perhaps with a separate sticker indicating the size, style, or fragrance. You might also be able to do your own packaging of items purchased in bulk, such as candies, seeds, beads, or soaps. Use a distinctive package, and add a fancy sticker or ribbon giving the store name.

You might also consider some products that can be personalized with a name or monogram, or customized for the consumer. Many shoppers are looking for products that express something about who they are. If you can give the customer choices (think Build-a-Bear Workshop), it will

Merchandise Buying: Gathering the Goods

help set your shop's offerings apart from those of the mass merchants. Examples range from a Christmas ornament or frameable sketch of a pub that can be personalized to a piece of fine jewelry designed around a stone of the customer's choice.

TARGETING TOURISTS

Someone once said that the best souvenir is an item that is a good buy and not readily available back home. As all products become more widely distributed, it gets harder to find something to offer tourists that is not available elsewhere.

One solution to this problem is to buy merchandise that has been *souvenired* or *name-dropped*, personalized with the name of the area or tourist attraction. Many t-shirt manufacturers will add the name of the city or state to any of their designs for a small additional charge. Another option is to have products created for your store that reflect the topography or special features of your area. You may find that local residents as well as tourists want goods that reflect their pride in their home town or state.

Young visitors are a prime market for souvenirs, especially at attractions visited by school groups. Be sure to carry a good selection of impulse items aimed at young buyers. Open acrylic bins, well labeled with price signs, are an effective way to display these small items, although shoplifting can be a problem. Plan to have at least one employee other than the one behind the cash register available to assist young shoppers when a large group comes in the store.

Not every tourist wants to buy an inexpensive souvenir. A selection of handmade items or regional specialties will help make the shop look more sophisticated and can lead to larger sales. Look for merchandise representative of the area, preferably locally made.

You may also want to stock guidebooks and other educational materials relating to the local attraction and have snacks and bottled

Screencraft Gifts of Lincoln, Rhode Island produces custom clocks, coasters, trivets and other gift items using local images, such as these nautical maps of the Seattle area. (Photo courtesy of Michael Pezza)

water as impulse items. Keep in mind that visitors may have to walk some distance to their car, so heavy or bulky items may need to be shipped or delivered to the customer's hotel.

Higher Margins through Direct Importing

Goods ordered to be shipped from the country of origin right to your shop or a port of entry nearby are said to be ***direct imports***. Merchandise purchased this way is almost always less expensive than goods bought from an importer or dealer, but importing has its own headaches. You must, as a rule, purchase in quantity, especially if you are ordering factory-made goods.

Merchandise Buying: Gathering the Goods

Unless you have an agent working on your behalf in the other country, you will be trusting the company you buy from to send you merchandise in perfect condition. You will need to pay for freight and often customs fees and the services of a broker. Freight claims for merchandise damaged in transit can be difficult to resolve.

Direct importing has two main advantages: paying a lower price gives you a better margin when you set your retail prices, and you sometimes can find merchandise that no other store in your area offers. Another advantage is that there are many trade shows abroad, offering the retailer who can afford it (it may be deductible, but it's not free) the opportunity to travel.

Finding lines to direct import can be a challenge for a small shop, especially as most goods with a well-developed market in the United States are already brought into the country by large wholesale importers. We once ordered some hand-painted Christmas ornaments at the Frankfurt Trade Show in Germany, only to find out that the exclusive US importer of the line visited the booth a few minutes later and tore up our order. Nevertheless, there are small suppliers in other countries still willing to export to individual shops. For many years, until her retirement, we bought dressed felt bunnies from a woman who lived on an island off the coast of England. Our customers knew spring was coming when these adorable bunnies arrive at Orange Tree Imports.

Large shipments of heavy goods are usually shipped by boat and may require a letter of credit in payment and the services of a broker to process them through customs. You may have to pay to truck the merchandise to your shop from the port of arrival, where US Customs may have held the goods for some time while levying the customs charges. All of these factors and costs need to be taken into account when deciding whether to import a line of merchandise directly from overseas. It helps if the vendor has an agent in the United States representing them and helping take care of import issues.

If you are already buying an item in large quantities through an importer, ask about getting better pricing by doing a direct import of the goods. Some suppliers, especially those dealing with discount stores and large chains, are set up to assist you with overseas shipments if your order is large enough.

A professional freight consolidator combines large orders from several stores and arranges to ship them in from overseas. The consolidator brings the goods through customs and then sends them on to the individual businesses. While not practical for small orders such as felt bunnies, the services of a freight consolidator can be the key to doing direct imports of larger items for shops not large enough to do huge orders on their own.

Many countries maintain trade offices in their embassies or consulates in the United States to assist buyers in planning business trips abroad and arranging for direct imports. It is in the economic interest of other countries to encourage exports of their goods to the United States, so they are happy to provide information about trade shows, visas, buying offices, export regulations, and so forth. State and federal trade offices here can assist with customs and other import regulations.

Keeping Inventory Under Control

It is easy to make the mistake of buying too much or buying without enough thought as to whether there are enough customers for certain items. In fact, it is much harder to say no to a line, especially when it is presented with a convincing sales pitch, than it is to say yes. New merchandise invariably looks fresher and more exciting than the stock on hand. Learn to stand your ground and turn down goods you don't need. Excess inventory has been the downfall of many a retailer.

You should also plan to routinely clear out old goods that haven't been selling well so that you have the money and space for fresh stock. Some experts even recommend budgeting a certain amount for mark-

Merchandise Buying: Gathering the Goods

downs each month. It is certainly helpful to track your markdowns, so you know whether the high sales in a line of table lamps comes from the fact that most of them are being sold at 50% off. You'll also want to know what you've marked down as clearance so that you don't reorder these items.

There is a saying in retailing that the first markdown is the most important. One Dallas gourmet shop had a rule that anything that hadn't sold in a year went into a trunk in which every item was $10.00—no matter what its original price had been. You can bet that its clearance items moved out quickly because the trunk was the first spot every customer checked on entering the store. Take a less Texas-sized discount than this retailer as soon as you realize that an item isn't selling so that you can recoup your investment and not sit on "dead" merchandise, as it is so colorfully described in the trade. Keeping slow movers on the move allows you to continue buying new goods with a clear conscience.

Dated price tags will help you determine how long the merchandise has been on your shelf. To make this system work, you need to make sure that the shipment of merchandise arriving first is displayed before the next reorder of the same items (this is known in the trade as *FIFO, first in, first out*—as opposed to *LIFO, last in, first out*). If you notice that an item has been around too long, use a color-coded sales tag to mark it down 10 to 20%. Track how long it has been on display at the sale price and mark it down an additional percentage until it sells.

Consider what you will do if a line doesn't sell well before you place an order. Most items can be marked down and sold, but if you have invested in special fixtures, you may not be able to reuse them. Be especially cautious with programs that involve stocking items personalized with a range of names, initials, zodiac signs, or months or years of birth. It is notoriously difficult to sell down to the last pieces of these items or to display them when there are not many left.

Few items continue to sell well forever. The fluctuations in an item's popularity is called its *product life cycle*. New merchandise that is well received by your customers may demonstrate a marked increase in sales every time you reorder, until suddenly sales drop off. Pay close attention to customer buying patterns, and listen to what sales reps are saying about an item's popularity. When you begin to sense that the sales of an item are slowing down, reorder cautiously or not at all. It is better to bring in new merchandise than to continue carrying an item just because it has been popular in the past.

TRACKING SALES FOR REORDERS

Every store has certain categories of steady sellers, called **bread-and-butter** items, that should never be out of stock. Most other items get reordered a few times, until sales slow down. Still others are ordered once and then replaced with something new.

A POS system will compile records of what merchandise has been sold, alerting you to dangerously low inventory levels. You can set a minimum inventory level for each item, based on how long it usually takes to receive a reorder and how many units you are likely to sell each day or week. The POS system can even generate a reorder; in fact, many chain stores use a system called **electronic data interface** (EDI), which provides a direct link between the store's computer and those of major suppliers. This technology may be practical for smaller stores heavily dependent on a few key vendors.

In a single-store location, you can control inventory levels by watching what is selling and doing manual counts. For items we reorder regularly, we use a perpetual inventory spreadsheet record with the quantity of each item received and the quantity left on hand a few weeks or months later. By tracking the number sold, we have an idea of how many to reorder. The quantity left from the first order, plus the quantity received on the reorder, become the new starting figure that we use to compare the amount left on hand the next time we are ready to order. A sample form is shown below.

A perpetual inventory can be taken weekly, monthly, or just whenever stock seems low enough to warrant placing an order. Many vendors have a fairly high minimum reorder, so you can't order just one item that is out of stock. It also helps to reduce freight costs if you order a large number of items at a time. The trick is not to wait so long that a popular item is completely sold out before the new stock arrives. Keep track of which suppliers ship in a few days and which ones need to receive orders a month or more before they can ship.

PERPETUAL INVENTORY

Product Description	Item Number	Retail Price	Wholesale Price	Starting Inventory	On Order Date:	On Hand Date:	On Order Date:	On Hand Date:

Many stores do not reorder exactly the same item of merchandise more than a time or two in certain categories, so even a simple perpetual inventory system may be more record keeping than is necessary for most lines. There is nothing wrong with checking to see how many teddy bears have sold by just taking a look at how many bears are sitting on the shelf and in the stockroom.

SPECIALTY SHOP RETAILING

Seasonal Planning Advice

Long before the first snowfall signals the start of the Christmas season to most shoppers, buyers who order seasonal merchandise will be turning their attention to Easter bunnies and Valentines. And while most people are anticipating the arrival of spring, retailers who stock seasonal goods will be pondering ghoulish jack-o-lanterns and wintry Christmas cards. Seasonal buying is somewhat like working the night shift; you always feel a bit out of step with the rest of the world.

Anyone would find it difficult to remember which Easter candies sold best while ringing up Halloween treats. If you add to this the fact that the buying season for holiday merchandise has gotten so long that Christmas ordering takes place over almost a nine-month period, it becomes clear that it is an ongoing challenge to keep track of whether there are enough (or too many, which is often worse) gift bags, tree toppers, or jingle-bell ornaments on order.

Many shop owners have discovered that some form of seasonal planning is a must. There are two real dangers in ignoring this need. The first, and more obvious, is that having too much merchandise on hand leads to excessive inventory at the end of a holiday that may have to be carried over in storage for a year. Some of these goods, of course, can be marked down and sold for cost within a few days of the holiday. Department stores have developed the after-Christmas sale into one of their biggest events of the year. But few small shops have the traffic to ensure that all of the post-seasonal merchandise is sold within a few days of a holiday. A post-seasonal sale should not be allowed to go on for very long; goods that haven't been sold while the holiday is still on everyone's mind are not likely to sell at all.

The second, less obvious, problem with not planning for seasonal sales is that you may have too little inventory on hand. You cannot sell 12 Santa figurines if you have only 4 in stock, unless you are lucky enough to find a supplier who can ship a reorder at the last minute. "You can't sell from an empty cart," the saying goes. Customers want what appears to be a full selection to choose from right up to the holiday itself. They usually will not buy the very last item on hand, even at closing time on Christmas Eve.

CREATING A SEASONAL PLANNING SYSTEM

A seasonal planning program can make life easier for anyone who buys holiday merchandise and should lead to better inventory turns and a more profitable operation. It is especially helpful to new buyers, including the hospital shop's volunteer who is asked to order seasonal goods without having any experience of his or her own to rely on.

The basic premise behind a seasonal planning system is that the buying patterns of customers can be predicted based on their past patterns. If you sold 30 dozen Valentines in 2017, you are more likely to sell 35 dozen in 2018 than you are to sell 3 dozen—or 300 dozen. And if hand-painted Easter eggs sold out early this season, you will probably want to make sure you have more on hand next year.

A large three-ring binder works well as a seasonal planning notebook because pages, including copies of orders and sketches of displays, can be added easily, and copies of these notes can be taken to trade shows. If you prefer to keep the records on your store computer, print out whatever data you need to take with you. A day or two before the holiday, take notes about how well each item sold —or just indicate "yes" or "no" as a reminder as to whether you should reorder it next year.

WATCHING FOR CHANGES

Although it is generally true that future sales can be predicted based on past sales, a number of factors can alter these predictions, and they should be taken into account when making buying decisions.

First are the local factors. Are the store's sales increasing or declining? How is your community's economy and that of your particular mall or shop location? Do you know of any special factors, such as a feature story in the news about your shop or bad weather that influenced your sales figures last year? Do you know of anything that will have an impact on this year's sales? The opening of a competing store or roadwork in front of your shop may influence what you will need to buy.

Look closely at any changes in the holiday you are buying for. Easter, for example, can fall in March or in April, and an early Easter is generally an indication of a slightly weaker season because of the shorter sales period. Halloween and Valentine sales are influenced by whether the holidays fall on a weekday or weekend. And, finally, be alert to trends in consumer holiday celebration and buying. Fashions in holiday decoration, cards, and gifts all change to some extent from year to year.

Despite these variables, all of which contribute to making retailing a constant challenge, it is possible to significantly increase your chances of doing a good job of holiday buying through consistent seasonal record keeping.

Buying for Displays and Promotions

Keep display and advertising in mind when you do your buying, always staying on the lookout for items that will be good draws when featured in ads or store windows. Advertising, promotion, and display should be coordinated, with any item featured in your advertising prominently displayed in the store.

Never have the last one of an item in the window. Plan ahead so you will have an adequate quantity of every item being highlighted. You may also wish to order a few oversize items to use mostly as display props, but priced in case a customer wants to buy them.

When you order a new line of merchandise or even just a new item, have some idea where you will display it in the store. If special fixtures will be required, order these to arrive at the same time as the goods. In addition to working toward a full and interesting variety, think about

Merchandise Buying: Gathering the Goods

Shoppers enjoy viewing the full Nancy Neill Designs line at a trunk show held at The Little Traveler in Geneva, Illinois. (Photo courtesy of Nancy Neill)

how the various lines you order will complement each other, and look for colors and textures that go well together. The merchandise you order will become the basic material you will use to create in-store and window displays to excite customers and make them want to buy.

Special events often call for additional merchandise, which makes it important to have a calendar of upcoming promotions with you at trade shows. One that does not involve an inventory investment is the ***trunk show***, a sales event during which the vendor or sales rep presents a wide range of their products on consignment. This allows customers (and staff) to see a much wider selection than would normally be in stock, and your store only pays for what is sold.

Buying Trip Tools

One of the joys of retailing is being able to travel while scouting out new goods. Even visiting gift shops in some popular resort area can yield samples of items that would sell well in your shop (although the IRS would probably still not consider a day at the beach to be a business trip).

We used to make a game of memorizing the name and address of a supplier before leaving a shop because it seemed impolite to write it down in front of the shopkeeper. But now we're more likely to pay full retail for a sample of the product, as much as this hurts when you are used to getting items wholesale. Unfortunately, not every item is labeled with its source—in some very competitive locations, retailers actually go to the effort of obscuring any information that could give away the source of an item. But you may find some friendly retailers who are willing to look up information and share it with you, as long as it is clear that your shop is outside their trading area.

Visiting arts and crafts shows is an excellent way to find small suppliers with handmade wares, which can be a wonderful addition to the merchandise selection of many specialty shops and are rarely carried by mass merchants. Artists who have never sold merchandise wholesale may need some help developing special products to sell to a store. We ask that artists selling to us not sell the same merchandise directly to the public—for example, at an art fair—at prices much lower than our retail price. This often means they need to decide which items they will sell to stores and which they will sell themselves.

There are several special trade fairs of crafts where artists already familiar with selling goods wholesale exhibit their wares for shop buyers. These artisans have already developed a line of crafts that they can produce or have made by others at a low enough price to be viable when retail markup is added.

Most buying trips involve visiting large wholesale trade shows that are often a combination of temporary exhibits by suppliers and sales reps and permanent showrooms of merchandise. Trade shows are an excellent source of merchandise, display ideas, and contact with fellow shopkeepers. A retailer who does not feel any need to go to trade shows is one who is not interested in growing a thriving business.

Some specialty shop fields, such as the bookstore and museum shop trade, have one national show each year. But for broader categories such as gifts, there are trade shows held two to four times a year all over the country. Some of these shows are large and thus offer more potential suppliers, but a small show, especially one in another part of the country, can be the source of items that other stores in your area may not have discovered. To make your shop unique, you'll want to find some products your customers can't find elsewhere.

Sales reps may not get any credit for orders written at a trade show out of their territory, so it is important to attend the show nearest you, in addition to any in other parts of the country. If you have a good working relationship with a rep, you might also ask if the rep gets full credit for the orders at the show in your area. When this is not the case, they will appreciate your taking notes on new items and writing the order with them in your shop later.

TIPS FOR TRADE SHOW ATTENDANCE

Perhaps the most valuable hint anyone can give a new trade show attendee is to wear comfortable shoes. If you are not used to standing on your feet all day, you will find that your buying decisions are being impaired by foot fatigue before the day ends.

Come to a show well prepared to place orders, with a sheet of credit references (see Chapter 3) and a business credit card for making any purchases that are cash and carry or need to be prepaid. In addition, you will need the proper business identification for getting into the show or your show badge and an ID if you have preregistered. Preregistering saves time when you arrive and can save you money on registration fees, if there are any. If you haven't preregistered, check the show's website before you leave home to find out what credentials are required to get an admission badge at the door. Be sure to look into the show's special offers on airfare and hotels. Trade shows reserve large numbers of hotel rooms and make special deals with airlines to be able to offer attractive prices to those attending their shows.

One trick of trade show attendance that seems simple, yet is always appreciated, is bringing along a sheet of stickers with your store's name, address, email, and phone number on them to put on the sold to and ship to sections on purchase orders. Harried salespeople who still write orders on paper (instead of using a handheld device) seem inordinately appreciative of this time saver—and you can be sure that your name and address will be legible.

If you are attending a trade show in advance of opening your shop, it would also be a good idea to use your computer to make stickers that state "Opening on _____" in large print. You want to make sure that the goods are shipped in time for your first day of business, and this is one way to ensure your order stands out in the pile of show papers to be processed. You can always put one of these stickers on the back of your business card if the order is taken electronically.

Many trade shows are a good source of catalogs, price lists, and even samples (although merchandise usually may not be purchased and taken with you from a wholesale show), so be sure to bring a bag big enough to carry these items, as well as your credit references, pens, business cards, and a notebook. Sticky notes, a calculator, and a highlighter are also useful, as is a folder for purchase orders. Many trade show exhibitors will allow you to photograph display ideas using your smartphone, but always ask permission first.

It is always good to bring some notes so you have a clear idea of what you need to order at a show. Don't overdo it—I once saw a buyer at the Atlanta Gift Show hauling a luggage cart behind her with a file box of all

Merchandise Buying: Gathering the Goods

of her store's inventory records. It is usually enough to have a general idea of what you have on hand and perhaps some specific inventories of lines you know you'll be reordering.

Bring copies of customer special-request cards and a list of new items you hope to find. Write down the booth numbers of your key suppliers before you come to a show so that you don't miss seeing them. You can find this information in a preshow directory and on the trade show app. You'll want to be sure to walk those aisles where your current vendors are located, although it would be a mistake not to browse other areas as well to look for new suppliers.

If you work with an open-to-buy budget, bring a chart of your monthly figures, and make a note of purchase totals by category and delivery month as you place your orders. You can use your smartphone or an iPad for this record-keeping as you go, or enter it in your laptop at the end of the day.

You might want to bring along a granola bar or two. Food at trade shows can be hard to come by when you are in the middle of a long aisle of exhibitor booths. And although the food may not be great, it's a good idea take a break occasionally and eat something. If you are lucky enough to be attending a show where food and drink are provided by the permanent showrooms, by all means take advantage of this hospitality. You may want to pass up offers of alcoholic beverages, however, until your buying day is over.

Be sure to keep receipts for meals, transportation, and lodging when you are on buying trips. Although the IRS doesn't allow meals (at either McDonald's or The Four Seasons) to be fully deducted, 100% of all other legitimate travel costs are considered business expenses. If you drive to a trade show, you can even reimburse yourself for mileage.

We like to occasionally take our full-time staff members to trade shows. It gives them an opportunity to learn more about our merchandise, to see what other products are available, and to participate in buying decisions. The excitement of going on a buying trip to another city can be a good motivational tool, especially if you treat everyone to restaurant meals and stay at a nice hotel.

Having additional staff at a show can sometimes be distracting, but it can also be beneficial to have more people looking for new merchandise ideas. You can split up and ask staff members to look for certain items you might not have time to research and have them report back to you before the show is over so you can visit the booths they recommend. When you take staff members to a trade show, have business cards made for them beforehand so they feel like professionals. You can easily print a single page of business cards on your store computer using special perforated sheets.

Allow enough time at a show to walk past as many booths and showrooms as possible. After all, you've come to the show to look for new merchandise, and unless you see everything, you may miss out on a potentially popular item.

Try to attend shows on weekdays rather than the more crowded weekends so that you will have the undivided attention of the sales representatives. If at all possible, stay long enough to be able to visit some stores in the area. No matter how long you've had your shop, you can always learn something new from other retailers.

WRITING ORDERS AT THE SHOW

There are two schools of thought about writing orders at a trade show. Some buyers like to order merchandise as they see it, selecting from samples rather than pictures in a catalog. Others want to see everything first, so they pick up literature to study later and then make their decisions. Exhibitors are often hesitant to give out expensive catalogs to those who don't write an order because experience has shown them that most people who take a catalog don't order later. And if an order is sent in to the home office, the salesperson in the booth usually does not get

Merchandise Buying: Gathering the Goods

credit for it, which makes it in their interest to encourage you to write the order at the show.

Request a catalog only if you are fairly serious about a line and unable to place an order on the spot. If you do request a catalog and the exhibitor promises to send one to you, make a note of the company's website in case it doesn't arrive.

Companies sometimes offer *show specials* to encourage customers to place orders, including free freight, a discount, special delayed dating on the payment of the invoice, or free goods. As with any other sale, it is well worth taking advantage of the offer if you really need the merchandise. But don't feel pressured to order a line you aren't quite sure about just because the show special is valid only for the few days of the show. If you show serious interest, you may be able to get the special terms extended until you have returned to your shop to count stock on hand or review other factors.

Exhibitors offering show specials don't always consider the fact that their sales reps may lose a sale on the road because of an attractive special offered only at a show. They are trying to cover the high cost of renting a booth by maximizing the orders written on the spot. If you know your rep will not get full credit for an order written at a show, you might ask if you can get the same terms on an order placed with your rep within a few days of the show. This considerate attitude toward sales reps will be much appreciated by reps who have developed a mutually beneficial working relationship with a shop.

The exhibitors at trade shows are often weary by the end of the day as well, because standing is even more tiring than walking. Buyers who know how their customers like to be treated in their shop should extend this same courtesy to those who are selling merchandise at a trade show. If you are not interested in a line, say so politely. If you do want to place an order and you have brought a number of staff members with you, confine the actual decision-making to one or two people. This is a courtesy to others who may wish to look at the same merchandise while you are ordering, and it makes it easier on the order taker as well.

You may feel nervous about placing orders at the first trade show you attend, especially if your shop is not yet open. But stores go out of business every year, so new stores are vital to the future success of every vendor. Let the experienced guidance of the exhibitor help you select the merchandise most likely to sell well in your store.

Using Purchase Order Forms Efficiently

For orders written in your shop, especially those faxed or emailed to reps or suppliers, you may want to produce your own purchase order form with the store's name, address, phone and fax numbers, and other pertinent data already listed. A sample form is shown opposite.

Leave room for the name of the supplier and its address and phone number. It is also useful to leave a space for the name of the sales rep, if there is one, and the account number assigned to your shop by the vendor. If the line is new to your store, you will need to send a copy of your credit references. You would then write "references enclosed" on the line for the account number.

The body of the purchase order form is the space for the quantity, item number, description, and wholesale price of the items being ordered. Because we use the purchase order to check in the merchandise, our form has room to the left of the quantity ordered for checking off the number received. The column to the right of the wholesale price shows our retail price and category code, both usually written in after the order is placed.

If you email or fax an order to a sales rep, you will ideally receive back a confirmation copy. This copy is usually created when the rep enters the order into a computer system or copies the order onto his or her own form to get credit for the sale. After comparing the confirmation copy with your copy for accuracy, you may choose to staple it to the original purchase order.

We file purchase orders alphabetically by company name, which sometimes necessitates writing it in above the rep group's name on the top of a purchase order. Other stores file purchase orders by ship date, especially if they place orders with only a few suppliers.

PURCHASE ORDER

To: _____

Please bill and ship to:
STORE NAME
Address
Phone | Fax
Email Address

Fax# or Email _____	Order date: _____
Telephone: _____	Ship date: _____
Address: _____	Cancel date: _____
_____	Ship via: _____
Our sales rep: _____	Account #: _____

No substitutions, please.   Backorders OK? ❏ Yes ❏ No   Ordered by: _____
Please note that we accept backorders of under $50 only when the vendor pays the freight.

Member _____ **Buying Group | No deliveries after 2:00 p.m. and no trucks over 30'please.**

Quantity Ordered	Item Number	Description	Wholesale Cost	Retail Price

Page 1 of _____ Note: _____

Please confirm receipt of order and pricing today via fax or email.

Sample purchase order form.

Professional Ordering Procedures

In addition to specifying the items and the quantities being ordered, the buyer specifies when the order should be shipped and the method of shipping to be used. If the merchandise is needed by a certain date, state a ship date a week or two earlier. If the goods will not be of any use to the store if received after a specific time, specify a cancellation date for the order. If the supplier ships the goods after that date, you have the right to refuse the order.

You may also want to place a series of orders, called **program orders**, with staggered ship dates. In this way, you plan your purchases for many months at a time and can cancel orders if the line does not sell as well as expected. Some vendors like having an idea of your needs far in advance; others find the cancellation of orders very problematic. Check with the vendor to find out whether program orders are welcome.

Suppliers often have a set minimum dollar amount for a wholesale order. This minimum order discourages individuals from buying wholesale for their own use and also assures the vendor that the orders are large enough to be handled efficiently. The minimum order is usually larger on the first order, as the vendor will have to go to the trouble of establishing a new customer number and account for the store.

Companies also want retailers to order enough of their line to show a good representation in the store. Reorder minimums are often lower to encourage shops to reorder the best-selling items as soon as they have sold. For customer special orders, companies sometimes waive the reorder minimum or allow a small order if you pay an extra charge.

Vendors are often out of certain merchandise, especially imported items, and may choose to ship them when they arrive. Items that are out of stock when the first part of the order is shipped are referred to as being **on backorder**. If you don't want to receive any items later, be sure to specify no backorders. You can also set a minimum for the size of the

Merchandise Buying: Gathering the Goods

backorders you will accept. Small backorders often have high freight charges, so we tell vendors not to ship backorders of less than $50.00 unless they are paying for the freight. If you have established special terms for the original order, such as free freight or a 10% advertising allowance, these terms should apply to backorders as well. When reordering a line, specify whether you want any items still not shipped from your previous order kept on backorder or canceled.

Some suppliers prefer to substitute items that are in stock for those that are out of stock. We specify *no subs* if we want our selections or none at all, especially when it comes to greeting cards. Suppliers sometimes ask if a shop uses a purchase order number, and we find that using the date the order is written as the purchase order number helps track the order if there is ever any question about it.

If you have already established an account with a company, you may be asked to specify the terms (when you will pay the invoice). Usually the terms are dictated by the company's policy, and are net 30 or sooner. A discount may be offered for paying earlier than the due date, for example 2%/10 net 30, which means you can take 2% off the invoice if you pay within 10 days of the invoice date. A discount of 2% may not seem like much, but when calculated over a long time period, these discounts add up. By paying a $1,000 invoice 20 days before it is due, you save $20.00. If you were to invest that $1,000 in a bank for 20 days instead, you would have to make more than 35% interest to get a better return on your money in that time period.

After I gave the new-buyer orientation talk at a gift show, a man came up and shyly asked me, "What's dating?" It took me a moment to realize he was asking a legitimate business question. Vendors sometimes offer more than the standard net 30 days to pay, especially on seasonal merchandise that they want to ship as soon as they can. It is not uncommon to find seasonal dating on these lines, with the invoice due close to the holiday or season in question. *Delayed dating* means you have the merchandise to sell for a longer period before you have to pay for it, always a plus.

Terms such as net 30 and beyond give the store a grace period in which to sell the merchandise before paying for it—a great help to the store's cash flow and a nice benefit provided by the supplier. Taking excessive advantage of this situation by paying bills late is called *leaning on the trade*, and is an unfair way to generate cash flow. Big chain stores are notorious for not paying bills on time, which gives the specialty shop that is a prompt payer an advantage over these pokey giants in the eyes of a supplier. Many suppliers belong to trade associations that share information about delinquent accounts, another reason to stay current on all bills.

Specifying Shipping Preferences

More often than not, your store will pay the freight on an order, so it is your right to determine how it is shipped to you. Freight costs can have a significant impact on the profit margin of your merchandise. Consider shipping options and distance when selecting merchandise. Shipments from companies in your part of the country will almost always have lower freight costs, but some vendors offer to pay part of the freight cost on large orders so that they can compete with companies in other regions.

Freight cost will not vary so much on small orders or lightweight merchandise, so the location of the vendor is not as important with jewelry, for example, as it is with jams and jellies. Heavy, inexpensive merchandise such as marbles may incur freight costs almost equal to the wholesale price of the merchandise. Ordering a larger quantity at a time helps reduce the freight per item. (Dean marks the percentage of freight cost prominently on the front of any invoices with high freight, so that he can take that into account on reorders.)

Merchandise Buying: Gathering the Goods

Many shops simply put *cheapest and best* under ship via. This allows the supplier to choose whether to send the goods with a *less-than-truckload (LTL)* trucking company (also called a *common carrier*) or with a small-package service, such as UPS or FedEx Ground. The size of the cartons and the total shipping weight usually determine which type of service is most economical.

There may be some special considerations to take into account in selecting the most economical way to ship merchandise. Small shipments of books, for example, may be sent inexpensively by parcel post's media rate. Bulky items, such as piñatas, must be shipped by common carrier, adding two or more dollars in freight costs to each burro or bull. Merchandise that is urgently needed by a customer may require shipment by the overnight service offered by FedEx and UPS, and customers may be willing to pay extra for this speedy delivery.

To minimize freight costs, try to avoid placing small, fill-in orders for heavy items. Remember to add more markup to the retail prices of items with high freight costs. Look for special shipping terms from suppliers, such as free freight or a partial freight allowance, terms often available when an order reaches a certain size or if it is prepaid.

When calculating freight allowances, keep in mind that a 2% discount for freight means 2% off the invoice total for the merchandise, whereas *half-freight* or *full-freight* refers, respectively, to deducting half or all of the amount of the actual freight charges.

A purchase order sometimes states at what point paying for shipping becomes the responsibility of the store. FOB means that freight costs must be paid by the store after the merchandise has been delivered to the shipping company— FOB stands for free on board, a throwback to the days when a supplier might actually deliver a bundle of goods shipside, instead of handing the package over to a friendly delivery person.

Developing Beneficial Vendor Relations

The suppliers you buy from should be partners in your success. Your store cannot thrive without good quality merchandise for customers to buy, and vendors cannot get their merchandise to the buying public without retailers as the link. Ideally, this partnership works well for both parties.

Retailers help vendors in the following ways:

♦ Ordering conscientiously

♦ Not canceling orders capriciously

♦ Displaying all merchandise well

♦ Reporting damage and defective claims fairly

♦ Paying invoices promptly

♦ Giving the supplier feedback from customers about the merchandise

Vendors help retailers in the following ways:

♦ Providing quality, fashionable merchandise

♦ Communicating regularly with retailers about new merchandise and specials

♦ Filling orders completely and on time

♦ Settling damage and defective claims quickly

♦ Not selling the same goods to discounters and neighboring stores

♦ Offering special terms such as free freight or early payment discounts

It stands to reason that a good retailer will favor suppliers who make a sincere effort to support specialty shop accounts. Some stores track vendor compliance to see how many orders are received close to the date

Merchandise Buying: Gathering the Goods

> Country Chic Paint of Vancouver Island, British Columbia, Canada, provides promotional materials, consumer samples and training to its retailers, and even allows them to create their own line of signature colors. The company helped retailers in Minnesota put together a special bus tour for their top customers, stopping at four different stores carrying Country Chic Paint for crafts demonstrations and a chance to win a gift basket of paints.

specified and how many items are defective, incorrect, or on back order. It is also important to note which suppliers are selling to other stores in your area, especially mass merchandisers, by shopping your competition often. When goods become commonplace or are discounted, they are usually no longer as viable for a specialty shop.

The speed with which a vendor can ship reorders, called the **replenishment time**, is important in determining how much merchandise you need to keep on hand. If suppliers can furnish you with new goods quickly, you will have fewer dollars tied up in stored inventory. Some suppliers, especially those dealing with imported goods, have great difficulty shipping promptly and completely, but it stands to reason that you should favor those that make an effort to do so. Your life is certainly easier when goods arrive just when you want them.

Because specialty shop customers expect high quality, the condition of the merchandise when you receive it is also important. We inspect items carefully upon receipt and expect our vendors to take back merchandise that arrives broken or does not meet our reasonable quality standards. If a customer returns an item as defective, we often contact the supplier for credit. It is usually only by hearing from us about a problem that the vendor will know if the consumer is dissatisfied with a product.

It doesn't hurt to ask if special terms or pricing are available from a vendor, especially if you are placing sizable orders. Be sure to find out from the supplier what items in the line are selling best as well as what items are new. Order writing should reflect the partnership relationship you are working to establish with each vendor.

How many vendors should you buy from? Having too few vendors puts your store in jeopardy should one of them fail or begin selling to mass merchandisers. Too many can be difficult to keep track of and can lead to an unfocused look in the store's merchandising. Some buyers also point out that by concentrating on large orders to a number of key suppliers, stores can become important to these vendors and will receive preferential treatment in return for their loyalty.

We are always looking for new, unique merchandise, so we open many new vendor accounts each year. This becomes somewhat of a headache for our bookkeepers, but it means we constantly have new goods to offer our customers. We favor certain exemplary vendors with larger reorders, but we rarely drop a line of really wonderful merchandise just because of poor performance in shipping. We want our store to feature the very best selection of merchandise available, and working with many vendors is one way we are able to do so.

CHAPTER 6
PRICING STRATEGIES:
CAPITALIZING ON YOUR INVENTORY

Merchandise must be priced for profit if you don't want to fall victim to that old retailing joke: "I'm taking a loss on every item, but I'm making up for it in volume!" It is a common misconception that consumers know exactly what the correct price is for every item and that they comparison shop so much that it is impossible to take extra markup. If consumers were really this savvy, there wouldn't be much excitement in the TV game show *The Price is Right*, would there? In actual fact, most consumers only have a vague idea of what most things should cost. They buy because the value of the item to them matches what is on the price tag.

Setting Prices: Keystone Doesn't Cut It

In many cases merchandise is purchased at a wholesale, or net, price that is half the retail price. This means there is a 100% markup (or 50% margin) on each item. The 100% markup that has been the standard for many years is referred to as *keystone*. Most experts agree, however, that keystone markup is no longer enough to keep a store profitable. Some items must be sold at a higher retail, at least at keystone plus a portion of the freight cost. Unfortunately, merchandise that is pre-priced, such as books and greeting cards, allows no fluctuation in retail pricing.

Luckily most items—even if the vendor has stated an MSR, or *manufacturer's suggested retail*—can be priced however you wish.

SPECIALTY SHOP RETAILING

Policies requiring you to adhere to the company's recommended prices are usually written to prevent discounting, not additional markup.

We are always looking for closeouts and other items on sale from our vendors, or available with special terms such as free freight, that will allow us to take markup that is higher than keystone and still offer prices customers will find attractive. We also look for "blind items," unique merchandise that customers don't have any preconceived idea about, so we can price these items slightly higher without hurting sales.

One way to create blind items is to bundle several items together, such as a soap dish and soap, and sell them as a set. Conversely, you can buy items in sets and then price them separately at a slightly higher total retail than the set price. Selling items individually that are normally prepackaged is a service to the customer who doesn't want a large quantity.

Keep markdowns and perishability in mind when setting retail prices. A nursery, for example, will price plants as high as 300% above wholesale cost. Plants require high maintenance until sold, and a certain percentage will not survive. Seasonal or trendy fashion apparel often needs to be cleared out at a reduced price after just a month or two in the store. Added markup is necessary to maintain some profitability when selling a significant amount of merchandise at clearance prices.

I write the retail prices on the purchase order soon after I've written an order, so the merchandise is still fresh in my mind, and I can remember which items I feel can be sold for slightly higher than keystone. When I place orders at trade shows, I try to get all the orders retailed before the end of each day. I occasionally catch errors when reviewing orders to price them and will contact the rep to make a correction before it is too late.

In determining retail prices, I pay close attention to even price points like $5.00, $10.00, and $20.00. If an item wholesales for $2.50, I almost always keep it at the $5.00 price point. (It may seem silly, but we do use

Pricing Strategies: Capitalizing on Your Inventory

$4.95 instead of $5.00—and I'm surprised how often a customer will refer to the price as "about $4.00" because of this.)

An item that wholesales for $6.00, however, will sell just as well at $12.95 as at $12.00. This type of discretionary pricing requires using some consumer psychology. You need to look at each item and try to determine how much above keystone you can go without acquiring a reputation for high or, worse yet, unfair prices.

Customers love a bargain, so when we are able to offer a lower price because of a quantity purchase or manufacturer's special offer, we often draw attention to the price by using a white price tag to indicate the regular price and a fluorescent red one preprinted with the word *Special* to flag the lower price.

Competing with discounters will require you to occasionally settle for less than keystone on some items and to make up the difference on other merchandise. There are also categories, such as books and electronics, that traditionally are sold at a lower standard markup. To protect your profit margins when going up against a discounter or when featuring low markup merchandise, you need to buy very carefully, looking for volume discounts, dating programs, and other special offers. It is essential to have a diverse product mix so that some of your merchandise will compensate with a higher potential margin.

PRICING SHORTCUTS

When placing an order, I figure out the retail price in my mind before deciding whether to order an item. Here is a quick trick: since many items are sold wholesale by the dozen, I calculate the approximate retail price per piece by dividing the dozen price by six. Although I may eventually price the item at slightly higher than keystone, this mental calculation tells me what the minimum retail price will need to be.

It is more complicated to determine the retail price of items of graduated sizes wholesaled as a set. If three baskets, nested inside one another, wholesale for $17.00 and you want the set to retail for $36.00, the individual baskets will range from $8.00 to $16.00 in price. Here's a shortcut for calculating nested set prices:

1. Starting with the number 2, add one consecutive number for each item in the set. For three baskets, add $2 + 3 + 4 = 9$.

2. Divide the retail price by that number. Because $36 \div 9 = 4$, the factor in this example is $4.00

3. Multiply the original numbers you started with (2, 3, and 4) by the factor: 2 x $4.00 = $8.00, 3 x $4.00 = $12.00, 4 x $4.00 = $16.00

At this point, you may want to adjust the figures to take into account facts such as the greater desirability of the largest size. Starting with the evenly spaced prices, add to one what you subtract from another. The price of the largest size could be adjusted up to $18.00, for example, and the smaller two down to $7.00 and $11.00.

MARKING THE PURCHASE ORDER

In addition to noting the retail prices on the purchase order, we indicate the code for the merchandise category of each item. Some vendors carry merchandise in only a single category, such as soaps; others may sell a range of products requiring a variety of category codes. This category information will be useful for pricing the merchandise, if you use codes on your price tags, and also will assist the bookkeeper in tracking merchandise purchases by category. If you are using an open-to-buy budget, total each order by merchandise category, and subtract the amount spent from each category's budget for the month when the order is expected to arrive.

Any special terms, such as dating or return privileges, should be specified in writing on the purchase order. We also attach a note to the

Pricing Strategies: Capitalizing on Your Inventory

purchase order with the names and phone numbers of any customers waiting for specific items from the shipment. Use a highlighter pen to emphasize special instructions or pricing so this information will catch the attention of those checking in the order when it arrives.

If you are using a POS system, you will want to prepare the data necessary to enter the merchandise into the system when it arrives. Each item will need a unique *stock-keeping unit* (SKU) number, reflecting what vendor it comes from and *price-look-up* (PLU) amount.

Check-in Time for New Arrivals

Buying for your store can be like shopping for a living, and sharing the exciting new merchandise you've found with your customers is enjoyable and rewarding. But in between these two stages comes a task that is crucial to the success of your store: the goods need to be accurately and efficiently checked in, inspected, and priced.

Precision in checking in merchandise can have an important financial impact on the store's operations. Not only is it essential that items be priced correctly, but also shipping errors on the part of vendors are not unusual; these can be costly if not caught and reported. You must be certain that what you receive is what you ordered and that the vendor's invoice matches the purchase order.

Some stores hire employees especially for stock work; others add this to the duties of the sales staff. If your sales staff is going to check in merchandise, it is best not to have them do this at the checkout counter, where it may distract them from serving customers.

In the front of our file of purchase orders is a lined sheet, the Arrivals Chart, with spaces to write in information about the shipments that arrive each day. We find the purchase order for each one and then list the vendor name, the date the order was placed, and how many cartons were in the shipment. This chart helps us track all packages that come into the store and can be useful if there is a disagreement later about what we received. Below is a sample arrivals chart. It is also available for download at www.specialtyshopretailing.com.

Once the shipment is listed on the arrivals chart, the purchase order is then labeled with a sticker, printed on our computer, with spaces for the date of arrival, number of boxes received, and the initials of the staff member unpacking the order. Most shipments include a list of contents,

ARRIVALS CHART

Date	Total # of Boxes in Shipment	UPS, FedEx, Truck, Parcel Post, Drone?	Supplier's Name	# of Boxes from this Supplier	Original Date of Order	Backorder? (yes or no)

Sample arrivals chart.

called a *packing list*, which we staple to the back of the purchase order. If an actual invoice is enclosed, it is forwarded to the bookkeeper. Invoices and packing lists often look the same, but an invoice has the shipping costs added and is totaled.

Ideally, the wholesale price on the purchase order is the same price you will be charged for the goods. We calculate retail prices when we place an order so that the merchandise can be checked in and priced as soon as it arrives. Other stores wait until the invoice arrives in order to see what the shipping costs are and whether there have been price changes. Some vendors, however, are rather slow in sending out invoices, which might mean that merchandise sits in the store for days without being priced and put out to sell. The sooner merchandise is displayed, the better.

DEALING WITH BACKORDERS

If you have elected to have backordered merchandise shipped to you when it arrives, you will receive shipments that do not have a purchase order on file. The reason is that the original order was processed when the first part of the order arrived; it is necessary to find this order and check to see whether the back order is correct.

We use a special form to check in backorders, and you can download a copy at www.specialtyshopretailing.com. When a backorder arrives, we begin by looking up the original order date and then enter the date the backorder arrives. The wholesale and retail information is taken from the original purchase order. This is a rather tedious process, which makes it even more inviting to specify no backorders. Not accepting backorders, however, might mean that you are unable to get certain popular items that are often out of stock. Most stores put up with some backorders to get the choicest merchandise, but it is smart to encourage suppliers to consolidate your backorders rather than sending out numerous small ones.

If you have merchandise on backorder and are writing a new order with the supplier, be sure to note if you want items kept on backorder (which may mean that you'll be first in line to get them when they arrive) or if you will be reordering these items on the new order. The latter is sometimes advantageous when you need to get your new order up to a certain minimum dollar amount or if you don't want to have to look up information on previous purchase orders when the merchandise arrives. Simply write *cancel backorders* on your new purchase order. You might want to contact the supplier first and find out if the backorder has already been shipped.

Coping with Problem Shipments

Ideally, when you open a shipment to check it in, every item looks exactly the way it did in the showroom or catalog, and the quantities match those on the purchase order. The prices on the invoice are the same as the prices you were quoted, and the terms are the same as the ones promised. Nothing is broken, and the order doesn't include pizza unless you ordered pizza. (The partially eaten piece of pizza, sent to us with a shipment of picture frames by a well-respected manufacturer, is legendary in our receiving area.)

Instead of pizza, the incorrect items in an order are usually pieces of merchandise from the line that are not on our purchase order. The person packing (or picking) an order may transpose the item number, sending us #5462 instead of #5426, or perhaps the company was out of #5462, so they sent #5461 without checking with us first to see if the substitution is okay. If we order 12 of an item, we may get 6, or 18, or 120. Items sometimes arrive broken, cracked, or crushed. All of these problems are common, and they are costly to deal with.

We have a two-part *problem slip*, shown opposite, which we use when there is some complication with an order. One part of it is stapled to the order, and the second part can be put with any incorrect items

Pricing Strategies: Capitalizing on Your Inventory

while they await pick-up by the vendor. We have a policy of ignoring problems on orders if the wholesale amount is less than $10.00 because they just aren't worth the time and effort.

When there is a problem with an order, we contact the vendor immediately, usually by email or phone, to ask for a *carrier call tag* to pick up items we did not order or that were defective. This means that the vendor pays the return shipping. If the merchandise is heavy and the cost of shipping it to the store was significant, it is reasonable to ask that some of the freight charges on the invoice be deducted as well.

NEW ARRIVALS PROBLEM

Vendor: _____   Date: _____

Purchase Order Date: _____   Staff Member: _____

A) _____ (quantity) of _____ (item #)
_____ (description)

     ❑ is/are defective or broken
     ❑ was/were not ordered (subbed for _____?)
     ❑ is _____ more than we ordered
     ❑ Was/were not received, but show as shipped
     ❑ Other _____

B) _____ (quantity) of _____ (item #)
_____ (description)

     ❑ is/are defective or broken
     ❑ was/were not ordered (subbed for _____?)
     ❑ is _____ more than we ordered
     ❑ was/were not received, but show as shipped
     ❑ Other _____

Please staple the top copy to the purchase order,
and attach the second copy to the incorrect or defective merchandise.

Sample new arrivals problem slip.
Print this form on two-part carbonless carbon paper.

Broken merchandise may lead to a freight claim being placed with the carrier. Depending on the type of carrier, the goods may be automatically insured for $100.00, as is the case with UPS, or not insured at all, as is often the case with the US Postal Service. Common carrier trucking companies base their liability for damage on the released value of the goods, which varies from one type of merchandise to the next. The more fragile the goods, the higher the freight cost due to the higher liability.

When making a freight claim, you are supposed to keep the broken goods and both the outer and inner cartons for inspection by the freight company. As a supplier once pointed out, UPS will not pay claims for freight damage unless they can visit the injured box personally. Keeping the cartons may be impractical if you have limited storage space or if, as once happened to us, the goods have been damaged by someone else's shipment of pickled pigs' feet leaking onto them. Freight claims are a headache for everyone and, luckily, are less common than they once were. Perhaps carriers are handling goods more carefully or vendors are packing them better.

Some suppliers take out additional insurance on a shipment, adding this cost to the freight charges for which you are billed. The freight charges on the invoice should reflect the actual cost of shipping the goods to you, plus any insurance charge. Another hidden shipping cost might be for inside delivery if a common carrier is being used. Otherwise truckers are not even required to bring a shipment from the truck to your door, although many will.

LATE AND LOST ORDERS

Vendors sometimes ship later than the desired ship date, but unless you have stated a cancel date, you can expect the merchandise to eventually arrive on your doorstep. If an order without a cancel date is late and you decide you can no longer use the goods, be sure to notify the vendor in writing that you don't want it shipped. You are under no obligation to accept goods that arrive unreasonably late if you have specified a cancellation date or written to cancel the order before it is shipped.

Periodically reviewing all orders still open is a wise idea. Call or email vendors to find out why merchandise due in the store has not arrived. Sometimes a supplier will have no record of receiving an order, and sometimes the supplier will not have been able to ship the merchandise for one reason or another. Good vendors will notify you of delays, but many do not. Open-to-buy budgeting depends on shipments arriving during the month specified, and, unfortunately, many of our suppliers are rather hit and miss in their delivery times. Some ship the day after receiving an order, and others take a month or more. Some ship every order complete, and others let the goods dribble in on numerous backorders. Dealing with these variables is one of the challenges in acquiring an optimal selection of merchandise for your specialty store.

Pricing the Merchandise

Once a shipment has been received and checked against the purchase order or invoice, the goods need to be labeled with price tags. If you are using a bar code scanning system, price tags may not be necessary, but you will need to make sure the price on the shelf and in the system are correct. One of the most frustrating experiences for shoppers is getting stuck in line waiting to check out while someone up ahead is arguing that the scanned price is not the same as the one on the display.

If you are selling expensive items such as antiques, you might consider having your logo printed on attractive hang tags (tags that tie on with a string), with someone with nice handwriting putting in the prices and any additional information useful to the shopper. These tags are especially useful if you have expensive items you don't want handled. A shopper can see the price of a fragile vase by turning over the tag rather than the item itself.

Using a price gun to print and apply self-adhesive price tags saves time and usually guarantees legibility. You can purchase labels that have your store name already printed on them, and the price gun can be used to add more data, such as date of arrival and a vendor or category code. We use a letter of the alphabet to indicate the category and a jumbled number code to indicate the date of arrival. An item marked 181505, for example, means that it was received on May 15, 2018. This system allows us to make sure stock doesn't linger too long, but customers (we hope) are not aware whether the goods are new.

Try to include some type of date code on your products, and establish a markdown plan for merchandise when it reaches a certain age without selling. For clothing, markdowns may need to be taken at 60 or even 30 days, whereas for other categories, between six months and a year may be acceptable.

The alphabet codes we use correspond to the 26 categories on our cash registers and are intended to help the staff remember what category an item gets rung up under. (If we were using a POS system, this would not be an issue, of course). We probably no longer need to code wine glasses G for glassware, but some items, such as plastic drinkware for picnics, are harder to place. Do they get rung up with glassware or with picnic baskets? The codes on the tags make sure that everyone rings items up in the same way and that the cash register category matches the inventory purchase category for that item on the invoice.

Be aware that some items won't hold a sticker for more than a few minutes, no matter what you try. The porous and oily surface of many wooden items, for example, refuses to take a price tag. If taping the tag on doesn't work, the only other option is a tag that ties on. Fabrics can be labeled using a Tach-It, or tagging, gun that pierces the item with an inexpensive plastic fastener that holds the tag in place. If even that fails, put an attractive price sign with the merchandise, and keep a list on or beside the register of unmarked products and their prices. You can also use this system for little items like toffees that are too small to tag.

Pricing Strategies: Capitalizing on Your Inventory

We use "dog bone" tags to label hanging Christmas ornaments and some jewelry. These tags are shaped like dog bones, or barbells, with adhesive under the large round ends so that they can be pressed together after the tag is wrapped around the item. The tags can be imprinted with the store logo and are available in a no-tear material for jewelry stores concerned about customers removing the tags instead of paying.

In addition to tagging merchandise with prices, consider adding a small, attractive label with the store name to consumable items such as candles, and bath and body products. They will help remind customers or gift recipients where to go to replace the item when it is used up.

PERSONALIZING YOUR PRICE TAGS

It may seem redundant to put your store's name on all your price tags, but this serves two purposes. It is an inexpensive form of advertising, reminding customers over and over again of the store's name, and it helps with identifying returns (if the consumer has left the tag on).

If you are using price guns, order rolls of labels with your name printed on them. Allow several weeks for the labels to arrive. For handwritten price tags, the store computer can print your name and logo on sheets of stickers or on business card stock to use as hang tags.

TIPS FOR REMOVING PRICE TAGS

The flip side of putting price tags on is taking them off again, especially when gift wrapping a purchase. Some self-adhesive labels are divided into little sections to discourage customers from switching the price from a less expensive item to a more expensive one. No matter what type of tags you use, removing them from certain products may be difficult. Lighter fluid and rubbing alcohol work for this purpose on some surfaces, and Goo Gone and Elmer's Sticky Out work on others.

Price tags put onto plastic wrap may tear the wrap when removed, so they should be applied to an inconspicuous spot. If it is very important to take a tag off without tearing the surface it was applied to, try a quick pass under a hair dryer to dry out the adhesive and release the sticker. You can then remove the sticky residue with a pencil eraser.

Good to Go

New arrivals need to be safely stored until they are ready to be put out. We will usually transfer the priced merchandise into cardboard totes, flattening the shipping cartons to be recycled unless the box is in good enough condition to be reused for shipping. Our system of participative democracy, described in Chapter 9, means that the staff member in charge of each department is responsible for getting the new goods on the shelves. The merchandise is put in different employee's section of the basement storage area in anticipation of being displayed as soon as possible. New arrivals in their areas often generate the same kind of excitement among our staff members that we hope customers will experience when they see the goods on the sales floor.

CHAPTER 7
VISUAL MERCHANDISING: DESIGNING DISPLAYS THAT SELL

Books about retailing—and I've read more than my share—are full of mathematical tables and formulas to help shopkeepers figure out where all the money is going, but few of them devote much space the artistic side of retailing, which is called "visual merchandising." The ability to display even commonplace goods in an attractive and effective manner is a skill every bit as important as being able to calculate return on investment, and I think it's one that's a lot more fun. Many of us go into retailing because we love the merchandise we sell, and we want to show it to our customers in a way that will make them love it, too.

Presenting the Products

Once the merchandise you have purchased is priced and ready to sell, it is time to give some thought to how to display the goods to their best advantage. A successful display makes merchandise look appealing and makes it easy for customers to purchase it—if a display is too nice, customers are afraid to remove an item in order to buy it.

As a general rule, most items should be put in displays that allow customers to handle them. Shoppers always prefer to touch an item before deciding to buy it. You may choose to put a large quantity of each item on display or to highlight the uniqueness of a piece by displaying just one.

SPECIALTY SHOP RETAILING

Merchandise that is easily shoplifted or broken can be displayed in locked cases, but customers are often reluctant to ask to see an item that is under glass. Stores with locked cases of merchandise need alert sales staff to offer help as soon as they see someone interested in a closed display.

When arranging merchandise on your display fixtures, keep the principles of color harmony in mind. Highlighting many items of the same color, called "color blocking," makes a strong statement. Products that come in a variety of colors sell best when arranged in a pleasing order, such as following the color spectrum or progressing from light to dark. Color harmony has a positive effect on the eye and enhances the sale of the products.

In addition to color blocking, you can create visually harmonious displays through repetition, that is, having a large quantity of the same item (or related items) neatly arranged *en masse* or interspersed with a few other products. When done with whimsy or creativity and using attractive merchandise, the result can be very appealing—especially in contrast to the "cram it all on the shelf" approach of mass merchandisers. As visual merchandising expert Linda Cahan says, "Repetitive images are one of the strongest, simplest display techniques available to retailers. All you need is a bunch of the same stuff and a good sense of spacing."

Often shops have so many items for customers to look at that the result is visual confusion. Help draw shoppers' attention to individual items on a shelf by using a mirror or a small piece of fabric under a display or by placing pieces of merchandise on a small riser to display items at slightly different levels. Plexiglass risers are available from display fixture suppliers, as are cubes made of cork, mirror, plexiglas, and wood. Make your own inexpensive risers to match a display by covering cardboard boxes with fabric or gift wrap. Plate stands or easels are versatile accessories for displaying many different items upright and can also be used to hold signs.

Visual Merchandising: Designing Displays that Sell

FOCAL POINT DISPLAYS AND CROSS-MERCHANDISING

Many stores are designed exclusively around fixtures that hold merchandise, with little thought to special areas that can feature changing displays that highlight new or seasonal merchandise. Often the only display that changes from month to month is the end panel, or *end cap*, of the traditional *gondola display* (a freestanding rectangular unit with shelves or hooks on both sides). When we expanded our store, we neglected to allow enough space for seasonal displays and for *cross-merchandising*, the technique of displaying merchandise from different departments together, such as placemats shown with holiday china, brass candlesticks, green glassware, and a Christmas cracker.

Our store atrium, originally conceived of as a restful area with a bench and a hibiscus tree, was soon pressed into service. We now change the atrium displays as often as we change the main window, with seasonal merchandise dominating in the fall and spring and featured items from one or more departments being highlighted the rest of the year.

Clothing stores often have mannequins or body forms positioned throughout the store, on platforms or on the walls above the hanging rods, showing coordinated outfits and accessories. Other types of specialty shops can make use of small areas of floor or wall space to create displays that can be changed periodically. Your store's regular customers should be rewarded for their loyalty by seeing something new each time they come into the shop. A focused display, even one using merchandise that is not new, draws customers' attention to the featured items.

Displays can be used to give decorating, gift, and use suggestions that customers find very helpful. Showing scented candles with bath salts, for example, evokes the image of a sensuous bath and suggests that candles, which customers may think of as a living room accessory, are also appropriate for the bathroom. Displaying a number of different apple-related gift items together, such as bags of potpourri, apple-shaped cookie cutters, an apple corer, and towels with an apple design, gives customers the idea of putting together a fall gift basket.

Cross-merchandising can also be done on the basis of color, leading to some unusual and interesting display combinations, for instance, red casseroles displayed with red Christmas ornaments and teddy bears with big red bows. Some stores display all their merchandise in cross-merchandising settings rather than having a separate area for each category. This is perfect for leisurely impulse shopping in a tourist area, but not ideal for shoppers hoping to find a specific item quickly.

Props can be used in store displays to add color and interest. A display for suitcases, for instance, might also feature maps of Africa, binoculars, a pith helmet, and a top-quality plush lion. Some of the prop items might be for sale, whereas others can be discreetly marked "*For display only.*" If the prop is on loan from another retailer, a sign should mention where it can be purchased.

The area near any checkout counter, even in the finest specialty shop, is a prime spot for impulse merchandise. (We all know what a strong draw the candy display can be in most grocery store checkout lanes.) Leave room near the register for a compact display of add-on accessories, treats, or any small new items to which you wish to draw attention. Because checkout counters can become cluttered with impulse merchandise, it is important to limit and frequently change the items that are featured there. These displays may be the final impression that customers have of your store, so be sure that the merchandise on the counter looks as enticing as the goods shown elsewhere in the shop.

Visual Merchandising: Designing Displays that Sell

Visual merchandiser Debi Ward Kennedy created this display cross-merchandising wine, ceramic serving pieces, and table linens for the shop at Columbia Winery in Woodinville, Washington. A faux pear tree and traditional furniture pieces help set a sophisticated tone. (Photo courtesy of Debi Ward Kennedy)

Maintaining Merchandising Excellence

It is more work and less fun to maintain existing displays than to create new ones. As merchandise sells, it must be replenished. Customers will unfold the folded shirts, move items around, tear packaging, and put merchandise they've changed their minds about in the wrong place. Straightening and dusting the merchandise and shelves is no one's favorite job, but it has to be done regularly if displays are to look fresh and inviting. Merchandise and display fixtures must be kept clean, and all displays should be kept full. A full display always sells more than one that is half empty.

We divide up the task of maintaining displays by having a staff member in charge of every department, which is part of our participative democracy management approach discussed in Chapter 9. This employee does the merchandise display and also dusts and straightens that area. Standing items are turned to face the same direction, and soiled or damaged merchandise is removed. Folded items get refolded and restacked in a standardized manner. Ideally, someone on the staff should straighten and dust every shelf several times a week. When things are quiet, we give employees flex time away from the counter (but within easy contact, using our intercom system) to dust their departments, which brings to mind another old retailing saying, "If you have time to lean, you have time to clean."

The employee in charge of an area in our store also restocks the displays. We encourage employees to restock from the storage area, looking to see what is in back stock and then making sure everything is on display. If the fixture seems full, those who restock from the display may not notice that an item is missing or that a new item has arrived.

Staff members in charge of a department also do inventories for the buyer of that area, and in many cases, they eventually do routine reorders of merchandise and perhaps even new merchandise buying. Even part-time staff members and our two bookkeepers are in charge of

Visual Merchandising: Designing Displays that Sell

small departments, so that maintaining the attractive appearance of the store is truly a team effort. With many stores offering the same items, we all realize that the way we present our merchandise is an important factor in our store's success.

Using Store Windows Effectively

The concept of store window displays is not very old; until the invention of plate glass, windows were very small and intended just to allow light to enter the shop premises. Early plate glass window displays took advantage of the larger space to cram in a sample of almost everything in the store, and some merchants today still follow this "more is better" philosophy. Others err to the opposite extreme, with so little in the window that it seems dubious that there is much inside. Good window displays take a certain amount of artistic talent, as well as organized planning.

Window displays should be changed at least once a month, and in high-traffic areas, every two to three weeks. Establish a calendar that identifies themes and responsibilities for creating the displays several months in advance, and share this information with the store's buyers in case they need to order any special merchandise for a display.

One of the cardinal rules for putting merchandise in a window is that there must be a reasonable amount of back stock for customers to buy. A customer who wants something displayed in a window will be frustrated if told it is out of stock. The goal of a window, after all, is to bring customers into the store to buy the merchandise.

It is helpful to set up a notebook or computer file with display plans, listing each of the next 12 months of window and in-store displays. Describe the proposed theme and add sketches, notes about sources for the tools and props to be used, and information about the merchandise to be featured, including when it will need to arrive. Take printouts along when doing the buying for the season to be sure that all the items needed are ordered. When a window has been completed, keep a photograph of the finished display, along with an evaluation of which elements worked well and which ones did not.

SOURCES OF DISPLAY IDEAS

A good window combines the elements of both visual display and creative advertising. There should always be a unifying theme, although the theme can be as simple as a single color or texture. Other themes might be a season or holiday, a product category, a color combination, an in-store event, or even an individual new item. Sometimes display themes are small vignettes, or realistic home settings, such as a dining room table or a bedroom dresser complete with all the accessories. The theme, which is sometimes referred to as "the story the window is trying to tell," determines the materials, merchandise, and signage to be used.

Where can you find ideas for window displays? A walk through your store should give you some ideas to start with: look for products that are visually exciting or hot sellers. We keep a photo album of all past window displays to inspire future designs. We also watch for good displays in the wholesale showrooms from which we buy merchandise. Some companies allow retailers to take pictures of trade show and showroom displays they wish to replicate and will even provide information about their sources for props and background materials.

Trade magazines often feature photographs of successful store windows you can adapt for your own use. There is even a special magazine devoted to display ideas, *VM+SD*, which stands for Visual Merchandising and Store Design (www.vmsd.com). Every year, *VM+SD* conducts an international visual merchandising competition and carries photographs of all the winners both in the magazine and on its website.

Visual Merchandising: Designing Displays that Sell

Look for window display opportunities outside your store. Seaside Silks draws customers to its shop by doing colorful displays of scarves in the leased display cases of a nearby luxury resort. Convention centers, meeting halls, and even airports sometimes have display cases available to rent, or you could offer to spruce up a vacant storefront by temporarily filling its windows with goods from your store.

Do You Do Windows?

In larger cities, there are professional window dressers, or visual merchandisers, who can take your design concept and bring it to life. You may also be able to find an artist who can translate his or her talents into store displays. We have always done our own displays, encouraging staff members to pair up and take turns doing a window. Near our main window is a sign giving the window dressers credit for their work. Some of our employees have turned out to be gifted designers, and it is nice to share the opportunity—and the challenge—of creating new window displays.

Art students, and even floral designers, are taught how to use complementary colors and geometric shapes to create a pleasing design, skills that retailers often have to learn on their own to do effective window displays. Merchandise alone does not make a display. Consider the aesthetics of the display in addition to the lighting, backdrops, props, and possibly signage. Good window design should take into account five key elements: balance (symmetrical or asymmetrical), proportion, contrast, harmony, and focus.

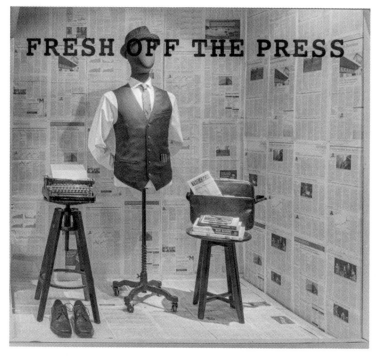

This menswear display window by students of the visual merchandising program at Toronto's Seneca College is an excellent example of the five key elements of design, with the addition of a witty play on words. Design and installation by Maro Lee, Sun Yoo and Heylee Kim. (Photo courtesy of Seneca College Toronto, Visual Merchandising Arts Program)

THE TOOLS OF THE TRADE

Enticing window displays often create an illusion, for example, an imaginary garden or jungle. A number of materials that fool the eye but are lightweight and inexpensive are ideal for creating this magic. The first of these is foamcore, a stiff board made of Styrofoam that can be cut into any shape using a sharp blade. Foamcore can be painted and pinned into, and it will not warp as easily as other stiff materials. It can be used to create a smooth floor, an archway, or a palm tree. Create a starry night background by punching holes through foamcore painted dark blue and inserting small Christmas lights from the back. Foamcore is available in large rectangular sheets from most craft stores and some home improvement centers. It comes in different thicknesses, from 1/4-inch sheets to 2-inch insulation foamcore that can be carved with a knife. Gatorboard, a much stronger and more expensive synthetic material, is ideal for permanent signs and other display applications. Its surface takes paint well, and it will not warp.

Fishing line is an essential tool for window dressers. This sturdy monofilament, available in hardware and sporting goods stores, allows items hung in a window to appear to be floating. Fishing line is also useful for reinforcing standing items so that they don't tip over during the time the window is on display.

I am a big fan of the use of small, white Christmas lights to outline window displays, especially during the holiday season. There are other colors of little lights available as well; we have used orange ones in the Halloween window and pastel lights at Easter. Strings of lights can be woven through a glassware display, intertwined in a floral garland, or even used on a Christmas tree.

PROP MASTER

"Display and visual presentation are the theater of retailing," wrote designer visual merchandising expert Martin M. Pegler. As in the theater, backdrops and props can be used to make a display come alive. These materials need not be items you sell, as long as the focus remains on the merchandise you do stock. You should constantly be on the lookout for inexpensive items that can be used in displays. Buy props at antique stores or rummage sales or borrow them. Many organizations are willing to loan out items in exchange for a credit in the window. Over the years, we have borrowed costumes from the *Nutcracker* ballet, a cast-iron bathtub, an antique table, a bicycle, and a baker's sample of a wedding cake.

SPECIALTY SHOP RETAILING

It is wonderful to have storage space so window props can be reused. This storage can be located off the store's premises, as it does not need to be accessible on short notice. Over the years, you can build up a useful collection of fabric, window shades, silk flowers, greenery, pedestals, and display props, such as fake rocks and mannequins. Some prop items that can be purchased inexpensively or borrowed to make an original window display include the following:

- Toys, such as beach balls and hoops
- Masks
- Musical instruments
- Theatrical costumes
- Trellises and garden fences
- Terra-cotta pots
- Ropes and rope ladders
- Standing mirrors
- Shopping bags with the store name and logo
- Silk trees and plants
- Plush animals
- Gift-wrapped boxes
- Sporting goods
- Paper or silk kites
- Life-size cardboard cutout figures
- Plastic flamingos or other lawn ornaments
- Natural materials (e.g., hay, vines, wood chips)

Visual Merchandising: Designing Displays that Sell

THE BACKDROP

The background of the window is not important if the window opens up into the store (although even in this type of window, some kind of railing, net, or grid may be helpful to keep customers out of the window). Closed windows, however, allow a backdrop to be an integral part of the display. We often use window shades made of bamboo, rice paper, or pleated fabric as a background, lowering the last shade carefully as we back out of the completed window. Fabric panels and woven throws are also useful as focal points in the background of a window.

Many other items can be used to form an interesting background in a display window:

- Flags and banners
- Panels covered with wallpaper or gift wrap
- Posters
- Fishing net
- Sheet music
- Photographs mounted on foamcore
- Shower curtains
- Window frames, shutters, doorways
- Fireplace mantles
- Large paper fans
- Sheets and woven throws
- Maps
- Wooden folding screens

Photographs, clip art, and other graphics can be enlarged for use in a window display by a local office supply store or printer. Be sure to have signed permission to reproduce any photographs or artwork that is not free of copyright restrictions. Dry mounting the enlargement on foamcore will keep it from warping although it may still fade when exposed to direct sunlight.

WORDS IN THE WINDOW

Signage can often pull a window together, announcing the theme or the customer benefits of the merchandise. Chain stores often apply the words directly on the inside of the window, a sophisticated technique that makes the words an integral part of the display's foreground. Vinyl letters and screened graphics to be applied to the inside of the glass can be created by many sign companies. Request letters that are reverse cut, or self-adhesive on the second surface, or front side. Keep in mind that light-colored letters show up best against a dark or colorful background, and dark letters work fine against light colors. Once the letters have been applied to the window, you will need a razor blade to remove them. Vinyl static cling letters are easier to apply, but are best for short-term use as they may lose their ability to cling over time.

Special events can be effectively announced using custom-made vinyl banners available through office supply stores and FedEx Office. We use this technique twice a year for a bright window announcing our fall street festival and our spring clearance sale, sometimes combining the banner with a window of air-filled balloons tied to our shopping bags with colorful ribbon strings. The balloons are slightly underinflated, to allow for heat expansion. They appear to float but actually are hung from the window's ceiling using a piece of fishing line taped to the top of each balloon.

HOW MANY WAYS CAN YOU SAY SALE?

In addition to using banners to announce a sale, there are many other creative ways to get this message across. Chain stores sometimes print special sale shopping bags and show mannequins carrying them. You can make use of this idea by creating fake sale shopping bags using color photocopies of the sale message attached to the front of five or six of your regular shopping bags. Shopping bags can also be spray painted to match the color theme of other windows, with a highlighting color of tissue or fabric tucked into the top of the bag.

In Denmark, we saw a window full of mannequins, each wearing a t-shirt featuring a single letter to spell out the word *udsalg* (sale) in giant type. One could also print the word SALE on balloons, flags, kites, umbrellas, or any other eye-catching prop.

This magical window display at Pufferbellies Toys of Staunton, Virginia featured six faux gingerbread house versions of local landmarks. "Staunton is known for its beautiful architecture downtown, and we wanted to do something in our windows to honor our special city," said Pufferbellies co-owner Erin Branton. "Our 'gingerbread' houses were built by Robbie Lawson using foamcore, hot glue, latex caulk, and plastic candy. The first year we had six landmarks—we subsequently added two more buildings and did two totally different window designs in following years." (Photo courtesy of Robbie Lawson)

MEMORABLE WINDOW DISPLAY IDEAS

Whimsy and imagination are often effective elements in a window. I remember a shoe store in Chicago's Water Tower Place that was holding a pre-inventory clearance sale. Rather than just showing shoes with sale prices, the window dressers created a vignette with an imaginary manager's desk overflowing with inventory forms, adding machine tapes, and spilled cups of coffee. Crate & Barrel in Chicago stopped passersby with a display of glassware hot glued onto shelves angled dangerously to look as if they were about to fall.

DISPLAY MISTAKES TO AVOID

Window designers sometimes try to communicate too much through one window display. Remember that you have only a few minutes of the viewer's attention in which to make your point. Don't make potential customers work too hard to figure out what you are trying to tell them, like the book on window design from 1970 that suggested promoting liquor-colored clothing by having "a mannequin dressed in an 'intoxicating color' pushing a baby carriage with a lovely setup of matching accessories and a few bottles of the genuine article peeping out from beneath the covers."

Avoid window displays that are too cluttered or contain too many props in comparison to the amount of merchandise featured. Conversely, windows should not be too sparse, although there has been a trend toward minimalist displays featuring very little in the way of product, props, or background. This requires a truly artistic eye to make it look intentional and not just unfinished.

A number of years ago, a store near ours read that the latest trend in window displays was the use of real food. The owners put together an attractive food display promoting the napkins and glasses they sold for tailgate parties. It wasn't long before the window also featured an impressive collection of dead bees and flies.

Visual Merchandising: Designing Displays that Sell

We have been guilty of putting candles in the window without thinking about what would happen to them on a hot day (they droop) and have used paper backgrounds that quickly faded in the bright sunlight. After a display has been completed, check it daily for items that may have fallen over, melted, or self-destructed. Windows should be washed regularly on the outside and cleaned on the inside whenever the display is changed.

Seasonal windows create a holiday spirit and are an important part of the marketing plan for many retailers. One of the greatest display challenges, especially during a busy holiday season, is making sure that no seasonal display remains up more than a day after the holiday is over. Don't let Easter chicks or Halloween ghosts outstay their welcome. Plan ahead so that a seasonal window can be dismantled immediately after a holiday and replaced right away. An empty window can quickly start rumors that your store has gone out of business.

Visual Merchandising in the Future

The press has frequently speculated that the Internet will replace traditional retailing, but as long as retailers do a good job of displaying merchandise in an attractive and inviting setting, this is unlikely to happen. Customers like to see and touch most types of merchandise before buying. Good displays can also give customers ideas of how to use products in their home or how to combine and accessorize fashions. At its best, a display can be as interesting or aesthetically pleasing as a work of art. You can't say that about a bunch of products shown on a smartphone or computer screen.

CHAPTER 8
STELLAR SERVICE: EXCEEDING CUSTOMER EXPECTATIONS

E xceptional customer service is one of the areas in which a good specialty shop should be able to outperform all of its competitors. Customer service begins with the basics: greeting each customer, being available to offer assistance, ringing up a purchase promptly and correctly, and saying "thank you" when the transaction is completed.

Yet how many times have we all experienced a lack of even these basics? We have been ignored by salespeople who text with their friends, waited in endless lines in stores with 12 checkout lanes but only 2 in use, and tried to get assistance in shops where staff members are vacuuming, even though closing time is still half an hour away. A store owner or manager who really cares about customer service would never permit these behaviors.

This emphasis on good customer service comes at a time when it is harder than ever to attract employees eager to serve. Putting someone else's needs before your own doesn't seem to come naturally to many people. It must be demonstrated by example, taught in training programs, and reinforced by recognition and rewards.

Fortunately, a shop with a reputation for fine customer service has a better chance of getting applicants interested in providing service, especially if it is willing to pay more than the going rate for its staff. Disney has shown how successfully customer service can become a part of a company's corporate culture. Cheerfulness and helpfulness are the norms at Disneyland and Disney World, which means that Disney undoubtedly attracts more than the average number of applicants comfortable with that expectation.

Customer Service Essentials

In *It's Not My Department*, Peter Glen's diatribe against poor service, he points out that "when customers have an adequate experience, they're satisfied, and they usually forget it. But people remember bad service forever. They form their opinion of entire companies or careers based on their worst customer experience. They remember every name and detail and they love to tell you how they suffered. The simplest secret of selling and serving customers is: Find out what they want, and how they want it, and give it to 'em, just that way. Talk to customers about the thing they are most interested in: themselves. And that means it will be different with each customer. There is no one right way to approach the customer: there are as many different ways as the number of people who ever stand before you." Listening to what the customer really wants is essential.

A key part of the training of any staff who will come in contact with customers—and this may not be limited to sales personnel—is this emphasis on placing customers' needs first. All employees should know that they are to put aside whatever they are doing when a customer approaches. Shoppers should never have to wait while employees chat or unpack merchandise. Employees should greet customers as they enter the store and offer assistance when appropriate. They should always try to find an answer to a customer's question, even if it requires calling a competing store. And a customer asking for a certain product should be shown where it is located, not just pointed in the right direction.

You need to decide if you want your employees to be salespeople who wait on customers or clerks who mostly just ring up sales. Because self-service is the norm in most stores today, be clear about your expectations. Salespeople need to be trained to give customer service that is attentive—but not overbearing. There is a fine line between being available to help and ruining a customer's shopping experience by hovering excessively.

When approaching a shopper to offer sales assistance, employees need to remember that the question "May I help you?" almost always receives the reply "No, just looking." Encourage staff members to begin a conversation with a customer by making a positive comment on some general topic or about the merchandise he or she is examining. Once a conversation has been initiated, it is easier to find out what the customer is shopping for and to point out the positive points of any products the customer is considering. Sometimes customers need assistance in making a purchasing decision. Employees should be taught that reinforcing the fact that the customer is making a good choice or offering to go get the item in a box can help close the sale.

When ringing up a sale, the sales assistant might ask the customer, "Did you find everything you were looking for today?" or suggest an add-on item, such as extra batteries to go with a new toy. Some stores have contests to see which employees can sell the most add-on items at the time of purchase—which is fine if the additional items are products the customers really need and want.

Motivating Employees to Give Great Service

Merchants everywhere try to motivate employees to give the kind of customer service that will win repeat business. Even in little Banffshire, Scotland, the government sponsored classes in "customer care," in the hope that more tourist income will result from sales clerks smiling and speaking slowly for foreign visitors.

There are four basic components to having employees who provide exceptional service: 1) hiring people with a positive attitude; 2) training them thoroughly so that they know all about the store, its merchandise, and its policies; 3) giving them the authority to do what is necessary to make the customer happy; and 4) rewarding them when they do well. Training and rewarding need to be ongoing processes because people don't usually stay motivated on their own. As Carl Sewell said in *Customers for Life*, "Even when people know what they are supposed to do, sometimes they forget. That's why they hold church every Sunday."

CONTINUOUS STAFF TRAINING AND COMMUNICATION

New employees are usually given training in procedures and merchandise. They should also receive training in customer service standards. Do you want your employees to offer assistance after greeting the customer? To answer the telephone by the fourth ring? Clearly communicating your expectations can help employees live up to them.

It is unrealistic, however, to expect anyone to memorize every aspect of product knowledge, store procedures, and customer service in the first few weeks of employment, and, of course, a good specialty shop is constantly changing. Staff education must be an ongoing process if employees are always going to be ready to give exceptional service.

Some shops find it useful to have biweekly or monthly meetings an hour before the store opens to introduce new products, review upcoming advertising promotions, and discuss any problems with store procedures. If bagels and fruit are served and the tone of the meeting is informal, these meetings can also serve an important social function to encourage team spirit. Meetings should always have a topic or agenda, however, so that staff members feel their time is being well spent.

Because we carry many kitchen items that require some technical knowledge to sell, we sometimes have our sales representatives give hour-long staff seminars before the store opens. The reps are usually quite willing to come and demonstrate their products because they stand to benefit as much as we do from an increase in sales. They even donate door prizes for us to give away to those who attend, which has the added benefit of putting products into the hands of staff members who later will be selling them. Customers love to hear that a sales associate uses a particular item at home and really likes it.

Everyone concerned with the survival of specialty shops in the era of serious competition stresses that staff need product knowledge, but they rarely mention that employees also need to know about the other aspects of the store: what is in the windows and what is being advertised, plans for adding new lines, procedures for handling difficult transactions, and so forth. Sizable sales can be lost if an employee doesn't know how to change the tape on the cash register or can't find the earrings featured in Sunday's ad.

If you want staff members who act like professionals, you may need to invest in some professional courses for them. Training in sales techniques, display, business procedures, and even specialized lines of products, such as gemstones, may be available in your community. Consider paying for tuition for some of these classes for your staff—and yourself. Although you might not be able to fund an MBA, as some big businesses do, staff members will appreciate any investment you make in them. Be sure to pay them their hourly salary for the time spent in class.

Trade shows and conventions often offer seminars for free or at a low cost. Time at a show is always at a premium for those doing buying, so you might consider taking along an additional staff member or two to attend some of the programs. Have them report any exciting new ideas to you and the rest of your staff.

Subscribe to the trade magazines in your field, and share copies with interested staff members, or put them in the break room for everyone to read. Clip out pertinent articles from popular magazines, and place copies of product catalogs where staff can read them during slower times. And of course, it's important to feature product details in your employee newsletter (see Chapter 10). The better informed your staff members, the better your customer service.

Stellar Service: Exceeding Customer Expectations

REWARDING EXCELLENCE

If you truly value great customer service, consider ways to reward and praise it. We offer our staff "Way to Go!" coupons that can be redeemed for a bonus and encourage them to give these coupons to fellow staff members when they see someone giving exceptional service.

Zingerman's, an Ann Arbor, Michigan deli and bakeshop that trains other businesses in its customer service approach, awards its associates Service Stars Awards, X-Tra Mile T-shirts, and other recognitions of excellence. Both the service provider receiving the Service Star Award and the person doing the nominating receive a financial reward.

A Warm Welcome

When Walmart started to institutionalize friendliness by stationing a greeter by its entrance doors, it meant that small shops had to go one step farther in making the customer feel welcome. Creative retailers started offering valet parking, complimentary coffee and cookies, and play areas for children. In the process, they learned that customers have so few positive shopping experiences (can you remember the last time you received really exemplary service?) that they are appreciative of even the smallest welcoming touches.

TELEPHONE MANNERS MATTER

To the customer calling by telephone, the person answering *is* the store. A cheerful greeting makes a memorable impression. Employees should always answer the phone promptly, give the name of the store, and ask if they can be of assistance. Perhaps you'd like them to give their first names so that the customer knows to whom he or she is speaking. If they must put the customer on hold, it should be done briefly and with sincere apologies. Be sure your telephone system has a reminder tone so that no one is left on hold indefinitely.

If you decide to use on-hold music, consider music that is appropriate to your shop, such as classical instrumental music for an upscale menswear store. You might want to make good use of the hold time to provide a lively message that you change every few weeks. Make sure that no one waits long enough to hear the message more than once, and test the message periodically by calling your store's number.

Some stores use an automated system so that callers can first hear a message with the store's hours and address without taking up the time of a real salesperson. If you get lots of calls with this question, you might consider this option. However, I think all of us prefer a prompt and personal response to every phone call.

No customer likes to wait while a salesperson talks on the telephone to someone else. When you have a customer on the telephone and one standing in front of you, greet whoever came second and explain to the customer that you will be with him or her in just a moment. If it looks as if the call will take a long time, perhaps you can get someone else to help out or offer to call the customer on the telephone back in a few minutes.

Time to Shop: Setting Store Hours

Evenings, and especially weekends, are now prime shopping times in many areas, and your store may be in competition with a superstore open 24 hours a day. Small retailers can't possibly keep those kinds of hours, and they don't need to. But ignoring the importance of being open Sundays and some evenings is usually a mistake. Ask your customers what hours they prefer to shop, and talk to owners of other stores in your area to try to standardize open times for the convenience of everyone's customers. Add extra hours during your shop's busy season.

We list store hours on our website and mention that we offer "added holiday hours." One Christmas Eve, a woman called at 3:00 and was unhappy to learn that we had already closed. "It says in the phone book you have added holiday hours," she sputtered. I tried to explain patiently that we had indeed been open until 9:00 every weekday evening the whole month, but that on Christmas Eve, we closed at 2:00 so we could enjoy the holiday with our families. She hung up angrily, only to call back a few minutes later to get the last word: "I just want you to know that it's people like you who turned Mary and Joseph away from the inn!"

Shopping centers usually require standardized hours, and customers like knowing all the stores in the mall will open and close at the same time. It is always important to open promptly at the hour promised, and to make sure your staff understands that shoppers arriving close to closing time deserve the same courtesy and attention as those coming in earlier in the day.

Because many of today's customers place great value on their time, they must be able to make their purchases in your store as quickly as possible. This means having an adequate number of well-staffed checkout lines whenever you are open and calling in more help from elsewhere in the store as needed. Indicate where customers should queue for the next available register to avoid misunderstandings about whose turn it is to check out.

It has been said that the average customer doesn't mind a 2-minute wait, but after that, he or she will become impatient. An important element of providing excellent customer service is constantly monitoring how well you are doing, and certainly your average wait time is an easy factor to track.

A Customer-Friendly Return Policy

There are some services that most stores offer, such as the opportunity for the customer to pay by credit card or check and to make a return. Be sure your staff understands your payment and return policies so they can be applied fairly. All sales and return transactions should be pleasant for both the customer and the sales staff member. Clear policies help avoid unnecessary misunderstandings, and employees empowered to make exceptions to the rules can often turn a difficult encounter into a positive experience.

KAZOOS ARE FOR KEEPS: HANDLING RETURNS AND EXCHANGES

A return policy may not seem like a positive customer service, but according to Susan Ward in a blog for *The Balance*, "How small business handles customers' complaints and store returns defines its customer service. It shows whether or not that company 'gets' that customer service is not just about making a sale, but about nurturing a relationship, a relationship that a small business keeps sweet by making a customer's every experience with the company a positive experience." Employees also want a return policy that will reduce the stress of returns, which can be one of retailing's most unpleasant regular transactions.

Lands' End offers a return policy that is "Guaranteed. Period." Nordstrom, the department store chain renowned for its customer service, is said to have given a refund on tires even though it doesn't sell tires. The fact is that no one really wants to give a customer his or her money back, especially new businesses that need every dollar they receive to stay afloat. But Lands' End and Nordstrom have figured out that the increase in sales that comes from a generous return policy outweighs the cost of occasionally being taken advantage of by an unscrupulous customer. The vast majority of people are honest, and they have a valid reason for returning a purchase or a gift.

Some items, however, can't be returned for hygienic reasons. The Magic Flute Music Mall lets customers know at the time of purchase that kazoos, harmonicas, and mouthpieces may not be returned. Stores selling swimwear, jewelry, and lingerie may also need a policy regarding returns, and some states have special regulations about this issue.

Stellar Service: Exceeding Customer Expectations

"I bet Nordstrom would have taken them back!"

YOUR WRITTEN RETURN POLICY

In fairness to your customers and your staff, post your return policy, and be sure it is usually followed. Some states have mandated that stores have a policy and follow it, although the actual terms are left up to the individual business. Big retailers have led customers to expect a liberal return policy, so specialty shops need to be at least as accommodating as their competition. Here are a few guidelines to keep in mind in setting a return policy that is equitable to consumers and the store.

The merchandise should be from your shop. Even Nordstrom, famous for taking back tires when they don't sell tires, sets limits. (The returned tires had actually been purchased from an Alaskan store, the Northern Commercial Company, which Nordstrom had recently bought.) You may choose, however, to take back an item you do carry, even if it was purchased elsewhere.

The purchase should be recent. Many stores set a 30-day limit on refunds and offer exchanges after that time. It is hard to sell items that are not from current stock.

The refund should be for the amount paid. This may be difficult if the customer has no receipt, and the item may have been purchased on sale. For some clearance sales and second-quality merchandise, you may want to have a no-return policy. If you do, clearly explain it to each customer at the time of purchase.

Credit card purchases should receive credit card credits or merchandise exchange. Since you have paid a service charge to the credit card company, giving the customer a credit card credit or store merchandise credit is the only way to recoup that charge.

Large cash refunds should be paid by check. There may not be enough money in the till to give out a large amount of cash, especially early in the day. And occasionally a thief will take an expensive item from the back of the store, remove the tags, and present it at the cash register, demanding a cash refund. Using a cash refund form that asks for the customer's name, address, telephone number, and signature to mail the refund will discourage this practice.

Decide if you want to wait for the check to clear before accepting a return paid for by check. If you have a lot of trouble with bounced checks or if the refund is for a large amount, you might want to wait until the check clears the bank before issuing a cash or check refund.

Establish a policy about the need for a receipt. It is always more convenient for the store if the customer has a receipt with a return so that you know the date of purchase, the amount paid, and the method of payment. But it is awkward for someone giving a gift to give the recipient the receipt, so many returns are without a receipt. Many POS systems will create a gift receipt; we avoid this problem by filling in a coded return slip to be put in the box with the gift. The pretax price of the item is hidden by writing it backward, with a number 7 added in front of the reversed price and a number 9 after it (e.g., $19.95 becomes 759919).

The fairest way to handle returns without a receipt is to offer a store credit, applicable on an immediate exchange or future purchase. But there will always be those who are unhappy with this policy, and it is probably worth avoiding their anger by authorizing staff to make exceptions and give a refund.

Keep on hand a supply of store credit forms, possibly on two-part carbonless carbon paper, with one copy for the customer and one for the store. Ready-made forms can be purchased at an office supply store, or

---

DEFECTIVE ITEM

Please place this item in the area for defectives right away, with the top copy
of the form attached. The second copy goes to the merchandise buyer.

Item: _____ Date: _____

Vendor: _____ Category: _____

Nature of problem: _____

- ❏ This item was accidentally broken, or found to be defective, in the store.
- ❏ This item was returned by a customer, who received:
    - ❏ A replacement
    - ❏ A cash or credit card refund
    - ❏ A store credit

Salesperson: _____ Retail price: _____

_____

Recommended action:
- ❏ Request replacement or credit from vendor
    Done by _____ on _____
- ❏ Discard, put in the staff "free box," or donate to charity
- ❏ Mark down for clearance sale, label "as is"

Sample defective item form.

you can create one that matches your store's branding. You can also use a gift card for credits.

Always take back defective merchandise. If something you sold is clearly defective, the first thing you should do is apologize. After all, the customer was disappointed in what you sold and has had the inconvenience of coming back to the store. Then ask what would make the person happy: a refund, a replacement, or a different item. Make it right, and then apologize again. You want the customer to come back.

Remove defective merchandise from the checkout area immediately and attach a form identifying it as defective (see next page). You will then want to decide whether it is worth pursuing a claim against your vendor for the faulty item.

Post your return policy. Signs clearly stating your policy should be put where customers can see them. We also keep pads of 3-by-5-inch slips with our policy on them by the registers so that we can give one to anyone who asks.

For Customer Convenience and Comfort

Many little touches can make the shopper's visit to your store more enjoyable. I am always happy when customers comment that coming into Orange Tree Imports cheers them up because it means we are providing a pleasurable shopping experience. We try to think of customers as our guests and to make their time in the store as relaxing and enjoyable as possible.

CREATURE COMFORTS

There are now apps to help customers find the cleanest restroom in the vicinity. But when was the last time you were in a small store that even allowed shoppers to use its bathroom? A clean, well-lit, and well-stocked bathroom is a delight and a relief to the customer who needs one. If you send a shopper to use the restroom in a restaurant across the street or around the corner, chances are good the person won't return.

There are dozens of excuses for not providing bathrooms for customers. Some are legitimate: an older shop without plumbing or a store in a mall where the restrooms are in a central location. But many shops have a bathroom for their employees and choose not to allow customers to use it because it is in an inconvenient location, or management is afraid thieves will shoplift items by concealing them while there, or no one wants to bother cleaning it regularly.

Anyone who has shopped with a small child knows that a convenient bathroom can be the ultimate and most appreciated customer service. If you can, make one available to your customers, and make sure it is clean and attractive, not a storeroom for cleaning supplies. If you sell hand soap, put some in the restroom, perhaps with a small sign indicating that it is available for purchase. Decorate the restroom with posters or prints that relate to your store theme. And make sure it is cleaned at least once a day, and is well-stocked with toilet paper and supplies. If you do not want customers to take merchandise into the restroom, provide a small shelf or rack near the door for their convenience.

In many areas, stores are required by law to provide a customer restroom that meets access codes for disabled shoppers. A wide doorway and grip bar make the restroom easier for all customers to negotiate. And, in designing your restrooms, don't forget mothers—and fathers— who may need to change a diaper while in your store. If you have room, provide a safe diaper-changing area. Fold-down changing tables are a practical solution used in many small restrooms.

Spouses and tired shoppers always appreciate a place to sit down. It is especially important that stores offering services that customers must wait for, such as prescriptions, repairs, or gift wrapping, provide a comfortable seating area. If customers are likely to have a long wait, be sure to advise them of this at the start. Some stores use electronic pagers so that those who are waiting are free to browse around the store while they wait.

If you have the space, offer coffee or hot cider in cooler weather. Shops selling specialty foods may wish to have regular samplings of the foods they sell. And stores that have customers who sit down to be waited on, such as a florist conferring about wedding flowers, might plan to offer hot tea in china cups to make customers feel really special.

KEEPING CHILDREN CONTENT

Shoppers with small children often feel particularly stressed by trying to get their errands done. They will be grateful if you offer a small play area or have some toys or coloring books that you bring out when a child needs entertainment.

My own children suggested that store employees make an effort to greet the child, as well as the adult. I often start a conversation with an adult customer by saying something nice to their child or baby. This opener puts the adult at ease and is a welcome change from talking about the weather.

SPECIAL CUSTOMERS, SPECIAL NEEDS

Traditional retailing wisdom suggests putting the most commonly purchased items, such as milk in a supermarket, in the back of the store to encourage shoppers to go past the maximum number of displays on their way to find it. This advice ignores the fact that the growing market of older and physically challenged customers need stores to make shopping as easy as possible.

If you think that this market segment is a small portion of your customer base, consider the fact that the 2010 census shows an estimated 56.7 million Americans have a disability, and about 30 million shoppers use a wheelchair or have difficulty walking or climbing stairs. "As Americans age and live longer," said Larry Paradis, co-founder of the

Stellar Service: Exceeding Customer Expectations

Oakland-based Disability Rights Advocates, "the number of people using wheelchairs can only rise."

"We want to be able to shop like everyone else," Paradis said. "We want to be able to shop independently and not have to rely on the increasingly beleaguered sales staff to retrieve merchandise. Crowded merchandisers, spaced closer than 32 inches apart, and tall, vertical displays make it difficult for those in wheelchairs to browse without assistance."

Look at your store from the perspective of someone who has trouble getting around:

- Are the aisles wide enough for a wheelchair?
- Is signage large enough to be read by someone with less-than-perfect vision?
- Are there any unnecessary steps up or down?
- Is there a place for someone who needs a rest to sit down?
- Are there baskets or carts for customers to use to carry their purchases?

We are happy to open early for anyone who has difficulty shopping when the store is crowded. (We've also extended this offer to celebrities who are performing in our area, but so far none of them has taken us up on it.) We offer telephone and email shopping service any time for those who can't come to the store in person.

Additional Opportunities to Impress

Services you offer customers can be every bit as creative as your displays and promotions. Specialty stores that offer services beyond the usual and expected show an eagerness to please customers that sets them apart from the crowd. A unique service will also be something customers will talk about, and that positive word of mouth is worth more than any paid advertising.

SPECIALTY SHOP RETAILING

There is no limit to the types of services your shop can offer if you use your imagination. Here are a few suggestions:

- Repotting house plants
- Antique appraisals
- Cleaning and repairs
- Loaners for customers while an item is being serviced
- Party planning
- Cooking classes or food sampling
- Additional gift with a purchase, such as batteries with a clock
- Valet parking or validated parking in a nearby facility
- Free recipes or crafts instruction sheets
- Elegant wrapping of gifts from other stores
- Complimentary installation or assembly of purchases
- A lending library of books and DVDs
- Trade-ins on used items
- Personalization or other custom work
- Birthday and anniversary reminders
- Storage of out-of-season items
- Craft parties for children's birthdays
- Office or home sales calls
- Rentals of tools or items for entertaining
- Coffee or juice bar, possibly run by an outside firm
- Guided tours led by a specialist from your shop
- Tourist information

Stellar Service: Exceeding Customer Expectations

Be sure to advertise your special services on signs in the store, as well as on your website. Make these services part of your brand image advertising in all media, especially if they help distinguish your store from competitors.

PERSONAL SHOPPERS

Stores with many regular customers should consider offering a personal shopping service. Department stores such as Nieman Marcus do this with great success. Print business cards for your salespeople, and encourage them to develop a list of customers who will work with them each time they come in or call. The salespeople should maintain records of their customers' purchases so that they can assist them in wardrobe planning, for instance, or offer reminders of special occasions requiring gifts. When new merchandise comes in that they feel will be of interest to their customers, staff members can call, email, or send a note.

Not everyone appreciates this type of assistance, and not every store can offer it. Those that do may find a rivalry developing among sales staff members, especially if compensation is based on a commission. To avoid competitiveness, some stores have employees take turns "being up," or taking care of the next new customer.

Many shoppers are grateful for service with a personal touch and appreciate being recognized when they shop in a specialty store. Encourage everyone to address customers by name, starting with whatever level of formality seems best, and make an effort to remember something about their interests, occupation, likes, and dislikes.

Employees should also be encouraged to send thank-you notes to important customers, telling them how much the store appreciates their business and inviting them to come in again soon. A coupon for a discount on the next purchase or a small gift could be enclosed. Provide your staff with attractive note cards with the store name on them, and keep a supply of cards and stamps near the checkout counter so that employees can fill them in during the quiet times between customers.

Co-owners Traci Lyden and Alana Turner (right) of Poopsie's in Galena, Illinois provide their sales staff with cute t-shirts proclaiming "Hello, I am a Poopette – Your Personal Shopper." (Photo courtesy of Alana Turner)

Stellar Service: Exceeding Customer Expectations

IT'S A WRAP

One advantage to customers in most specialty shops is that the merchandise they purchase will be packaged nicely and possibly even shipped or delivered. When the items the customer is purchasing are handled respectfully, the customer feels well treated.

Many shops package items by putting them in an attractive bag, possibly wrapped in tissue. For this type of packaging, the bag and the tissue should be color coordinated and should have the store's name on them (as in the photo from Poopsie's). But in most cases, especially if the item is being purchased as a gift, boxing and wrapping are services customers expect from a specialty shop. To paraphrase one box company's ad, if it's a gift, you'd better have a box for it.

Having boxes of many sizes and a variety of papers and ribbons requires a great deal of space and expense, but wrapping and boxing are services that are a good investment, providing an excellent means of advertising your store image to both the customer and the gift recipient. Your store packaging should be in keeping with the branding you are creating for the shop. Remember to order these supplies, especially those that will be custom imprinted, at least six weeks before the store will open.

If you incorporate your name or logo into the packaging in a subtle manner, no one will object. Tiffany, for example, has such a prestigious reputation that customers actually want the store's name on the outside of the package, but most of us need to be more subtle. We use tissue paper printed with our store name and logo in heavy white ink on white tissue. Other stores use an overall repeat of their logo in colors to match the gift box, or they seal solid-colored tissue with a sticker with the store name. The store logo can be hot stamped on the outside of a gift box. However, many customers will not consider a package wrapped if the store name is on the outside.

SPECIALTY SHOP RETAILING

At Leonardo, a gift and decorative accessory shop in Copenhagen, small purchases were treated to a simple but elegant wrap: the item was wrapped in a bit of tissue and placed in a pretty floral gift bag, which was folded over at the top and sealed with a store logo sticker and a swirl of curled gold ribbon. Some shops use a paper gift bag as their store wrap, lining it with colorful tissue and tying ribbons to the handles.

How do you select gift boxes for your store? There are inexpensive, lightweight white boxes available, although they may not be strong enough to hold heavy items securely. Choose boxes that are in keeping with the style and quality of the products that you carry. Measure your most popular gifts, and try to select an array of boxes that will accommodate most items.

The cost of boxing and wrapping can be charged to the customer or included in the store's markup. Consider taking a little extra margin on items likely to be wrapped and offering gift wrapping as a complimentary service. As an alternative, you might offer free wrapping on purchases above a certain minimum, such as $5.00. A box, bow, and wrap can easily cost more than $1.00, so it can be prohibitive to wrap every small item at no charge.

If you offer wrapping, make it as attractive as possible within your budget, and offer a choice of papers for different occasions. If you want to offer extra touches, such as a little ornament tied into the bow of a Christmas package, you might make this deluxe wrap available at a slight extra charge. Wrapping can be a wonderful creative outlet for you and your staff.

Delivery and Shipping Service

Some specialty shops, such as florists, are expected to make local deliveries, often the same day the purchase is made. If you are one of these, having your own vehicles and delivery staff may be essential for prompt service. A delivery vehicle presents another opportunity to

Stellar Service: Exceeding Customer Expectations

advertise your shop, so be sure that your truck or van is attractive, clean, and well-marked with the store name, tag line, logo, website, and address. (It's been said that an attractive sign on the side of a delivery truck can be one of the best forms of advertising.) Staff members making deliveries will be representing your store and should be as polite and neatly dressed as anyone in the shop.

When delivering gifts, don't miss out on the opportunity to let the recipient of the delivery know about your business. Be sure there is a card or sticker on the item with your store name, address, and telephone number. You might even follow up with a call, asking if the gift was received in good condition and saying you hope the recipient enjoys it.

Delivery service is essential if you are selling corporate gifts or bulky items such as furniture. If you do not have your own delivery vehicle, a local courier or taxi service, or even ride share companies such as Uber and Lyft, may be able to help you on a per-delivery basis. You might also consider cooperating with a noncompeting store that has its own vehicles and would like to make fuller use of them.

Many shops offer to ship a customer's purchases via a parcel service. For a small charge, UPS and FedEx will make daily stops at your store to see if there are any packages to go out. The customer usually pays the UPS or FedEx charge and perhaps a small packing fee. The store needs to have an area set up with packaging materials, such as bubble pack or Styrofoam peanuts to wrap the purchases. You will also need a system for tracking these shipments in case of problems.

When a customer orders an item to be sent to someone else, a thoughtful touch is to send a thank-you note to the person making the purchase stating the date the package was shipped. If the order was placed online or by phone rather than in person, enclose the credit card receipt as well. You can use the following forms for shipping and shipping acknowledgments. They are available to download from www.specialtyshopretailing.com.

SPECIALTY SHOP RETAILING

SHIPPING FORM

Date: _____   Ship: ❑ ASAP   ❑ On _____

Items:

_____ Price: _____
_____ Price: _____
_____ Price: _____

Ship to:

_____
_____
_____ State: _____ Zip: _____
Phone: _____ (If address is a P.O. Box, phone number required.)

From:

_____
_____
_____ State: _____ Zip: _____
Phone: _____

❑   Gift wrap: _____ ❑ None
❑   Enclosure (Circle: Receipt   Card   Gift Enclosure)
❑   None
❑   Enclosure is where: _____

For phone and email orders only:
❑   Check   ❑ MasterCard   ❑ Visa   ❑ American Express   ❑   Discover
Credit card number: _____
Exp: _____ Code: _____ ❑ Rung up (date, initials)

Shipping Charges: Weight: _____ UPS Zone: _____ UPS Charge: _____
                                           Packing Charge: _____
                                           Total Shipping Charges: _____

Reminder: Be sure to include the residential charge if applicable.

Salesperson: _____

_____

For shipping department use only:
Shipped on: _____ By: _____ Shipped weight: _____

Sample shipping form.

Stellar Service: Exceeding Customer Expectations

TO BE SHIPPED

Date: _____   Staff initials: _____

Item/s to be shipped:

_____

_____

_____

To be shipped to:

_____ individual (customer)

Or

_____ company (vendor)

From:

❑   Store returning item to vendor

❑   Customer

Gift Wrapping:

❑   To be wrapped?   ❑ Yes   ❑ No

     Choice of gift wrap: _____

❑   Enclosure?   ❑ Yes   ❑ No

     Enclosure is: ❑ Inside of Box   ❑ With shipping form

Miscellaneous:

❑   Waiting for address

❑   Does not ship until _____

❑   Other: _____

Sample "to be shipped" form
to attach to item awaiting shipping.

THANK YOU FOR YOUR BUSINESS!

Your order was shipped on: _____

We are enclosing your receipt and look forward to serving you in the future.

Store Name
Mailing Address
Phone   Email   Website

Sample shipped-order acknowledgment and thank-you note.

SPECIALTY SHOP RETAILING

Added Sales through Wedding Registries

Wedding registry started with the tradition of the bride (assisted by her mother, not the groom) selecting a china and silver pattern, but today both members of a couple put together their wish list for wedding gifts—and that list is by no means limited to dinnerware. We've had couples register for picture frames, Christmas ornaments, and even fancy soaps. Many stores, such as REI and Home Depot, now offer wedding registry service. To stand out, a specialty shop must offer something special.

Whether you use a computerized registry (particularly practical for shops with multiple locations) or a paper system, the key to gift registry is to make it as easy as possible for the people registering and for the person selecting a gift. We have a preprinted form listing lots of suggestions by category, following the layout of the store. After an introductory chat, the couple is given a clipboard and pen and encouraged to select as many items as they want. The more the merrier, in fact, because guests want a variety of merchandise and prices to choose from.

Other stores have a wedding consultant walk through the shop with the couple and make note of their selections. Traditionally, the consultant would offer advice to the bride and create a table setting showing how the bride's choice of china, crystal, and silver would look together. The table setting would then be displayed in the store together with the engagement picture of the happy couple. In lieu of this, some other listing is needed to show who is registered and the wedding date. We use a framed wall sign holding an elegantly printed registry announcement that we create on the store computer.

A store using a POS system may be able to give couples a bar code scanner and allow them to create their registry by going through the store and "zapping" the items they like. This is the system used by stores like Crate and Barrel and Target, and it is easy to understand its appeal.

Stellar Service: Exceeding Customer Expectations

After a couple has registered at our shop, we give them a small thank-you gift (usually a picture frame) and then post their gift list on our website. When a guest comes in to select a gift, we go through the list of items the couple has selected, offering to show some of the items in the person's price range. We offer to gift wrap every wedding gift purchase for free and then mark it off as sold on our registry form.

At most chain stores, guests can go to a self-service computer terminal and read through a wedding registry, printing out any information they need—or they can shop at home. The wedding registry information is updated instantly whenever a purchase is made anywhere in the country. You will need to decide whether you want to offer this level of service on your website.

The amount of time you wish to devote to this will be a major factor in determining whether you want to post the entire wish list on the website, and either updating it manually as purchases are made, or linking it to your store's POS system to do so automatically. Posting the wedding registry online allows you to reach the couples far-flung family and friends, with the couple providing a link to your store on their wedding site.

Many children's stores offer baby shower registries, and others encourage children to register their birthday gift wishes. We tried a general gift registry at Christmas one year, providing customers with a handmade Christmas tree magnet that said, "Santa, I've been very good. To find out what I'd like for Christmas, stop at Orange Tree Imports." But most of our customers seemed reluctant to write down what they hoped to receive, perhaps associating letters to Santa with unfilled wishes from their childhood.

One Size Fits All: Gift Cards

Even with a gift registry, some people can't quite decide what to give or want to let the recipient have the pleasure of visiting the store and selecting something. Every shop should have gift cards available for these occasions, and they should look as festive as any gift you sell. Design a gift card that reflects the nature of your shop, and when opening a new store be sure to order them enough in advance that they will be on hand when the shop opens.

Gift cards have become one of the most popular holiday gifts. They have the advantage of being able to be displayed for impulse sales like any other merchandise, because they have no value until activated by a POS system or special terminal. Stores with several locations find gift cards especially appealing because they can be purchased at one store and used at another.

Another advantage of gift cards is that they can be used to give customers store credits when they make returns, and low-denomination cards may be given to thank customers and bring them into the store again soon. Instead of a 10% off promotion, some stores offer customers a $10.00 gift card with a $100.00 purchase, or a $5.00 gift card with a $50.00 purchase. They can either use this card on a future visit or give it to someone else. Many companies offer gift cards, including most POS system providers, and there are firms offering gift card systems that can be managed through the Internet.

Customers enclosing the gift card with a greeting card will not need any packaging. But consider offering an alternative, such as a fancy "pillow puff" gift box with gold star glitter in it, for those who want something fancier. Some lingerie stores go all out to make their gift certificate packaging attractive because a significant percentage of their gift cards are reportedly never redeemed. Even those that are redeemed usually cost stores less than it might have cost them to box and gift wrap a large item. And two more positive features of gift cards are that shoppers redeeming gift cards often make more than one visit to the store before the card is used up, and card redeemers are more likely to buy items at full price than other shoppers.

Don't forget to promote your gift cards at your cash register and throughout the store. We also offer ours on our website, and they sell well to shoppers located in other parts of the country looking for something special for a friend or loved one in our market area.

Special Orders and Holds

Can you imagine walking into a discount store and asking the clerk to order something for you that the store normally doesn't stock? Most specialty stores will do special orders for their customers whenever possible. Suppliers sometimes make this service difficult by having high minimum orders and minimum packs on specific items. Before promising to get an item you don't stock, make sure that the customer is serious about buying it, perhaps by requesting a deposit. Check with your supplier about availability and minimums as soon as possible, and keep the customer informed about the status of the order.

In addition to special orders, customers sometimes request items we are out of and expect back in, or something we don't have a source for but will try to find. We use a two-part, 4-by-6-inch carbonless carbon customer request card for all these requests (sample on next page). The card is given to the buyer for that department, who staples it to the purchase order when the item is ordered.

When the requested item comes in, we notify the customer by telephone or email. The item is then put on hold for two weeks, with the top copy of the card attached to it. The back copy of the card goes into a file at the register to be pulled when the customer comes in. If someone hasn't turned up by the time the on-hold period has expired, we try to re-contact the customer to find out if he or she still wants the item.

```
┌─────────────────────────────────────────────────────────────┐
│                    Customer Request Card                    │
│  Name:_____Date:_____     │
│                                                             │
│  Address:_____  │
│                                                             │
│  Email:_____Phone:_____   │
│                                                             │
│  Item requested, incl. quantity:_____   │
│                                                             │
│  _____Source:_____ Price:_____  │
│                                                             │
│  Date needed by, if any:_____ Salesperson:_____  │
│                                                             │
│  ❒ Deposit paid? (If so, please list on back.) To be put on hold? ❒ yes ❒ no │
│                                                             │
│  Date ordered:_____ Date Received:_____ Hold Until:_____ │
│                                                             │
│  Notified via ❒ email ❒ phone ❒ by _____ on_____ │
└─────────────────────────────────────────────────────────────┘
```

Sample customer request card.

Sometimes customers phone for an item and want it held; sometimes they select it in the store and are not ready to buy it right away. We attach a version of the special order form to the item to go in the file at the register with the cards of items on hold. When a customer decides against an item on hold, we have been deprived of the opportunity to sell that item for the time it was being held, so we do set a time limit of one to two weeks.

Evaluating Customer Service

Good customer service is giving your customers what they want. And how do you know what they want? By asking. If a customer compliments you on your store, thank the person and ask if he or she has any suggestions for how you could improve it. If a customer complains about something, look at the complaint as an opportunity to learn how to do things better.

Make it easy for your staff to pass customer complaints and ideas on to you, and track them so that you can see if any trends develop. As the owner or manager, you should personally follow up on all customer problems immediately, by telephone or by email. Thanking a customer for bringing a complaint to your attention is often enough, but you may want to enclose a gift card to encourage an unhappy shopper to give the store another try.

Keep a notebook handy to list items that customers regularly ask for that you don't have, and try to fill in the gaps. Having the widest possible selection of merchandise on hand is one form of good customer service. Customers like to shop at stores where they can count on finding what they are looking for.

Many stores have a suggestion box for customers. Some food co-ops make their suggestion boxes the source of an ongoing dialogue with customers by publicly posting all suggestions with a written reply from a staff member. Even children's suggestions are answered respectfully by someone in the store and put up on the bulletin board.

A more formal way of finding out what customers want is by conducting a customer survey. This can be done briefly at the checkout counter, if it is limited to a few questions—for example, "How did you hear about our store?" "Did you find everything you were looking for?" and "Is there anything we can do to serve you better?" You can also post a survey on your website, send out an email questionnaire, or use an online survey service such as www.surveymonkey.com. Online survey services will also compile the data for you, which is very convenient. Remember that in order to attract responses, your survey needs to be short, with straightforward questions.

A longer survey can be sent to your email list, with a small gift to reward those who complete it, or filled in while a customer is shopping in the store. Other possible questions include asking where customers live, what radio and TV stations they like, and what newspapers and magazines they read—invaluable information in planning your advertising.

For the ultimate amount of customer feedback, consider forming a customer council. We did this when we were planning a major expansion and found that our best customers were pleased to be consulted and happy to give us an evening of their time. We presented the group with specific questions to discuss and invited our staff to join us for the session. Refreshments were served, and the customers were rewarded with a gift to thank them. As a bonus, the local newspaper found the idea so novel that it featured the story on the business page.

YOU CAN'T DO IT ALL

When employees make suggestions, they realize that we can't implement them all. Customers also have ideas that we may choose not to act on. We know, for example, that if we asked customers what hours they'd like us to be open, they would probably want us open earlier every morning. We are able to operate a successful business without being open at 9:00 a.m. so we choose to meet their needs in other ways. We offer the services we feel are most important to our customers and are economically feasible for our shop, realizing that in the future we may have to change in order to stay competitive. But the cornerstone of customer service, polite attention to the customer's needs, always remains the same and is essential to the success of every specialty shop.

CHAPTER 9

HELP WANTED: FINDING AND KEEPING GREAT EMPLOYEES

Conversation at a cocktail party turned to the subject of retail stores. A guest asked Linda Alanen, our employee and neighbor at the time, the secret of Orange Tree Imports' success. "The staff, of course," she replied. I must admit that had I been asked, I would have been tempted to take some of the credit myself, but her answer made me realize that in the eyes of our staff and many of our customers, the employees are the store. Your customer service is only as good as your staff. The selection, training, and positive reinforcement of good employees are key to creating a winning specialty shop. And because you will be spending countless hours in your store, it is important to surround yourself with people you like to be with.

When Do You Need to Hire?

Some new shop owners try to postpone hiring employees, hoping to avoid the expense and the many government regulations and forms. But this approach is shortsighted. Not only is it impossible to grow a business without employees, but going it alone exacts a heavy toll on the business owner's personal life. The total cost of an employee is not too much to pay to provide better service for your customers and to buy yourself some free time. Without employees other than your spouse or children, you cannot afford to be sick, go on buying trips, or take vacations. This lack of time off can take be difficult on you, your family life, and your business. If your shop is very small, consider starting with a staff of perhaps just one or two part-time employees, provided they can work full days if you are absent.

You will undoubtedly also discover that there are some tasks that you are well suited for and others that you would do best to delegate. Hiring those whose skills and knowledge make up for your weaknesses makes your business stronger.

When you decide to hire employees, you commit to meeting a weekly or biweekly payroll, no matter how slow sales are. There may be times when you must go without a paycheck yourself or borrow money in order to pay your staff. As an employer, you have a moral obligation to provide your employees with a dependable income and a safe work environment—not a responsibility to be taken lightly—but creating meaningful jobs can also be a source of great pleasure and satisfaction.

Enlightened Leadership: Participative Democracy

Being the boss may be new to you. In case you think this role as the boss is unimportant, remember this classic quote from Dickens's *A Christmas Carol*, in which Scrooge says about his kindly first employer, Fezziwig: "He has the power to render us happy or unhappy, to make our service light or burdensome, a pleasure or a toil. Say that his power lies in words and looks, in things so slight and insignificant that it is impossible to add and count 'em up: what then? The happiness he gives is quite as great as if it cost a fortune."

The role of boss may initially be an uncomfortable one for you, especially if you did not like your last boss. But owning or managing a retail store is an opportunity to show just how effective a leader you can be: educating, motivating, and rewarding your employees. Keep in mind that a good boss does all of the following:

- Treats employees as individuals, caring about their success

- Routinely spends time on the sales floor

- Is always available to employees when they need guidance, support, or just someone to talk to

- Welcomes the input of all staff members

- Praises the contributions, large and small, that each employee makes to the store's success

- Is as generous as possible in rewarding employees for their efforts

Even a good boss cannot always please everyone, but as a leader, you need to make sure all employees can count on being treated fairly and with respect.

If you have never managed employees before, read some of the many books available on personnel policies and business management. Enlightened management techniques can have an enormous impact on your employees' level of job satisfaction, and you will find that a happy and enthusiastic workforce is essential for providing good customer service.

We use an unusual but effective approach to store management. The technique *participative democracy* is a form of business management based on the concept that employees should have a voice in all aspects of running the business. In addition to being in charge of one or more departments of merchandise, our staff members are privy to all our financial data and give input on major decisions, from hiring to visual merchandising and remodeling. The final decisions still rest with us, but in order to make this technique effective, we realize we must share some real power with our employees.

Delegating Effectively

"Giving away responsibility and authority is the ultimate expression of leadership," according to Jammie Baugh, author of *The Nordstrom Way*. It may be particularly difficult for a novice boss to learn to delegate responsibility, especially if you are used to doing everything yourself. An employee will rarely perform a task exactly the way you would have, but in order to be an effective leader, you must learn to give employees the authority to own the jobs they are doing.

Changing a display or second-guessing a customer refund decision undermines staff members' confidence. There is a fine line between wanting the very best in window displays, customer service, restocking, and product selection—for the sake of the store and its customers—and wanting to let employees set their own standards for their job performance. We continue to struggle with this issue.

The day may come when you begin to delegate buying responsibility beyond just the placing of routine reorders. Staff buyers need to understand the focus of the shop and the criteria you use to evaluate merchandise so that the store will retain your personal touch. It is helpful to review all orders initially, especially if you do not provide a buying budget. Don't expect every item on every order to sell well. All buyers, even you, make some mistakes.

Being able to delegate effectively is an enormous advantage. The skills and ideas that our 25 employees bring to Orange Tree Imports allow us to do much more than we could if Dean and I were trying to run the store alone. The variety of ages and interests of our staff members reflects the diversity of our customer base, and their varied opinions help us keep in touch with different perspectives. And because we encourage them to take on as much responsibility as possible, our employees' many talents are reflected in creative touches throughout the store.

Help Wanted: Finding and Keeping Great Employees

Hiring for Special Job Functions

Chances are good that the first employees you hire will be salespeople. Some stores call them clerks or cashiers; we use the term sales associates because it has a professional sound. A dignified title is an inexpensive perk that can make staff members feel more important. This may seem insignificant, but consider the attitude reflected by a department store chain's decision to refer to its sales staff as "hourly units."

As your store grows, you will need more staff to supplement your own efforts. As you develop specialized job functions, write job descriptions stating exactly what responsibilities you want these employees to take and what skills the employees will need to have. Specialty shops often employ people with the following job functions:

- Housekeeper
- Stockperson
- Bookkeeper
- Manager
- Assistant manager
- Personnel/HR (human resources) manager
- Buyer or purchasing agent
- Department manager
- Advertising manager
- Display coordinator/visual merchandiser

If you decide to branch out, you will need a store manager, and probably an assistant manager, for each location. If you have many branch stores, you may wish to have a division manager to oversee a group of stores in a specific geographic area.

When looking for employees for special job roles, experience and training become primary concerns. Almost anyone with a friendly personality; average reading, communication, and math skills; and a willingness to learn can be trained to be a sales associate, but it is preferable to hire managers with managerial experience and bookkeepers with bookkeeping experience.

Skills testing may be useful for qualifying candidates for these specialized positions. Some businesses also find that personality testing is helpful in finding which candidates are best suited for a certain job. The more you can find out about each applicant, through testing or extensive interviews, the easier it will be to choose the best person for the job.

THE ROLE OF THE STORE MANAGER

Many store owners find themselves overwhelmed by the endless amount of work to be done: waiting on customers, buying merchandise, dealing with personnel issues, filling in government paperwork, and on and on. If you find there is never enough time in the day to get everything done, it is probably time to hire a manager. Having someone to help run some aspects of the day-to-day operation will allow you to concentrate your time and energy on those tasks you do best and enjoy most, as well as freeing you up to work on the long-range, big-picture issues facing your business.

Hiring a store manager is a special challenge because this person will represent you to your staff, as well as to your customers. It is important to hire a person who shares your values and your vision of what you want your store to be. Look for someone with a level head, good listening skills, and a consistently upbeat attitude. As the owner, you need to share real responsibility and authority with the manager. Encourage the manager to be a role model, providing excellent customer service. A manager who supervises other employees should work to earn the respect of his or her coworkers by treating everyone as benevolently and fairly as you treat your staff members yourself.

It is essential to establish open communication and an easy rapport with the one or more managers you hire, creating a strong leadership team for the store. In order to keep a positive attitude, despite the challenges of the job, a manager needs your ongoing support and encouragement. Having a manager means being able to delegate many store responsibilities, but there is still a real need for you as the store owner to remain enthusiastically involved. Don't let yourself get out of touch with your customers and their needs, or with your staff and their concerns.

Appealing to a Shrinking Workforce

The dwindling pool of candidates, especially for sales positions, has long been of grave concern to all retailers. In some areas, stores compete fiercely for employees, luring staff members away from each other with the promise of higher pay and better benefits. And yet surveys of employees show that the opportunity to do meaningful work, the feeling of being appreciated, and a sense of job security are as important to most workers as the hourly salary and benefits. Of course, you should check to see what other stores are paying and offer as much as you can afford in order to attract the best candidates. But look beyond money and benefits to create jobs that people will enjoy. As a specialty shop owner, you are in a position to offer many things:

- ♦ A pleasant work environment
- ♦ A generous discount on merchandise
- ♦ Flexible yet predictable scheduling
- ♦ Opportunities to give input
- ♦ Seasonal employment

SPECIALTY SHOP RETAILING

- ♦ Social interaction with customers and fellow staff members
- ♦ Creative work, such as designing displays

These perks will automatically make your job listing more appealing to most people than job openings at a fast-food restaurant or discount store. If you can also provide better wages and benefits, who would choose to flip burgers instead? The main competition for quality employees, of course, comes from companies offering considerably higher salaries and opportunities for advancement. Retailing, especially at the sales-associate level, simply can't support the same wages as what my staff sometimes jokingly refers to as "real jobs."

A specialty shop has to work hard to retain employees by making their work more enjoyable than the alternatives. Although we do have turnover every year, I'm very pleased that we also have employees who have been with us over 30 years. We celebrate staff loyalty by presenting employees with an enameled orange tree pin on their fifth work anniversary and every five years beyond that. We commemorate the annual anniversary of each employee's date of hire with a thank-you in the store newsletter, and sometimes a special note or gift.

One way to keep employees is to offer opportunities for advancement. A small shop may have limited jobs to fill, but if branches are in the store's future, there may be opportunities for sales staff to advance to store management positions. Even with just one location, we are able to help employees train to do product buying or to take on new roles such as cooking school director or display coordinator. Employees who stay on can be rewarded with salary raises, especially as they take on more responsibility, and added paid vacation and sick days.

Help Wanted: Finding and Keeping Great Employees

The Importance of Flexible Scheduling

When your store is new, it may be difficult to predict how many sales associates will be needed at any one time or to know how many hours a week specialized jobs such as bookkeeping will take. Many startup businesses, especially restaurants, hire more people than they actually need on the assumption that a percentage will leave or be terminated within the first month or two. If they don't, everyone's hours get cut back.

It is better to hire a reasonable number of employees, favoring those who can be flexible in the hours they work. Employees willing to work 15 to 30 hours can start out at 15 and work more as the store gets busy. For many of our employees, flexible scheduling is one of the strong appeals of working at our store.

With time, customer patterns will develop that make it easier to know how many staff members will be needed on certain days of the week or even at certain times of day. We know that Saturdays are always our busiest day of the week, for example, and that we need extra help the day before Valentine's Day. These are all factors for the person doing the hiring and scheduling to take into account. Payroll is usually a store's highest operating expense, so it makes sense to schedule efficiently. Use cash register records to determine which times of day and days of the week are busiest and which months require extra sales staff.

Our staff is made up of both full-time and part-time employees. The full-time employees work 30 to 40 hours a week, providing a wonderful sense of continuity by being at the store so much. All of the full-time employees have duties beyond customer service, and, as a result, these staff members are paid at a somewhat higher hourly rate. We also have a number of employees who work 20 to 30 hours a week, a position we call "special part time." These employees have a real commitment to the store, despite the fact that they don't want to work full time.

SPECIALTY SHOP RETAILING

Some of our special part-time employees have been with us for many years, and most of them manage at least one department. Our part-time staff that works less than 20 hours a week is key to being able to offer flexible scheduling, because they fill in as needed and work more hours during vacations and the busy season. We sometimes hire seasonal help for late November and December, ideally getting started with their hiring and training in late October.

Setting up a schedule that makes everyone happy is a major challenge for the personnel manager. Many retail employees—even those who are full–time—have other responsibilities, so we try to set up a schedule that is consistent from month to month for their convenience. Employers who don't do this make life very difficult for staff members trying to juggle more than one commitment, according to a recent University of Chicago study.

We only make changes when an employee needs the schedule altered or when we need extra staffing for our busy season. Employees are invited to submit schedule requests, and we make every effort to accommodate them all. Weekdays are divided into two shifts, 10:00 to 2:00 and 2:00 to 6:00, plus the evenings when we're open late. These four-hour units allow us to schedule those who want to work partial days as well as those who want a full eight-hour day. Anyone working eight hours needs a lunch or dinner break, which is usually covered by having a half-day worker come in early or stay late.

Employees who have paid vacation time as part of their compensation package are encouraged to schedule their vacations early and to avoid taking them during our busiest months, November and December. We sometimes have a problem with too many employees wanting time off in August, and those years we ask that staff members try to schedule summer vacations in June and July. Some stores allow those with the most seniority to have first choice of vacation dates.

Help Wanted: Finding and Keeping Great Employees

Weekends are the busiest time for most retail stores, and Saturdays and Sundays can be very difficult to staff. We make working weekends more appealing by splitting Saturday into two shifts and by setting up an A and B weekend schedule, so employees have the option of working every other weekend. Dean and I work most Saturdays ourselves. Without the distraction of sales reps and telephone calls, Saturdays provide an excellent opportunity for us to have direct customer contact. We take Sunday and Monday off as our weekend together.

JOB SHARING

Almost all of our specialized job functions are job shared—we have two bookkeepers, two stockpersons, and a management team—and both the store and the employees benefit from this flexible arrangement. The essential work in one area does not come to a halt if someone is sick or on vacation, and staff members have someone to share their workload with. Parents enjoy being able to be home when children return from school or to stay home with a sick child. Usually those sharing a job develop a close rapport, working out on their own how to divide the tasks at hand and even sometimes setting up their own schedule.

Where to Look for Good Employees

Advertising for employees in the classifieds was once the most productive way of looking for new staff, but we now start with Craigslist. Since you're not paying by the word, which was the case with classified ads, you can allow yourself the luxury of writing copy that romances the excitement of working in your shop. We also usually add a photo of our staff or store.

Be sure to mention the benefits you offer, and to specify the type of experience and skills you are looking for. Not only will this help you attract qualified candidates, but a lack of experience can often be used to soften the sting of rejection to those who don't get hired.

There are other online job services that you might consider, and our shop local organization sponsors one to help reach individuals who want to work for small businesses. The national job boards may be especially effective if you are hiring large numbers of employees or have shops in several parts of the country. In addition, you can have a jobs available page on your own website and promote your openings in your social media and email blasts.

Facebook offers a "Jobs" bookmark that you can add to your page. It makes sense that someone who has "liked" your shop on Facebook might also like working there. Consider creating a targeted market of job seekers so that you can boost your Facebook post about the fact that you are hiring.

Colleges, technical schools, and local high schools may have job boards that will post listings for you or even provide work-study training programs that allow students to get credit for time on the job. Students placed with a store as part of a course in retailing or business may well be interested in staying on after graduation.

Use social media and your store email list to get the word out that you are hiring.

Help Wanted: Finding and Keeping Great Employees

Don't overlook organizations that target retirees, who often make excellent employees. For management positions, you might consider using an employment agency, although these services are often quite costly. And be sure to ask your current employees if they have friends looking for work. It is not uncommon for companies to offer a bonus to an employee whose lead turns out to be a successful hire.

One of the best ways to advertise a job opening is to post a notice in your store and on the door. Current customers who have shown an interest in your store and its merchandise may enjoy working in a shop they know they like. Some businesses put up large "Help Wanted" signs that are visible from the street, but I prefer something more discreet. You don't want to broadcast the fact that you are short staffed or that someone just quit.

Out of respect for your current staff, don't post the hourly salary. This is a matter that can be discussed with applicants privately or mentioned in a memo attached to the application form. We find it useful to also list the job description and hours on this memo so that applicants know specifically what we are looking for in terms of experience and availability.

Should you hire family members or friends? Some authorities say no, cautioning that the employer-employee relationship may damage the personal relationship and that any favoritism shown toward the friend or family member will be resented by other staff members.

Be sure that the person you hire is qualified for the job you offer and understands that you both will need to be able to relate to each other in a businesslike manner. You may find it difficult to criticize employees who are friends or relatives or to assign them tasks they don't like. Although we are guilty of ignoring this rule, most authorities advise, "Don't hire someone you can't fire."

The "How to Hire" Guide

Careful hiring can result in lower turnover of employees and a happier, more compatible staff. A written job application is useful for providing background information, and one or two in-person interviews will allow you to get acquainted with the applicant. For retail jobs, many people feel that attitude and aptitude are equally important. Skills and product knowledge can be taught—how to be pleasant and helpful usually have to be inherent traits, and are what you are looking for during an interview. Of course, even two face-to-face interviews cannot tell you everything there is to know about a prospective employee, but this process should give you some idea of each applicant's strengths and weaknesses and how interested he or she is in the job.

THE JOB APPLICATION FORM

The government doesn't care much about what merchandise you buy, how you display it, and whether you empty the trash each night, but it cares a great deal about almost all matters relating to employees. The application form you use to screen potential employees may not ask questions about age (if over 40), gender or sexual orientation, race, religion, birthplace, and military status. It is illegal to discriminate against potential employees on these grounds, so of course these same issues may not be discussed when interviewing candidates.

The US Equal Employment Opportunity Commission also points out that "Questions about marital status and number and ages of children are frequently used to discriminate against women and may violate Title VII if used to deny or limit employment opportunities." Some states and cities have "ban-the-box" laws that prohibit questions about whether applicants have ever been convicted of a crime. You can still run a background check after deciding to hire an applicant, but this legislation is intended to prevent discrimination against individuals with criminal records.

Help Wanted: Finding and Keeping Great Employees

What can you ask? Name, address, email and telephone number are basic. Past work history and education are also important questions. We don't require a certain amount of education or experience, but this information gives us an idea of the applicant's interests and whether they have successfully completed a degree or held a job for some length of time. You may also ask about limitations that specifically apply to performing the essential functions of the job. A stockperson, for example, needs to be able to lift packages weighing over 30 pounds, but a bookkeeper does not. Unless the job schedule is completely flexible, ask about available hours, so you will know if the applicant can work during the times you need to fill.

Applicants should also provide contact information for three references other than family members and friends. Past work references are seldom a source of much information since many companies are afraid of being sued if they give a negative reference. Nevertheless, most past employers will at least confirm the dates of past employment; if nothing else, this information proves that the candidate has told the truth about past work experience.

You may wish to create your own form customized for your store, but templates for application forms are available to download online, and can be purchased in printed form through office supply stores. These forms have the advantage of being revised constantly for compliance with federal and state regulations and are worth consulting periodically to be sure your form is current.

REVIEWING THE APPLICATIONS

A competitive job market requires you to act quickly on applications that look particularly promising. A delay of a few weeks may mean that the applicant has already been hired by another business. Look over the application for neatness and completeness, as well as content.

Any retail experience is, of course, a plus, as is any work or volunteer experience requiring interaction with the public. Very few applicants have academic qualifications that specifically apply to retailing, but a high level of education does reflect a capacity to learn and to commit to a program. Long-term commitment is something we value in an employee, especially as it is much more expensive to hire and train someone new than to retain a good employee.

Look for consistency in the education and job history. We once had an applicant with an unexplained 10-year gap in his work record. When we asked what he'd been doing those 10 years, he replied that he didn't remember. Needless to say, he didn't get the job. Another applicant said she had been working on a cruise ship for two years, but we found out she'd been in prison during that time.

The application doesn't reflect the most important qualities of an employee: enthusiasm and a willingness to learn the job, to work hard, to serve customers, and to be a member of a team. For this reason, all applicants who meet the basic qualifications should be interviewed in person.

PRELIMINARY INTERVIEWS

Our interviewing process reflects the participative democracy management style mentioned earlier. One of the most important elements in the success of this approach is the entire staff's involvement in the interviewing process, hiring, and employee training. We have used this technique for many years, so all of our current employees have been hired by their colleagues.

A preliminary interview of all the most likely candidates is usually done by the personnel manager, myself, and sometimes an assistant manager. The questions we ask during this 10-minute interview are similar to those that are on the application form, plus some open-ended queries such as, "Tell us about an achievement you are particularly proud of" and "Give us an example of how you handled a difficult situation in one of your previous jobs." The applicant is given a chance to talk informally and to ask us questions about the job. The key to good interviewing is to put the candidate at ease and allow him or her to talk as much as possible.

THE STAFF INTERVIEW

The three or four candidates selected for second interviews after this first round of screening are asked to come before the store opens for a staff interview. As many as 15 of our current employees usually attend these informal interviews, and all of those present have been hired in this way. We sit in a circle and meet with one candidate at a time, asking the applicant to tell us a bit about him- or herself. The staff is free to ask anything they want, except of course about topics prohibited by law. Questions sometimes range from, "What book would you take to a desert island?" to "Do you like to cook?" In the interest of fairness, we try to ask every candidate a few of the same questions.

One employee usually tells the candidate a bit about what it's like to work at Orange Tree Imports and describes what the job entails. After the last candidate has left, the staff discusses the notes they have taken and then votes by secret ballot (if it looks like it will be a close vote) or a show of hands.

Some candidates find it very intimidating to face this large group, and we take their nervousness into account when evaluating their interview performance. We look for indications that the candidate really wants to work at our store, as evidenced by a positive attitude and by good grooming for the interview. The stress of the staff interview is not unlike facing a number of customers all wanting immediate attention, so the process helps us see if the candidate is comfortable talking with strangers.

The staff has a vested interest in the success of the new coworkers they have selected. These employees come on the job having already met a number of the staff members and with the knowledge that their coworkers want them to be there. Of course, as with any other democratic voting process, candidates are sometimes selected by a narrow margin, but most staff members are comfortable with the concept of the majority vote ruling. I can think of one instance, however, when some members of the staff were so vehemently opposed to the final candidate for personnel manager that we started the process over again. (Yes, even the personnel manager is hired by staff interview.)

We check references after the selection process is completed, and offer the job to the chosen candidate as soon as we are able to get in touch with their references. Those not selected are given the courtesy of prompt notification via email, and often their applications are kept on file for future consideration.

REFERENCE AND BACKGROUND CHECKS

Ideally, a good job reference call can help you make sure you are hiring the right person for the job. Although many businesses now have a policy of revealing very little aside from dates of employment and possibly salary range, it is a good idea to confirm that the employee is telling the truth about their former employment. You may also be fortunate enough to get more information when you ask questions such as "Would you rehire this person?" and "Is there anything about this person's job performance that you think would be helpful for us to know?"

For a position of high trust such as bookkeeper or manager, you will want to do a background check. Some stores check on all employees because they will have access to cash and merchandise. Call your city police department or the Department of Justice for your state to ask what records are available online. There are third-party services that will conduct background checks for you; however, it is important to make sure the service is insured in case of a lawsuit. You will need to provide the potential employee's name and birth date and may have to show that the individual has given you permission to access his or her records.

Government Forms for New Employees

The first day on the job for a new employee involves a certain amount of paperwork. Your business will need to have obtained a federal Employer Identification Number (EIN) or form SS-4. Apply for the EIN online or contact the IRS at 1-800-829-4933.

You'll also need to have a W-4 Withholding Exemption Certificate form for each employee. This form is used to record the employee's marital status for federal tax filing purposes (same sex marriages are treated the same as marriages of couples of the opposite sex) and any exemptions they are claiming to withholding. If your state has its own income tax, and most do, you will need to withhold state taxes. The W-4 form provides a space for the number of deductions being claimed for state as well as federal taxes.

Employers must also see proof that the employee is legally entitled to work in the United States, as required on Immigration and Naturalization Service (INS) form I-9. Within the first three days of employment, you should ask to see the following:

- Unexpired US passport, or foreign passport with an I-551 stamp *or*

- Alien registration receipt card/permanent resident card *or*

- Unexpired employment authorization card or document *or*

- A Social Security card, US government issued birth certificate or other document to establish authorization to work in the US, together with proof of identity (e.g., driver's license, school photo ID, voter's registration card).

A number of other documents, such as a Native American tribal document, may also be used. If you have questions, call the U.S Citizenship and Immigration Services (USCIS) information line at 800-375-5283 or visit their website. You might want to take a look at their internet-based E-Verify program for determining whether an individual is legally eligible for employment in the US. The fine for hiring someone who is not can be stiff, and the employee risks deportation. The Immigration Reform and Control Act, which requires employers to establish their employees' right to work in the United States, does prohibit discrimination on the basis of national origin or citizenship.

You are required by law to annually report all wages paid and taxes withheld for each employee to the federal government. This report is filed using form W-2, and copies of the W-2s must be given to employees by the end of the following January and filed with the Social Security Administration.

The Employment Agreement

There is no government requirement that you have an employment agreement or contract, but it does make good business sense. Spelling out the compensation you are offering an employee can avoid future misunderstandings. Stating your expectations lets an employee know exactly what the job entails. There is a sample employment agreement shown on the next page, and you can download the form at www.specialityshopretailing.com. Many employee contracts include a noncompete clause in the contract, asking that employees promise not to open a competing store within a certain distance of the employer's store within a year or two of leaving.

Although these clauses often prove difficult to enforce legally, there is no reason not to request that at least those in managerial positions make this promise. Unfortunately, it does sometimes happen that an employee privy to inside information uses that knowledge to open a new business or to benefit a future employer.

EMPLOYMENT AGREEMENT

(After completing this form, make a copy to give to the employee.)

Employee's Name: _____

Starting Date: _____ Full-time/Part-time: _____

Job Title: _____

(See job description for details of duties and responsibilities.)

Usual Work Schedule:

_____

_____

_____

Compensation:

Starting Rate: _____ Pay Days Are: _____

Vacation Days: _____ Sick Days: _____ Personal Time: _____

Additional Benefits: _____

Periodic Performance Evaluation:

Seasonal employees will be evaluated: _____

All other employees will be evaluated: _____

Termination:

The first _____ weeks are a provisional period of employment.

After this time, the employee is expected to give _____ week's notice.

If dismissed, unless for behavior outlined in the Employee Handbook, the employee will receive

_____ weeks' notice or the equivalent in severance pay.

_____   _____

Employee's Signature, Date   Employer's Signature, Date

Sample employment agreement.

The employment agreement also usually states how often employee evaluations will be held and spells out the conditions for termination. It is standard to request that employees give two weeks' notice when leaving and to promise an equivalent amount of notice, or severance pay, if the employee is dismissed for reasons other than fraud, theft, illegal drug use, or unprofessional conduct.

In addition to the employment agreement and the W-4 and I-9 forms, we ask new employees to fill in an emergency contact form. These forms, kept in the employee's personnel files, give us the telephone number of a close relative or friend to contact if necessary. A sample of this form is shown below, and you can download the form at www.specialityshopretailing.com.

EMPLOYMENT EMERGENCY CONTACT FORM

Name: _____

Address: _____

City and State:_____

Phone numbers: _____

This information is current s of _____

Please remember to update this form if anything changes.

IN CASE OF EMERGENCY

Call: _____

Phone numbers: _____

Or: _____

Phone numbers: _____

Allergies, medical conditions, or other important information.

_____

_____

_____

Sample employee emergency contact form.

Help Wanted: Finding and Keeping Great Employees

TWO WEEKS ON TRIAL

Two interviews are better than one, but even after two interviews, you will still know very little about how well a new applicant will work out. Keep in mind that the process of dismissing an employee is difficult and often costly. Put your best effort into the hiring process, and if you don't find a candidate you and your staff are comfortable with, continue the search until you do. You can also insist on a two-week trial period for the new employee. This offers both the employer and the employee an easy out if the fit is not right. If a serious problem, such as tardiness, a negative attitude, or poor work habits, turns up during the first two weeks, the conditional period allows both parties to sever the relationship without having to give the usual two weeks' notice or written warnings.

It is essential to let the employee know at the time of hiring if the first two weeks will be considered a trial period. The new employee may have quit another job in order to take the one at your shop, so dismissal even during the short trial period can be very problematic. Be sure that you and the staff do everything possible to make the person a successful member of the team.

Training Staff on Store Procedures

After filling in the necessary forms on the first day of work, our new employees are taken on a tour of the store, introduced to some of the staff, and given their own copy of the store's employee handbook (see Chapter 10). The actual job training is spread out over a week or two because there is too much for anyone to learn in a few days.

We use a training checklist to make sure nothing is missed. This list varies from job to job, but for sales associates, it includes cash register training and information about a myriad of small procedures, from selling gift cards to calculating out-of-state shipping charges. We even include details such as what we want employees to say when answering the telephone. We cover important topics relating to customer service and

> Try reinforcing the teaching of product location during the initial training period by using a treasure hunt approach to see if new employees (or even existing ones) know where to find a list of different items. Be sure to provide prizes for those who get the most right.

help employees begin to be familiar with the benefits of all our products and how to find various types of merchandise in the store and stockroom.

Procedures are explained and demonstrated, and then the new employees practice them. Some of this training takes place when the store is closed, so the cash registers are available for practice. Role playing is used as a training method, with the personnel manager and new employee taking turns pretending to sell each other items, handle refunds, and correct mistakes. It is essential that these skills are practiced, not just explained. As the Chinese proverb says, "I hear and I forget. I see and I remember. I do and I understand."

After the initial training period, a sales associate is assigned to shadow an experienced staff member for several shifts. This buddy system allows the other staff members to get involved in training new employees and gives the new person a specific coworker to turn to with questions. We encourage new employees to ask questions. There is a lot to learn, and no one gets it all the first time.

After two weeks on the job, each new employee is given an evaluation. This is an opportunity for the personnel manager to sit down with the person and ask if there are any areas of the training process that need more work and to review the employee's first weeks of job performance. This is also a good opportunity to build the employee's self-confidence, pointing out how much he or she has already learned. Sometimes new staff members are a bit worried because they realize they don't know everything and can't remember some of the procedures they've been taught. We reassure them that it can take as long as a whole year to feel comfortable with all aspects of the store's operations.

CHAPTER *10*
PROGRESSIVE PERSONNEL POLICIES: MOTIVATING YOUR STAFF

To deliver the highest level of customer service, and to have your store run smoothly, you need to treat all employees fairly and with respect. The personnel policies that you put in place should make your expectations clear, and also spell out the way in which you will reward your staff for a job well done.

Creating an Employee Handbook

My informal poll of small shop owners revealed that a surprisingly low percentage have employee handbooks or manuals. I wonder how the employees of these stores know what standards of behavior and appearance they are expected to live up to and what the store's policies are regarding issues that concern the staff, such as sick leave, paid holidays, and salary increases. For the sake of consistency and clarity, many personnel issues should be addressed in a handbook that can be given to each new employee.

You can download programs to create a standardized retail employee manual; however, in keeping with our participative democracy mode of management, we developed our employee handbook with the input of a staff committee. A group of five or six of us spent several months hammering out the store's first policy statements on such issues as dress code, tardiness, employee evaluations, and maternity leave. The process could have been abbreviated by not seeking staff input, but then the policies might not have been as willingly followed. Employees will support policies they help to create.

Our employee handbook starts out with a brief history of the store and our mission statement (see Chapter 2), which help focus the staff on our shared goals. The remainder of the employee handbook is devoted to brief, clear statements about personnel policies and employee benefits, including, but not limited to the following:

- Payroll procedures
- Paid vacation and sick days
- Parental and adoption leaves
- Overtime policy
- Employee discounts
- Health, life, and other insurance
- Sales bonuses
- Opportunities for advancement and raises
- Breaks
- Use of cell phones on the sales floor
- Business trip reimbursement
- Termination and exit interviews
- Drug and alcohol use policies
- Dress code
- Scheduling
- Changes in part-time or full-time status

The information contained in the employee handbook is intended as a guideline for all staff members. We try not to be too restrictive in the wording; it is not intended to sound like the Ten Commandments. Staff members are invited to bring any policy up for review at any time.

Progressive Personnel Policies: Motivating Your Staff

DRESS CODES AND NAME TAGS

Customers appreciate being able to identify a store's personnel by the way they are dressed or by the name tags they wear. Some stores carry out the shop's theme in the employees' dress, for example, having all the staff wear referee shirts, lab coats, denim shirts and khaki slacks, or gardening aprons. I must admit that it took 30 years before my staff decided that aprons embroidered with our logo were a good idea, and they still don't wear name tags, as much as I appreciate it when salespeople in other shops use them. Some employees don't want customers to call them by their first names, and we respect that.

A store that chooses not to provide a uniform for its employees still needs to have a dress code for staff members. We keep ours very simple: no faded or torn jeans, no shorts, no T-shirts or sweatshirts with writing on them, and nothing low-cut or revealing.

The employee handbook states that everyone is expected to practice good hygiene, and male staff members are required to shave, unless they have a beard. Employees are not allowed to chew gum or smoke in the store. We have a facial piercing policy limiting such jewelry to one small stud worn in the side of the nose. By spelling out these details in the handbook, we hope to avoid having to criticize an employee's appearance. It isn't so bad to tell someone that they've priced an item incorrectly, but to ask an employee to go home and change is an embarrassment for us both.

Compensating Your Staff

There are two basic methods of compensating employees: salary and commission. Most stores pay an hourly salary, plus some benefits at least for full-time employees that might include life and health insurance, sick days, and paid vacations. Others pay their associates a commission based on sales, and some use a combination of the two methods. The commission approach is generally practical only for stores providing one-on-one customer service and selling high-priced items such as electronics, expensive clothing, and furniture. If your employees are paid by commission, remember to carefully monitor staffing levels so that everyone on duty has a reasonable expectation of earning a decent wage.

The advantage of paying commissions is that employees' income is directly tied to their job performance. Commissioned compensation encourages staff members to develop a customer base and to serve those customers well. But it does not always encourage team spirit, and commissioned salespeople can sometimes be too aggressive in their sales techniques. Some stores pay an hourly salary plus commission, requiring employees to achieve a minimum average amount of sales per hour to justify their base hourly pay. Those unable to live up to this standard are either terminated or moved into non-sales positions.

An alternative to the commission system is to offer special rewards or bonuses as incentives for exemplary sales and service. Some retailers treat employees to lunch or give staff members a day off with pay when they reach specific sales goals. We add an hourly bonus to the base pay of employees performing certain extra credit tasks, such as doing a main window display or assisting with a Cooking School class. To encourage sales assistants to substitute for each other, we give employees a sub shift voucher for every shift they take; five vouchers entitles the employee to a $20 bonus. We also allow employees to compliment each other on any exemplary job performance by giving a similar "Way to Go!" voucher (discussed later in this chapter), which is redeemable together with the sub shift vouchers.

Managers are often salaried, that is, paid a flat amount no matter how many hours they work. Sometimes a monetary bonus is added to the manager's salary based on annual sales or on achieving certain sales goals or increases. This is especially appropriate if the manager is in charge of a branch store's operations and can be a prime motivation in attracting and keeping good managerial staff.

Progressive Personnel Policies: Motivating Your Staff

MINIMUM WAGE ISSUES

There is a national minimum wage in the US, as well as state and local regulations covering this issue, which can be confusing. You will need to base your hourly wage on the highest amount required in your location—as well as what your competitors are paying. There is a movement in some municipalities and states to more than double the federal level, which may make it difficult for independent retailers to staff their stores. We have always paid a starting wage of at least $2.00 above the national minimum wage, and we know that when the law changes in our area, our employees will want to be paid a comparable amount above the new minimum.

It is tempting for shopkeepers to speak out against raising the minimum wage because of the hardships it will cause their businesses. However, this is an unpopular stance to take since most people agree that it would be very difficult to support a family by working full-time at the current minimum wage. The best we can hope for is an exception for part-time employees, especially younger workers who are still in school, because for them a retail job is often a flexible option for earning some income. And we can speak out in favor of more affordable housing, because the challenges of finding a place to live is often a driving factor in the effort to raise wages.

COMPLYING WITH OVERTIME REGULATIONS

It is required by law that almost every employee, salaried or hourly, be paid overtime, or time and a half (one and a half times the normal hourly rate), for all time beyond 40 hours in a seven-day period. The only exemption is for employees at a higher pay level than is offered by most retail stores.

Needless to say, paying time and a half increases payroll costs significantly. We have always tried to avoid overtime by requiring employees to notify us in writing in advance of going over the 40-hour limit. The government takes a firm line on making sure no more than 40 hours fall within a seven-day period. Your employees may not work 39 hours one week and 41 the next, even if you use a two-week pay period.

There are also special restrictions involved in hiring minors, and these regulations may be different at the state and federal level. Be sure to check how many hours high school students are allowed to work on school days and other restrictions.

PAYROLL PROCEDURES

Bookkeeping software and outside payroll services can take much of the headache out of producing payroll checks with the correct amounts deducted and paying the government all the taxes and contributions due in a timely manner. Payroll checks may need to have state, federal, and possibly even local taxes withheld, and as an employer you will need to match your employees' contributions to FICA (Social Security) and Medicare. You are also responsible for paying state and federal unemployment taxes. There are strict deadlines for reporting and paying all of these taxes, and it will save a lot of grief if you set up a tight system of payroll accounting from the start. Falling behind in tax reporting or, worse yet, in making the required deposits or payments on taxes can result in heavy penalties.

Whether you are doing your own payroll or outsourcing it to a service, you should be able to make direct deposits of your employees' pay into their bank accounts if they so desire. All of our staff members have chosen this convenient option. The payroll service still provides a receipt and a check cleverly labeled "this is not a check" for the employee's records.

You may choose to pay your employees once a week, biweekly, or even monthly. We have our staff members keep track of their hours on special time cards. The information gathered on these forms is essential for preparing the payroll, and it is useful for planning future staffing. We ask employees to give us a breakdown of how their time is spent, so we know what percentage of our payroll goes toward sales, restocking, meetings, bookkeeping, our cooking school, and other activities. Vacation and sick days are also noted on the time card and entered on the employee's file when the payroll is compiled.

This honor system has always worked well for us, but some businesses feel more secure using a time clock to track employee hours. Staff members are given a form or code number to punch into the clock when they arrive and when they leave, so work hours are recorded with minute precision. Many POS systems also provide this as an option, and there are also smartphone apps that include both a time clock and GPS tracking for making sure employees are where they are supposed to be. Automated timekeeping programs do not, however, provide much information about how the employee's time is spent.

Be sure to save all payroll records, including time cards, in the unhappy eventuality of a government audit. The IRS recommends that you keep records for a minimum of four years after you pay the tax or the tax is due.

Offering Attractive Benefits and Perks

Hourly pay or an annual salary is usually only one component of employee compensation. Some of the other benefits, such as paid time off for illness or vacation and health, disability, and life insurance, are commonly granted to employees in big businesses. A small shop may be hesitant to take on the cost of these perks, but without them it becomes more and more difficult to compete for quality employees.

In a society that in many ways values time as much as money, a generous number of paid vacation, personal, and sick days is very important, especially to full-time staff members. Paid sick days prevent employees from coming to work when they are ill and potentially contagious, which will help keep the rest of the staff healthy. Don't forget to include compensation for holidays as well, at least for all full-time employees who would have worked on those days if the store had been open.

One compromise that can help control the high cost of employee benefits is to offer a two-tiered system, with part-time employees receiving a lower level of benefits than those working at the store full time. Some of our part-time employees have full-time jobs elsewhere that provide them with insurance and other key benefits, or perhaps spouses with family insurance benefits. Our full-time staff may not have many other options if we do not have a decent benefits package.

INSURING YOUR EMPLOYEES—AND YOURSELF

It is ultimately in the best interest of employers to have a workforce that is protected by insurance against life's catastrophes. Some types of insurance protect your employees, such as workers' compensation, are mandated by state law. Workers' compensation insurance provides wage replacement and medical benefits to employees injured on the job. Fortunately, retailing is not inherently dangerous, so the premiums are not as high as they would be for, say, construction work. The amount of workers' comp is based on the total payroll, and coverage does not include the store owner in the case of sole proprietorships. In some states, workers' comp is sold through a government program; in others it may be obtained through your insurance agent.

Unemployment insurance is collected to provide payments to workers who are laid off temporarily. Each state administers a separate unemployment insurance program within guidelines established by federal law. The cost to your store will be based on your total payroll and the long-term record of how many of your employees have collected from the business's unemployment fund.

HEALTH INSURANCE OPTIONS

Having seen our health insurance costs rise astronomically over time, it is easy to understand the reluctance of many retailers to offer this coverage. But by the same token, the lack of benefits like health insurance makes retailing an unattractive field for some top-quality candidates. It is also a dilemma for a caring business owner to see an employee suffer through a serious illness without adequate health care coverage.

There are many choices of health care programs available today (although this may change depending on government actions), and most shops should be able to offer to provide some coverage for its full-time employees. The Affordable Care Act (ACA) currently offers incentives, such as tax breaks and tax credits via the Small Business Health Options Program (SHOP), to small businesses with the equivalent of fewer than 25 full-time workers, making less than $50,000 in average annual wages, to help them provide health benefits to employees.

One option you might look into is a managed care program such as a health maintenance organization (HMO) or preferred provider organization (PPO). This is the type of coverage we offer as it encourages our staff to get regular checkups and routine care by charging only a nominal co-pay for these services. Our company policy is to pay 100% of the health insurance for those who work 35 or more hours a week and 25% of the cost for those who work 20 to 30 hours.

Another option is the consumer-driven health movement (CDH), which the government allows to be funded by the employer and the employee with pretax dollars when used in conjunction with a high-deductible insurance policy. Current CDH options include the Health Reimbursement Arrangement (HRA), Medical Savings Account (MSA), Flexible Spending Account (FSA) and the health savings account (HSA). These programs permit employers to set up accounts with a financial institution in which money is deposited for medical expenses. Disbursements are tax-free when used to cover medical costs, and unused funds earn interest tax-free and belong to the employee. Information on these programs are available from the IRS.

You might want to consider instituting a wellness program at your store to lower insurance costs by encouraging healthy living. Some businesses offer a rebate to employees who join the YMCA or a gym or go to Weight Watchers. You could also bring speakers on wellness topics to your staff meetings and stock your snack area with healthy alternatives instead of sweets. We have a share in a CSA (community-sponsored agriculture) farm, and our staff takes turns being the recipient of our biweekly delivery of fresh vegetables.

DISABILITY AND LIFE INSURANCE

Disability insurance for staff members is sometimes overlooked by new entrepreneurs, but statistics show that a disabling illness or injury is more likely to occur than an untimely death. Policies with a relatively long waiting period before benefits are paid are less expensive than those that begin at 30 or 60 days, but it is important to look for a policy that will continue to pay benefits until retirement age or death.

Life insurance may not be a very attractive benefit in the eyes of young employees, but it is not expensive to provide a small amount of coverage, such as the equivalent of a year's salary. We provide disability and life insurance for all our full-time employees. Term life insurance can be purchased as part of a package of employee insurance benefits or as a separate policy.

When selecting disability and life insurance for your staff, don't forget to check about extra coverage for yourself. If you are unable to work or if you die, the effect on the business and your family could be catastrophic. Providing an adequate amount of insurance can cushion the blow. You might also consider key person or key executive insurance, which specifically protects the business, as the beneficiary, against loss in the event of your disability or death.

This insurance is especially important if you are in partnership with your husband or wife because your spouse might be unable to function efficiently for some time if you were to pass away or suffer a serious illness or injury. The premiums for this insurance are not deductible as a business expense; however, if benefits are ever paid, they are tax-free. Business loans often require a certain amount of this type of insurance in order to protect the interests of the lender.

Key person insurance is important to obtain for essential employees in your organization, such as branch managers. Businesses with one or more partners may wish to take out partner life insurance, which would provide the funds to buy out a deceased partner's share of the store without having to close or sell the business.

RETIREMENT PLANS

As the owner of a store, you need to save for your own retirement. At the same time, you have the opportunity to contribute toward retirement funds for your employees or to offer them a retirement plan into which they can put money from their salaries. Government regulations regarding retirement savings allow certain tax exemptions for plans that do not favor the employer at the expense of the employees.

There are currently three basic types of retirement plans:

1. A 401(k) plan allows employees to contribute their own funds toward retirement by means of salary deferral. This money is not subject to income taxes, but social security tax must still be paid on it. This plan can also be used by business owners with no employees other than a spouse.

2. In the Simplified Employee Pension Plan (SEP IRA) contributions are made by the employer only and are tax deductible as a business expense.

3. The Savings Incentive Match Plan for Employees (SIMPLE IRA) or simplified employee pension plan permits employers to make a

contribution matching the employee's contribution (up to 3% of pay) or to make a 2-% contribution to all employees. The funds can go into a 401(k) or an IRA account, and there are minimal reporting requirements.

Employees who are not covered by any pension plan at work may make tax-deductible contributions into individual IRA accounts. If you do not provide a pension plan, you should be making contributions into your own IRA or 401(k) each year.

Be sure to check with your tax adviser or CPA for the latest information about retirement plan regulations. You can also get information about current qualified retirement plans from the IRS. Whenever the rules for these plans change or you change your mind about your plan, administrative fees may be required in order to keep the business in compliance. Look for a plan you are sure you can afford and one that will appeal to your staff.

STAFF DISCOUNTS AND COURTESY CARDS

We offer our employees all merchandise at 10% above wholesale. This is our most popular perk, and, of course, it really doesn't cost us anything. We also do special orders for our staff members. Occasionally, one of our farsighted cookware or gadget suppliers will offer an even deeper discount to store employees, realizing that a salesperson who owns and uses an item can sell it more effectively.

As business coach AJ Sue points out, "Getting products into the hands of your employees can make them "true believers". . . and having a team of true believers is one of the most powerful predictors of your store being exceptionally successful."

For purposes of record keeping, and also to monitor potential employee theft, we ask employees to have another staff member ring up their purchases. Both parties initial or sign the receipt, which is kept in a ring binder near the register that has a pocket page for each employee.

Progressive Personnel Policies: Motivating Your Staff

We used to extend the staff discount to employee spouses, but not everyone on our staff is married, so we came up with a popular and fair alternative: the courtesy card. Each staff member is allowed to assign two annual 20%-off courtesy cards to a spouse or the friends or relatives of their choice. There are certain exceptions to the discount, and these are listed on the back of the card. We print the cards on the store computer, using sheets of pre-perforated business cards stock. If an employee leaves the store before the end of the calendar year, the card is invalidated.

GOAL SETTING AND BONUSES

One way to get the staff more interested in the sales and even profit figures is to involve them in setting goals for the business. When there are real rewards associated with reaching these goals, the staff have a natural motivation to work toward them. Bonus program goals should be announced with fanfare, followed in weekly or monthly progress meetings, and celebrated when met.

We pay our entire staff, including employees such as the stock person and bookkeepers, a quarterly sales bonus representing 10% of any increase in sales for that quarter over the same quarter the previous year. This bonus is divided among staff members (Dean and I do not partici-pate) based on their percentage of the total payroll during the quarter. Other stores share a percentage of profits with their employees at the end of each year or reward their employees with stock or a contribution to a pension plan. These methods all help give employees a vested interest in the success of the store.

It is important that the time period being measured is short enough to keep staff interested, which is why we do a bonus quarterly instead of annually. We have a calendar showing the figures to beat for each day: the sales figures from the same day a year ago. We adjust for the day of the week before setting up these charts each year so that the sales on Sunday, April 1, are not being compared to last year's sales on Monday, April 1, just because the date is the same.

In addition to measuring sales, you can set other goals, such as targeting two and a half inventory turns per year in certain departments, a certain percentage of gross profit margin on all sales, or an increase in customer traffic or the average transaction. Always target something that can be measured, and set goals that have a good chance of being met.

Using Open-Book Management

We used open-book management for years without knowing the name for it. With the exception of confidential personnel information, all the store's financial data is available to staff members. Jack Stack, author of *The Great Game of Business,* maintains that "the more people know about a company, the better that company will perform."

In a retail store, it is a good idea to teach all staff members how the income generated by sales is spent and how the cost of goods sold affects the net profit. Most employees aren't aware of the overhead costs in running a store and don't realize that most of the store's profits go to taxes and to fuel growth. They also need to know how their work fits into the big picture and how important their efforts are to the store's success.

We find it especially useful to share sales figures, broken down by merchandise category, with our staff. Those in charge of a department are eager to see how their area is performing, even though their compensation is not tied to these sales figures. We periodically review the additional data on the income statement and balance sheet with the store's management team, which is made up of our personnel, advertising, and operations managers.

We pay special attention to the payroll and advertising budgets, as well as sales figures and inventory turns. In a small shop, these are the main variables that we can try to adjust as expenses like rent and utilities do not fluctuate much. Although we do not focus a lot of attention on statistics, we do know a healthy bottom line is essential for the future of our business.

The Importance of Employee Evaluations

Employees and managers should be in continuous communication about issues of common concern, but a private annual evaluation makes sure that every employee gets an equal opportunity to be heard. This conference provides each employee a chance to bring up job-related concerns and to discuss future plans.

There is real value in having this special opportunity to listen to an employee, and by holding these conferences in a safe and quiet setting, you show each staff member how much you value his or her input. Try to use the occasion to praise the employee for past accomplishments. If there is room for improvement, list specific items under future goals. At the next annual evaluation, or sometimes a follow-up meeting a few weeks after the first one, check to see if progress is being made toward these goals. A sample Employee Evaluation form can be downloaded at www.specialtyshop-retailing.com.

Tying salary increases to the annual evaluation means that the money issue becomes the primary focus. An employee not receiving a raise may wonder why and may doubt the sincerity of any praise of his or her work. Ideally, salary increases should be given at other times of the year, such as when additional responsibilities are taken on.

CONFIDENTIALITY

All employee evaluations, and most conferences, should take place in a private setting free of interruptions. Arrange the chairs so that everyone is face to face, without a big desk in between creating a physical and psychological barrier. Everyone, management and staff, should be on equal footing. Encourage open discussion by promising that all matters discussed privately will be kept confidential if that is the wish of those involved.

One of the most difficult challenges facing an employer using the participative democracy style of management is keeping confidences. When openness is the norm, it is painful not to be able to explain to other staff members that one of their colleagues is feeling particularly emotional because of a personal problem or to know that someone is leaving soon without being able to mention it. But part of employer-employee trust is promising that when something is said in confidence, it will not be repeated. Thankfully, no one has ever asked that my husband, Dean, and I not talk to each other about staff concerns, so we always have someone to discuss an issue with without violating confidentiality.

Although we do ask employees to keep the store's financial information confidential, we are realistic enough to realize that everyone talks about their work at home. We have never had anything we were trying to hide from the outside world, so fortunately, it has not been detrimental to have our store's operations be somewhat publicly known.

Correcting Performance Problems

Stores should have clear performance standards, spelled out in the employee handbook, and should hold all employees to these standards equally. When an employee doesn't live up to the store's standards, a discussion of the problem and any consequences that follow a poor performance should take place right away. I usually make it a policy to overlook any problem if it occurs only once, but if the error is repeated, a conference is called for.

It is never pleasant to criticize an employee's behavior. Discussions of problems should be held in private—never in front of customers or other employees. Cushion your criticism with encouragement and praise of the employee's strengths (this is sometimes called the Oreo approach—beginning and ending with positive points, with the problem sandwiched in the middle).

Criticize the act, not the person. Make it clear that you are interested in helping the employee correct the problem, not in being punitive. Set written goals for better performance, and arrange for a follow-up meeting to see if these goals are being met. If an employee does not seem able to correct a problem, perhaps a different job function would allow the person greater success. A staff member who is not good at waiting on customers, for instance, might excel at stock work.

It is helpful to use an employee Job Performance Improvement Agreement, (see below) which can be downloaded from our website, www.specialtyshopretailing.com. Document any discussion with an

---

**Agreement for
Job Performance Improvement**

Employee: _____ Date:_____

Manager:_____

Situation:_____

_____

Reason this is a problem:_____

_____

Desired improvement:_____

_____

Consequences if improvement is not made by_____

will be_____

Timing for follow-up meeting:_____

Agreed to by:_____
(employee's signature)

Please keep this and all personnel matters confidential.

One copy of this form goes to the employee, and one is kept in the employee's personnel file. The file copy may be destroyed after one year at the employee's request if no further improvement agreements have been signed.

Sample job performance improvement agreement.

employee about a performance problem, and list the goals and dates for follow-up. Give a copy to the employee, and keep one in the employee's personnel file to add notes to during the conference to see if the required change has been made. The file copy may be destroyed after one year at the employee's request if no further job performance improvement agreements have been signed.

Written documentation not only shows the employee that the situation is being taken seriously but may also be necessary proof that you warned the employee of a problem before dismissing him or her. Progressive discipline is intended to ward off the necessity of firing an employee, but sometimes this action is inevitable.

THE LEGALITIES OF FIRING

Eventually you will probably face the unpleasant act of firing a staff member. We have learned the hard way that the laws offering employees protection against wrongful discharge are complex and can easily be used to bring a lawsuit against the former employer. No business can afford to fire someone without knowing the legalities involved, preferably far in advance of ever having to terminate someone. Check with your lawyer and other advisers for recommended sources of information, such as the local Small Business Development Center.

Problems should ideally be brought to an employee's attention, in verbal and written form, long before firing is considered. If an employee is chronically late, for example, have a private conference with the person and have him or her sign the job performance agreement described above spelling out the consequences for continued tardiness. Follow up on the deadlines set for improved behavior. Firing should be considered only after two or more written warnings. This progressive discipline can help prevent accusations of wrongful dismissal.

Some offenses nevertheless warrant immediate firing, and these should be spelled out in your employee handbook. Verbal or physical abuse, theft, drug or alcohol abuse, insubordination, and embezzlement are automatic causes for dismissal in most businesses.

Firing should always be done in private, with a witness present if you suspect that the employee may pursue legal action. Have all the necessary papers prepared ahead of time, including a final paycheck if possible, and details about severance pay, unused employee benefits, unemployment compensation information, and any optional continuation of insurance coverage.

Ask where the employee would like W-2 payroll tax information sent and what information should be provided to future employers asking for a reference. Collect the employee's keys to the store, and make sure the person has all of his or her personal possessions.

Escort the employee out of the store without going past customers and other employees if at all possible. If you have an alarm system code, it is good policy to have the code changed whenever anyone is fired, no matter what the circumstances. You might also plan to have the locks changed.

Expect tears, rage, or defensiveness when you dismiss someone. Even when the firing is humanely handled, the employee will feel rejected and unhappy. The lawsuit a former employee files after being fired may be motivated in part by anger at the wrong they feel they have suffered. A lawsuit may also be the result of greed; it is often less expensive for you as an employer to settle out of court than to defend yourself against a disgruntled former employee, even if you know you would eventually win the case.

Despite the unpleasantness of firing, do not put it off once you realize dismissal is necessary. The unsatisfactory employee may be a drain on the staff's morale, and the situation will undoubtedly weigh on your mind until you take action. If you have to fire someone for the good of the store and the rest of your staff, do it as soon as possible.

You should realize, however, that a sudden dismissal may be very upsetting to the rest of the staff. Staff members may be in touch with the former employee, hearing his or her side of the story. For reasons of confidentiality, you may not discuss the reasons for the dismissal, which frustrates employees who are used to open communication.

It is important to reassure the rest of the staff that their jobs are not in danger. Spending extra time on the sales floor may help to reestablish a feeling of trust and teamwork. In time, things will return to an even keel. Helping to hire and train a replacement employee can focus the staff's attention on the future instead of the past.

EMPLOYEE LAYOFFS

Occasionally a retail store will need to lay off employees because of a decline in sales or profits. These layoffs may be temporary, or they may actually be permanent terminations. Make it clear to the individuals involved that the action has nothing to do with their job performance. Be realistic about whether you might be able to hire them back again if the store's situation improves, and offer to write letters of recommendation for each employee.

State unemployment compensation is often available to employees who are laid off. Before taking action, find out what benefits your employees might be eligible for. This information may help soften the blow when you inform them of the layoff.

Saying Goodbye: The Exit Interview

Employees who leave for reasons other than termination should meet with the personnel manager or owner one last time for an exit interview. The employee can turn in keys and fill in a form giving information such as where their W-2 form should be sent. This is also an opportunity to ask the employee for suggestions regarding the store's staff training and management. Although it may be painful to ask an employee why he or she is leaving, the answers can lead to improvements that will increase the job satisfaction of the remaining staff members.

Below is an Exit Interview form available to download at www.specialtyshopretailing.com.

Exit Interview

Name:_____ Date:_____

Where would you like us to send your last paycheck and your W-2 form?

What information would you like us to release to future employers?

Status of health insurance coverage through the store:

Keys returned: ☐ _____ door   ☐ _____ door

Do you have any suggestions for us regarding staff training, communications, or other areas in which we could improve?

_____
employee

_____
employer

Sample exit interview form.

Creating Team Spirit

Establishing a sense of community is key to creating a workplace that is enjoyable to employees and welcoming to customers. Sometimes a group of people develop this camaraderie naturally, especially if united by similar interests and backgrounds. But many stores, including ours, have a very diverse workforce: our employees represent a 50-year age span and very different lifestyles. We present opportunities for staff members to get to know each other at parties, on our annual picnic and play outing to American Players Theatre, and during the social part of staff meetings.

We set up smaller teams to work on spring cleaning and other special projects. We encourage employees to do favors for each other, such as watching over a department while someone is gone or filling a sub shift on the schedule. Staff members are welcome to reward each other with Way to Go! vouchers, shown below, acknowledging a fellow employee who has provided special help or given exemplary customer service. A sample Way to Go! voucher can be downloaded at www.specialtyshopretailing.com.

WAY TO GO!

This coupon may be combined with Sub Shift vouchers
and other Way to Go! Coupons.

5 = $15 bonus

Awarded to: _____

By: _____

Date: _____ Approval: _____

Reason: _____

Sample "Way to Go!" voucher.

Progressive Personnel Policies: Motivating Your Staff

Part of establishing a team spirit is avoiding a gap between management and hourly staff. All managers should spend some of their time on the sales floor, waiting on customers and working with the sales staff. Managers' offices should not have closed doors. Dean and I don't really have an office or even a desk. We meet with sales reps and do paperwork at the customer service table in the upstairs sales area or at any free spot in the bookkeeping office, which doubles as the store's gift wrap area. We try to be accessible to customers and to staff and ask that the members of our management team do the same.

Employees want to feel a sense of pride in their workplace. Involving the staff in celebrating the store's successes is important. Be sure staff members know about charity donations the store is making and encourage employees to participate in fund-raising projects for nonprofit organizations. Instill a sense of belonging by providing the staff with t-shirts, jackets, or caps with the store name and logo. And most important, work with the staff team to create a successful business of which you can all be proud.

STAFF NEWSLETTERS AND OTHER COMMUNICATIONS

We send out an in-store newsletter via email on our biweekly payroll day covering important topics such as new lines of merchandise and any proposed changes in scheduling or policy. We feature staff birthdays and work anniversaries, new businesses on our street, and other lighter material. When we hire a new employee, we include a short biography in the newsletter so that the entire staff knows a little about the latest addition to our crew. Using clip art or product images from the Internet helps make the newsletter visually interesting.

Day-to-day communication is done in person whenever possible but otherwise is handled by notes posted on the staff bulletin board, which also features the ads we are running and various other messages. We also post a daily who's where schedule listing the stations we want each sales associate to cover during the day, rotating the staff through the upstairs and the two downstairs sales counters to give everyone a little variety in their day. This schedule also allows us to pair an experienced employee with a less experienced one.

At periodic staff meetings, which are important for staff morale, we always have refreshments and often give out door prizes or staff recognitions. At some meetings we brainstorm ideas for in-store and window displays; at others we discuss the season just past and how we can improve it next year. The agenda is kept informal so that the staff can bring up issues of concern to them. We arrange the seating in a circle if possible and make sure that the sales staff and management team members do not divide into separate groups. All ideas are given careful consideration, and we try to act on as many staff suggestions as possible. Employees need to feel that they have a voice in their workplace and that their work is more than just a job.

KEEPING IT LIGHT

One of my favorite quotes about small business is from Paul Hawken, the entrepreneur, author and activist who founded the Smith & Hawken garden stores: "If you aren't having some fun, you might wonder just what you are doing in your business life. Laughter and good humor are the canaries in the mine of commerce. If employees, customers, and vendors don't laugh and have a good time at your company, something is wrong."

Retailing should be fun, exciting, and interesting—at least most of the time. If things are getting too serious, set up a product trivia contest with real prizes, suggest a betting pool on some silly topic such as the next day's weather, or surprise your staff with a treat.

Employees are first and foremost people, and they need to feel the business cares about their joys and sorrows. Celebrate birthdays and other special events in the lives of your employees, and when things go wrong, send flowers or a note to let them know you are thinking of them.

For many employees, their fellow staff members form the community with whom they spend the majority of their time. Stories and photographs from past years are the group's family history and are important to preserve and share. We reminisce about former staff members, memorable customers, and other anecdotes that show we have a common history. We keep photo albums of all our past parties and window displays and a box full of clippings and other memorabilia. We want employees to feel that they belong to a corporate community with both a past and a future.

On the wall of our bookkeeping office is a family tree, shaped (naturally) like an orange tree. All staff members, from the earliest day of Orange Tree Imports to the present, are listed on the tree. Every five years on the store's anniversary, we host staff reunions, with our family tree, photo albums, and letters from former employees around the world displayed for everyone to enjoy. We've had about 225 employees over the years, and I'm pleased to say we've kept in touch with a majority of them. We certainly couldn't have gotten where we are today without all of our past and present staff members.

CHAPTER 11
ATTRACT MORE CUSTOMERS: ADVERTISING EFFECTIVELY

dvertising doesn't cost," the old saying goes, "it pays." The short-term dollar-for-dollar return on money spent for advertising may not be apparent, but in the long term, the money you invest in promoting your shop should be rewarded with increased sales.

Do you need to advertise? If you are running the gift shop at a national park, probably not. The best advertising in the world will not inspire the average customer to make a special trip just to visit a small store far off the beaten path. In fact, location alone is enough to draw customers to shops in many tourist destinations and in some other well-traveled, high-traffic places. For a shop like Dylan's Candy Bar, the Manhattan treat boutique owned by the daughter of Ralph Lauren, a busy city location, celebrity name, and colorful signage provide a strong appeal.

Most specialty shops, however, do need to advertise in order to attract new customers and to encourage existing customers to return. Good advertising increases awareness of your products and reinforces your store's total image, or branding, in the eyes of the public. Customers like to know what to expect, so consistency in your image is important. It should help differentiate your shop from the competition, especially the discount stores and category killers that focus on low prices. Use your advertising to let the public know about your style, service, selection, and knowledgeable staff.

There is no limit to the forms that advertising can take, from a website banner to a banner towed by an airplane. Signage, window displays, shopping bags, brochures, and public television underwriting can all be considered part of your advertising program. Online promotion and social media (discussed in the next chapter) are essential parts of all advertising programs today. How many different ways can you find to express the appeal of your store and your merchandise to the buying public? What is the image of your store that you want all your advertising to project?

Establishing an Advertising Budget

Many traditional forms of advertising are fairly expensive, so you must spend your dollars wisely, especially at first. Experience, based on the types of advertising that produce the best results for your store, will help guide your future decisions. (There are also numerous low-cost or free promotional opportunities discussed in Chapter 14.)

An advertising budget normally ranges from 3 to 5% of total sales, but can be as high as 10%. Several factors should be considered in setting the budget: (1) traffic, (2) marketplace awareness, (3) competition, and (4) price sensitivity. If you have high traffic, are well known in your market, have few competitors, and place little emphasis on price, you won't need to spend much on advertising. Conversely, if you are in a low-traffic area, are not well known, have many competitors, or want people to shop with you because of low prices, you will need to do more advertising. Stores that sell merchandise with higher markup, such as jewelry, can afford to spend more on advertising, and may need to match what others in their field are spending.

A new store needs to advertise more aggressively than one that is well established. Some sources recommend doubling your advertising budget for the first year you are in business. Of course, unless you are opening a franchise or branch store, you will have little way of predicting what this first year's sales will be.

Doubling an advertising budget based on a hypothetical sales figure can be dangerous. I spoke with a store owner who spent $10,000 on television advertising soon after opening, producing only $12,000 in sales. Had sales been $100,000, this might have been a wise investment. As it turned out, the store went out of business within a year. Check with other stores your size to get an idea of their advertising budget and the types of advertising that work best for them.

If your business is seasonal, budget more of your advertising money for the months when you are busiest. It is always tempting to run ads to bring in business during slow times and to try to increase sales of slow items by advertising them. But as a rule, you should follow the dictum to sell what's selling when it's selling.

How to Spend Your Advertising Dollars

If you've never done any advertising before, you may be surprised at how little you get for your money. An ad you barely glance at as you read your morning paper may have cost hundreds of dollars. It pays to give careful consideration to getting the most mileage from your advertising budget whether you are spending it on radio, TV, print or web ads or social media.

There are three basic types of advertising:

1. Image or brand marketing

2. Product promotion

3. Special event or sale advertising

Advertising designed to help make new customers aware of your store, including where it is located, what it sells, and the services it offers is *image* or **brand advertising**. This type of promotion is useful for building prestige and trust among existing customers as well as reaching new ones. A motto, or tag line, used in conjunction with your store name and logo can help create a memorable impression in this type of ad.

Try to define your store in a few well-chosen words that are relevant to the consumer. Erik's Bike Shop, for example, is well known for its clever tag line "We Pedal Good Bikes," and they have protected their use of this phrase as part of their trademark. If you use radio or television, your tag line can be part of a jingle to help listeners remember it. Repetition is the key to making a lasting impression, and you need to make sure your message is simple and consistent.

The second type of advertising is **product promotion**, which highlights individual items. Some vendors, especially national brands, do their own product advertising. Suppliers with an advertising program sometimes allow a store name to appear in their product ads or underwrite store advertising featuring their products by providing an advertising allowance.

The third type is **special event** or **sale advertising**, encouraging customers to come in during a specific time. A special event can create a sense of urgency that calls the customer to take action soon, although a sale may not get today's shoppers very excited -- there has been such a proliferation of sale advertising that consumers have become a bit jaded.

TOOLS FOR TARGETING YOUR MARKET

Who are you trying to reach with your advertising? This is the first question to ask in order to focus your advertising dollars. A fashion store for teens would do better to approach its customers through a popular radio station than print ads. The older, wealthy shoppers that a home design store wants to reach are likely to read a glossy city magazine. Try to establish a profile of your typical customer, just as you did when planning your first buying decisions. Imagine an average shopper walking through your front door. Is this person male or female? How old? Where is he or she most likely to live or work? These demographics will help you target your advertising.

In addition to your primary target market, you may wish to focus some advertising on specific segments of your customer base or your merchandise selection. We run ads for Hanukkah menorahs in the local Jewish community newspaper because we know this is a good way to reach our best customers for these products. Your store may appeal to several such small niche markets, as well as to customers who belong to a specific population group, such as the elderly, Latinos, or African Americans. Don't forget to allot some of your advertising budget to targeting these important segments of the market.

Research the best way to reach each targeted group. Before you open, you can solicit suggestions from your focus group. Once your store is open, you can do an informal survey of which media your customers favor. Make a list of local radio and TV stations, local magazines, and daily and weekly newspapers. Ask customers if they'd be willing to check off their favorites, but be sure to be gracious if they'd rather not participate. Offer a small gift to thank those who fill in the form.

Choosing the Best Media for the Money

Once you have determined who you want to reach through your advertising, three additional questions will help you decide what direction you want to concentrate on.

1. What is the message you wish to convey? Radio may be a better choice for timely information about a special event, whereas print advertising or television is better if you need to show an item. Stores selling home exercise equipment might do better promoting a YouTube video showing the features of their products than with direct mail.

Attract More Customers: Advertising Effectively

2. What type of advertising is most appropriate to your store? The choice of medium should be in keeping with your store's image. Don't do coupons if you are concerned about making an elegant impression. Stores that appeal to a narrow segment of the population, such as a bridal shop, can market directly to engaged couples. This would be more effective than ads aimed at the general public.

3. When do you want your message to reach the target audience? Time your advertising to create a sense of urgency, encouraging shoppers to take action soon. For example, you might consider using a drive-time radio program to influence shoppers to stop at your gourmet take-out shop on their way home from work.

Most retailers use a combination of several media in order to get thorough coverage. Whatever you decide, it is important that you commit to a long-term program and give it enough exposure to make it effective.

Having a clear idea of the who, what, and when goals of your advertising will help you work more productively with the sales representatives from the various media. In large communities there are so many radio stations and print options that meeting with these reps can take a lot of time. Instead of listening to a canned sales pitch, type up a list of your advertising goals, and ask media reps to give you ideas for reaching them. For example, you might state that your main goal is to promote your store's name recognition among males aged 30 to 50, and to increase sales of sporting goods to this target market over the next three months. Ads in a women's magazine would not be ideal for this purpose, but a cable TV sports program might propose an attractive package.

Stretching Your Advertising Dollars

There is never enough money on hand to do all the advertising that you would like, so here are three ways to get more advertising at low cost.

Let your vendors pay a share. Manufacturers benefit when retailers promote the vendor's products through store advertising. To encourage stores to promote their merchandise, suppliers sometimes offer to pay for part of the advertising through ad allowances, or co-op money. The manufacturer will often pay 50 to 100% of the actual cost of advertising featuring its product if the ad meets certain criteria, such as the inclusion of the supplier's logo. Usually the amount of advertising allowance available is based on the amount of merchandise purchased. Purchases are normally added up, or accrued, over a set period of time. One reason department stores are able to advertise so aggressively is that they earn huge advertising allowances through volume buying during each accrual period.

Do joint promotions with your business neighbors. If your shop is located near other stores, you can stretch your advertising dollars by cooperating with them to promote your shopping area. Customers who visit one store are likely to visit another. Bring more shoppers to your neighborhood by pooling some of your advertising money to produce general ads, especially in magazines or other media aimed at visitors, and to create a shared website and a guidebook to the businesses in your area. Our store originated the Monroe Street Shopping Guide, a full-color brochure that is distributed in local hotels and visitors centers as well as to convention groups. Ads in the guide pay for the printing costs, but every business, whether it contributes or not, is listed. Individual ads in newspapers or magazines have more impact when blocked together with ads from other shops in the same area. The periodical will sometimes contribute the space for a unifying banner across the top of the page, and offer lower rates to participating businesses.

This clever and colorful map of all of the locally owned businesses in their area was created by Johnny Carrillo of the kitchen boutique Mabel's on 4th in Tucson, Arizona. "We paid to have it printed to give to our customers for free in order to remain relevant in their minds," reports co-owner Nicole Carrillo. "We then ran it as an insert in the local paper, with coupons inviting customers to come visit our shop. As a result, our gorgeous local foodie magazine included it in a recent edition, at no cost to us!" (Courtesy of Nicole Carrillo)

Shopping centers usually require a certain amount of joint advertising, and management will develop the advertising campaigns. Other shopping areas can benefit from the merchants forming their own association to improve the area and develop some special events, such as an annual street fair or holiday open house. With many merchants sharing the cost, purchasing banners, flyers, radio spots, and ads to promote these events is not expensive.

Look for opportunities for fusion advertising. You need not limit cooperative advertising to neighboring merchants. Look for creative opportunities for what is known as fusion advertising, with the customers of one business getting a special gift or discount if they patronize another. Offer to give out coupons for a free dessert at a restaurant, for example, if the restaurant will give its patrons a discount offer for your store.

The World of Print Advertising

Print ads have been steadily losing ground to online promotions and social media (see Chapter 12), but this type of advertising is still often a viable option. Weekday and Sunday newspapers continue to be used by businesses appealing to the more mature segment of the population, and in many cities there are free alternative weekly newspapers that are an effective way to reach a younger demographic. Direct mail postcards, brochures, catalogs, magazines, and even business cards are additional options for print advertising.

DESIGNING NEWSPAPER AND MAGAZINE ADS

Take a look at the ads in your local paper. You'll probably notice that many of them are crowded, confusing, unimaginative, or otherwise visually unappealing. As a creative retailer, one of your jobs is to design ads that are as pleasing to the eye as your store displays. And if you want customers to find your store entertaining, make your ads entertaining.

Attract More Customers: Advertising Effectively

Good print ads usually feature a headline that catches the reader's attention or announces the benefit to the consumer; factual copy, or text, that invites action; and a pleasing balance of white space (open areas), and graphics. The graphics should be appropriate to the type of merchandise being sold; as a rule, photographs sell better than illustrations. Note that the trend today is towards ads that are mostly PR, with editorial or news content, or ones with large product photos and very little copy. Be sure that every print ad includes your logo and tag line, if you use one, and your store name in its logo typestyle, along with your address, telephone number, website and store hours.

All print ads should be carefully proofread by at least two people. Always allow time to receive a proof so that corrections can be made. Watch for odd hyphenations of words that are too long for one line and for errors in spelling, prices, and store hours (especially around holiday time).

Most print media provide free technical assistance in designing ads. Some of their artists are better than others, of course. It can't hurt to see what they come up with and perhaps take their concept to your own designer to be refined. You can also ask the newspaper or magazine to create a layout from your idea.

Advertising rates for newspapers and magazines are based on the size of the ad. Newspaper ads are usually measured by the column inch, which refers to the width of a printed column for that publication and a standard inch in height. Magazines often sell ads based on a percentage of the page, such as a half-page or quarter-page. If you want to select the location of your ad—for example, in the sports section of the newspaper or on the inside front cover of a magazine—there is normally an additional charge. Check with the sales representative about the savings available when you agree to sign a contract for multiple ads over a period of time. The open rate, or one-time rate, is almost always considerably higher than the contract rate.

Newspapers and magazines often also have the ability to deliver a separate advertising piece for you, either bound-in or loose (like all those supplements stuffed into the Sunday paper). With this service, you can reach every subscribing household in a certain area, or zone, or reach the entire circulation of the periodical. Consider using this method to distribute a flyer, an advertising supplement provided by one of your manufacturers, or your store catalog.

Effective In-Store Advertising

The most obvious goal of advertising is to bring customers into the store. But an important part of your promotional presentation reaches consumers once they have entered the door. Signs and handouts in the store influence customers' shopping experience and encourage them to return. The way the items purchased in your shop are packaged can help promote the shop after the customer leaves; in fact, a good shopping bag becomes a walking billboard. These in-store elements of your marketing plan should be as carefully planned as your media advertising and should be consistent with the branding of your shop.

In addition to framed shelf talker signs (see Chapter 4) describing your merchandise, you might want to have a supply of individual cards or handouts available for customers to take with them when they make a purchase. This is a particularly useful service if the items you carry require special assembly or care or if there is interesting information you'd like to share about the products, such as the biographies of the artists who made them or the folk traditions the items represent, and adds extra value when included with a gift. Be sure that your store name, address, website, and telephone number are listed.

Attract More Customers: Advertising Effectively

BUSINESS CARDS: YOUR SMALLEST AD

Have you ever thought of your business card as part of your advertising program? Customers appreciate being able to help themselves to a business card by the cash register, and it is surprising how much information you can fit on these little giveaways: store name, location, and telephone number, plus your tag line, hours, the names of the store's owners, website and email address, and so forth. At Music and Memories, a music box store, the back of the store's business card was designated as a wish list, with room for the stock number, description, and price of the items the customer liked best.

Take a stack of business cards with you whenever you display your products at a consumer show or anywhere other than in the store. You might also ask a related business to keep some on hand. An animal photographer, for example, might be willing to give out cards for a pet supply store that is willing to return the favor.

BAG STUFFERS, BROCHURES, AND OTHER PRINT OPTIONS

In-store advertising can be used to encourage customers to return. Customers love to take brochures and other literature with them, especially if they are undecided about a major purchase. Check with your suppliers about any free product literature that may be available to you, and be sure to put your store name and address on each piece with a stamp or sticker.

A bookmark, a small flyer, or a larger advertising piece can be sent home with every customer by using them as bag stuffers. Staff members can insert these items in the bags ahead of time or slip them in with each purchase. We have occasionally used this technique to help a local nonprofit group by bag stuffing a notice of a special event.

SPECIALTY SHOP RETAILING

PACKAGING AS ADVERTISING

Your store packaging is as much a part of your store image as the front display window, your logo, and the way your display fixtures coordinate with the merchandise you sell. All these components make up the branding of your shop—the identity you want the public to remember. A customer leaving your store carrying a bag with your logo on it is carrying your brand out into the world, and chances are good that if it is attractive, it will be noticed by other shoppers. If the purchase is a gift, the store wrapping will become part of the presentation, creating a positive impression of your store to the recipient and any other potential customers who are present when it is opened.

Good packaging need not be expensive. A small shop or kiosk might begin by rubber-stamping its logo and an attractive design on plain kraft bags or by adding a sticker to a patterned bag. As the business grows, one of the many suppliers of imprinted boxes and bags can help you to develop a program of matching shopping bags, flat bags, and other packaging materials. We offer flat paper bags, a small paper shopping bag and two sizes of plastic bags to our customers. We pay a premium so that the plastic ones are made of a recyclable material, because we know this is important to our customers.

In designing your bag program, keep in mind that consumer surveys have shown that "strong graphic design" is a factor in decisions about what bag to reuse. Shops selling more expensive merchandise should consider buying distinctive packaging to reinforce their sophisticated image. Jute, vinyl, or cloth bags can be imprinted with the store logo and given away with a large purchase or used as part of a gift package. Customers almost always reuse these bags, providing free promotion for the store.

Direct Mail: Making the Best Use of Your List

While media advertising reaches a large group of readers or listeners, direct mail advertising—and its younger sibling, permission-based email marketing (discussed in Chapter 12) allows you to target one specific customer. It also allows you to test every variable in your mailing by making minor changes in a piece each time you mail a batch and tracking the responses you get each time.

There are two ways of using direct mail: 1) to advertise to existing customers and 2) to solicit new customers by focusing on a selected list of likely prospects. Both US mail and email fulfill the first goal; however, it is difficult to seek new customers via email.

How do you develop your first mailing list? When your store opens, put a guest book by the front counter and encourage everyone to sign it. You could also put out slips of paper for a prize drawing, and enter all the names and addresses into your database. This method, however, can result in quite a few "unqualified" customers, because most states do not allow stores to require a purchase as a condition for entering the contest. Take time each day to copy the names and addresses on all the checks you receive. If you conduct a customer survey in the store, ask for an optional name and address. Be sure to add everyone to your list who fills in a request card or asks to have a package shipped, taking their names and addresses from these special forms.

Put out a stack of 3-by-5 mailing list cards and invite customers to fill one in. In addition to lines for the mailing and optional email address on these cards, provide check boxes for special interests, allowing you to subdivide your list and occasionally send out smaller, targeted direct mail pieces or emails. Your mailing list card can mention that customers signing up for mailings will be eligible for a monthly prize drawing and will receive special sale offers and invitations. Encourage everyone who comes in the store to sign up. It is much less expensive to cultivate an existing customer than to solicit a new one.

To get addresses of non-customers, you'll want to work through a mailing house or list broker. These companies rent out lists targeted at specific income levels, geographic areas, or topics of interest. This is an excellent way to seek new customers, especially if you choose the right list. We have rented the list of cooking magazine subscribers in our area and sent them our kitchenware catalog, with a special coupon inviting these potential customers into the store. In addition to magazine lists, it is possible to rent names and addresses based on occupation, group affiliation, and credit card use. The price for renting a list is based on units of 1,000 names and addresses and covers one-time use for a specific mailing piece. List brokers usually include a few hidden code names to find out if a list is used more than once or for a purpose other than that agreed on.

When using more than one mailing list at a time, try to track which one is most effective by using a numeric code above the customer's name and asking all those responding to the mailing to give you the code. Before your mailing piece is addressed, have the lists compared to one another to eliminate costly duplication. This process, known as a *merge/purge*, can be done by computer through a commercial mailing service.

Commercial mailing services have sophisticated methods for comparing lists and also for labeling mailings and sorting them for bulk mail according to the latest postal regulations. Although there are inexpensive programs that allow you to maintain your own mailing lists on your store computer, you may find that using a commercial mailing service ultimately saves you both time and money. The service can often handle every aspect of your mailing: printing, labeling, sorting, and even delivering the mail to the post office.

A general mailing list of your customers is essential and can become one of your store's most valuable assets if you use it often. It is also beneficial to be able to break this main list down into smaller targeted lists. If you sell a variety of products, you need to know which customers

Attract More Customers: Advertising Effectively

are especially interested in a specific area. A crafts store, for instance, might send out a mailing featuring knitting supplies that would not be of any interest to customers who do woodworking. Mailing list services and store computer programs make this type of tracking feasible for even the smallest store.

In our mobile society, mailing lists need to be cleaned periodically. Bulk mail is the most economical way of sending a quantity of pieces, but in most instances bulk mail is not forwarded if the recipient has moved. Check with the post office about updating your list at least once a year. This can be done electronically, especially if you are using a professional mailing service to maintain your list. You can also indicate on your mailing piece that you would like to receive address corrections, and the postal service will, for a fee, return all the undeliverable pieces to you with the recipient's new address if one is available.

WHAT TO MAIL: CATALOGUES AND FLYERS

Producing a catalogue to mail to your customers may only be practical if you are part of a buying group that makes them available to its members. In addition to the production of a slick, professional-looking catalog with your store name on it, the collective buying clout of the group helps convince vendors to grant generous advertising allowances, often in the form of a 5 or 10% discount taken right off the invoice. Priority may be given in shipping orders of catalog merchandise. Some catalog groups negotiate exclusive rights to a new item before it is made available to all other stores. New products that a shop tries because of the catalog may become steady sellers. Members in a catalog group often enjoy support and guidance both from the catalog company and their fellow group members.

Our store is a member of the HTI Buying Group, and once a year we send out a multi-page flyer offered to all the stores in the group. We use it mostly to pre-sell the customers on our mailing list, telling them more about each product than we possibly could in the store. There are also coupons on the back cover that are valid for one month each. We usually insert a quantity of catalogs in our local newspaper and also send some to a rented mailing list to bring in new customers.

To determine whether there is a catalog that is right for you, check with your major suppliers to see if their merchandise is featured in any group catalogs. If you find a good possibility, request a sample copy and compare the image it projects to that of your store. Are most of the items pictured ones that you normally carry? Does the look of the catalog resemble your shop in terms of quality and sophistication?

Once you have selected a catalog, call other retailers who belong to that group and ask about their experience. Many shops report significant increases in sales when they send out a catalog, but there are also some drawbacks. You will not have complete control over the merchandise selection and pricing, the catalog will not reflect your store's unique character, and you may find that your customer base is not large enough to support the considerable volume of catalogs you will need to buy.

POSTCARDS, INVITATIONS AND LETTERS

Letters and other mailing pieces that are delivered in an envelope can easily be produced on your own. Check with your printing house to see if they have suggestions for clever, effective direct mail pieces. We often send our top customers cards we have printed using the inexpensive photo card service available through a nearby drug store chain. We use a photo of the store, or of ourselves, and add copy that includes an offer of a free gift, as well as a thank you message.

A postcard is an effective way to make regular use of your mailing list, and a great way to deliver coupons to customers who respond to that approach. The cards themselves are not expensive to produce, and there is a considerable savings in postage in comparison to other mailing pieces. Check postal regulations for size and layout specifications, especially if you will be using a bulk mailing permit. We once had an 8,000-piece postcard mailing rejected by the post office because the layout failed to meet postal standards.

Broadcast Media: Radio and TV

The advertising images projected by radio and television are fleeting, so it is essential to commit to a campaign with a great deal of repetition in order to make broadcast media work effectively. The longer you run an ad, the more likely someone is to remember it. A consistently repeated message in a specific media market may need as long as four months to reach a level of familiarity with a public bombarded with auditory and visual messages every day.

APPEALING TO THE RADIO LISTENER

Radio allows you to speak personally to an individual. Use language that creates a vivid *first mental image* (FMI) and closes with an equally vivid *last mental image* (LMI). The listener must be a participant in your advertising, and ideally should imagine taking a specific action as a result of hearing your message. Music can be used to create a mood to augment the spoken copy. This text can be professionally recorded or read by the program announcer.

You might want to be your own spokesperson, especially if you have an interesting voice or accent. A good, recognizable announcing voice in radio commercials can help build a sense of trust in your business. A catchy jingle may also help customers remember your store's name, but you will need to repeat it many times to make it seem familiar to the public.

The immediacy of radio makes it ideal for announcing events with time value. The copy can create a sense of urgency, encouraging the listener—who may well be in his or her car already—to go to your store right away. Be sure that each ad mentions the store's name and location at least twice.

Selecting a radio station in a market that has more than one option requires some market research. Ask your customers what commercial stations they prefer, and see if a pattern emerges. You can also get demographics from the media salesperson that will show you whether the station's listeners are your target customers. You'll want to ask for the average number of listeners for specific programs in order to apply the standard method of measuring advertising's effectiveness: *reach times frequency*. For a radio ad, reach is the number of people who hear your message, and frequency is the number of times your ad is run.

Radio spots are sold in increments of 30 seconds. This may not seem like a long time, but it is long enough to read approximately 60 to 70 words of copy. Instead of buying 60-second spots, consider running 30-second spots twice as often. Select the times that your spots will run based on the listening habits of your customers as well as on your ad budget. Drive times, for example, are excellent for reaching commuters on their way to and from work.

If your store is busy during the first few months of the year, traditionally a slow time for other retailers, you may be able to buy radio time rather inexpensively. Business advertising drops off after the holiday season, so stations are eager for advertisers in January, February, and March. And with the lighter advertising schedule during these times, your ad will stand out.

Many radio stations offer the option of a live remote broadcast from your store. The public enjoys the novelty of seeing radio personalities in action, and announcers like to meet their listeners. To be truly effective, a remote should be tied to a contest, event, or special offer that will draw listeners to the store. The announcers should sound excited about being in the store and should mention free refreshments, entertainment, a sale, or other offers when they invite customers to come see them.

Attract More Customers: Advertising Effectively

AS SEEN ON TV

Streaming of television programs and the profusion of cable TV stations has made advertising on television a complicated proposition. In addition to the difficult decision about where and when to place a TV ad, production costs to create even a 30-second spot can be considerable. Because your locally produced ad may run before or after a sophisticated spot produced by a large national advertising agency, it is unwise to cut corners when creating TV ads. If you are going to use television, obtain professional production advice from the television station or your advertising agency. You may wish to create two or more ads at the same time so that you can rotate them during a heavy advertising schedule.

TV is a medium that is both visual and aural. It allows you to tell a story, demonstrate a product, or communicate an image of your store or products in a way that will delight the eye and the ear. Not everyone, of course, will be watching and listening. Your store name, location, and tag line should be shown in writing on the screen for those of us who hit the mute button whenever an ad comes on.

The major networks still have a somewhat dominant position in television, so if you can afford to advertise on these stations and wish to reach as broad a market as possible, they may be your best option. We have experimented with using cable television to reach our target market, running spots promoting our kitchen products on the Food Network. Our lively, 30-second ad took more than four hours to produce, and countless vegetables were sacrificed to the cause as we tried to demonstrate the use of as many gadgets as possible.

Retailers who have strong, likable personalities are often successful at starring in their own television ads. Customers like to buy from someone they know, and if you are usually present in your store, encouraging the public to identify your store with your trustworthy and familiar face gives you an advantage Kmart will never have. The down-side of regular TV appearances is being recognized wherever you go and realizing that whatever you do or say reflects on your business. Individual promotion also makes it difficult to share the responsibility (and credit) equally with the store's other partners or staff members, and, of course, it may make it difficult to eventually pass the business on to a new owner.

ALTERNATIVE TELEVISION AND RADIO PROMOTIONS

Public radio and television are prohibited from carrying commercials, but they are often able to give extensive descriptions of the businesses that sponsor them. Public television underwriting has actually been one of our most effective means of advertising. For years we have sponsored cooking programs by Julia Child, Jacques Pepin, and other chefs; this year we are underwriting the popular *Great British Bake-Off*. These shows have a loyal following among our customers who are avid cooks. Ask your public television and radio stations if there are programs that might tie in well with your merchandise.

Most public television stations raise funds through an on-air auction or membership drives that feature premiums to reward those who sign up. Donating merchandise for the auction or fund drives is an inexpensive way to gain exposure on your local public television station. And if you enjoy volunteering as an on-air auctioneer, you can gain additional recognition for your store. I am amazed at how many people mention seeing me during my annual two-hour stint as an MC during the Wisconsin Public Television auction.

Evaluating Your Advertising's Effectiveness

Many retailers view advertising as throwing money down a black hole because it is often difficult to see clear results from an advertising campaign. Consumers seldom mention seeing or hearing an ad, and, in fact, every so often a customer will mention coming in because of an ad that never existed. But it is possible to make an effort to track the

Attract More Customers: Advertising Effectively

effectiveness of an advertising campaign, beyond the obvious method of looking for an increase in either general sales or sales of the item advertised. There are several ways to track results:

- Include a coupon in your ad or in your mailing. Ask staff to keep all coupons and to write the total amount of purchase on them.

- For radio advertising, offer a free gift or special discount to anyone mentioning the ad.

- When doing consumer surveys, be sure to ask how the customer found out about the store.

- Query sales staff as to whether they think many new customers came in as a result of a promotional campaign.

Advertising when Sales are Down

It is tempting to save money when the store is not doing well by not advertising. That, according to advertising specialist Jay Conrad Levinson, in *Guerrilla Marketing: Easy and Inexpensive Strategies for Making Big Profits from Your Small Business*, is like stopping your wristwatch to save time. You need frequency and persistence in order to succeed in advertising. The store that discontinues its advertising and disappears from the public eye may soon disappear entirely.

Advertising that is well researched and designed should at least pay for itself. Even a store that has fallen on hard times should work hard to promote itself. An economical advertising program, coupled with an array of inexpensive creative promotions, social media posts, online marketing and some free publicity, can help attract new customers and bring the old ones back.

CHAPTER 12
DIGITAL MEDIA:
PROMOTING YOUR
BRICK & MORTAR STORE

The web offers many opportunities for retailers of all sizes. You may want to use the Internet just to promote your brick and mortar store, or choose to sell products both in the store and online as a bricks-and-clicks business. But in either case, a robust online presence is essential in today's business environment and should be part of your store's promotional plan.

This chapter will walk you through creating a website, making the most of permission-based email, and using social media to promote your business. Chapter 13 covers how to sell online, including the importance of setting up a secure shopping cart and efficient order-processing systems.

Staking a Claim to Your Home on the Web

As soon as you've determined your store's name, it's a good idea to reserve the domain name (web address) of your choice. There is a minimal cost to own the rights to a domain name even if you don't plan to set up the site right away. Register the domain name with a registrar, such as GoDaddy.com, NetworkSolutions.com, or BuyDomains.com. You may find your first and second choice already taken. If you can't get your store's name, try adding shop to the front of it—

www.ShopOrangeTreeImports.com would have worked for us if www.OrangeTreeImports.com had been taken. You can also use your domain name as part of your email address. Our basic email address, for example, might be info@OrangeTreeImports.com, and we could then add email addresses for key staff using their names instead of the generic "info." Domain name registration is usually valid for two years, after which time you will need to renew it.

Advertising Online: Website Essentials

The Internet is today the key source of information about businesses, so you need to make sure that your store's details are well represented on the web. Some stores decide to use a Facebook page in lieu of a website. While this may save time and money, it does not offer the same opportunity to present a full range of information—and the message you convey to consumers may be that your store is not a serious business.

You can create a basic website on your own using a platform, such as Squarespace or WordPress, that provides a range of templates that can be customized for your store. In addition, you should see if your business can also be featured on one hosted by your community, buy local campaign or shopping area.

More web pages are now viewed on mobile and tablet devices such as smartphones and iPads than on desktop and laptop computers, so it is essential that your website design (as well as your email blasts) be responsive, i.e., display well on whatever device and web browser the viewer is using.

Think of your website as an online brochure, and include basic information including name, address, zip code, phone number, email address, store hours, and some information about what the store carries. Many websites that don't offer merchandise for sale still show a variety of best sellers. Even a brick-and-mortar location can increase sales through "web-influenced" purchases. Be sure to update and change the information on your site regularly so that it is always accurate and has something of interest for the return visitor.

All websites should be visually clean and easy to navigate, and should load quickly. Remember that the graphic identity of your website is an extension of your store's branding. Consider showing the logos of major brands that you carry and linking to these companies' websites. Customers appreciate extras like this, but remember, when you link to any page outside your shop's own site you should make sure the page opens in a new window instead of carrying the customer entirely away from yours.

Here are some ideas beyond the basics to consider for your website:

- About Us: background information about you and the store (shoppers like to buy from real people)

- Special Holiday Hours

- Links to Local Visitor Information

- Special Offers, set up so that you can change them frequently

- Links to Neighboring Businesses and/or your Business Association

- Calendar of Special Events: listing upcoming in-store events

- Best Seller List, showing your most popular products (keep it current!)

- Store Photographs

- Join Our Mailing List

- Recent Awards

- Press—news features about your store

- Employment Opportunities

- Wedding or Gift Registry listings

Digital Media: Marketing Your Brick & Mortar Store

It's a good idea to have some photographs taken of your store's interior and exterior to use on your website, and also to give out when you get requests from the press. "Taking a photo at dawn or dusk with the store lights glowing from within can result in a particularly effective image," advised professional photographer Peter Patau.

The more variable information you feature, the more often customers will return. These topics should be set up as CMS, or *content management system*, fields that you can fill in and update from the store. Offering a special of the month or showing new products will encourage frequent visits by those who are particularly interested in what you carry.

If you want a sophisticated site that reflects the image of your store, you will probably need to have a professional web designer create it for you while you concentrate your talents on retailing. Be sure to get a firm idea in advance of what the costs will be and what the fees will cover. Ask to see samples of other websites by the same designer, and call these businesses for feedback. You should also find out what tools the web designer will use to attract customers to your site through SEO (*search engine optimization*), discussed in Chapter 13.

Making the Most of Email Marketing

Email blasts, which are advertising messages sent in a large batch via email, are a wonderful way to send customers information you think they'd be interested in. Once you have an email list of customers who have granted you permission to contact them set up on your store computer, sending out a group promotional message is almost free—unlike direct mail marketing, which can be quite expensive. The downside of using email for promotion, however, is the challenge of building a list of addresses. Junk email is even more irritating than junk mail, and at this time there is no way to rent a well-qualified email list of customers likely to welcome a message from you.

Good customers already have an interest in what you are selling, so you just need to show them the advantages of belonging to your email list. Here are some ideas of benefits you might want to mention on your website and a sign in the store:

♦ Coupons or discounts

♦ Sneak peaks at new arrivals

♦ Exclusive special offers

♦ Advance notices of sales

♦ Tips and information about your products

In addition to these perks, you should assure customers that you do not share or trade your email list. Privacy is an important issue to consumers today.

Once an in-store or Internet customer has agreed to be included in your email list, you are free to send them permission-based emails. One of the advantages of this type of marketing is that it allows you to send out large email blasts or to target mailings to a very specific group if you've segmented your mailing list by interest. This is one component of *relationship marketing*, discussed in Chapter 17. Because the customer has volunteered to receive email from you, hopefully the message will be read. However, the open rate for emails is declining as many people feel overwhelmed by the daily influx. If you achieve an open rate of 30%, you will be doing better than average. The CTR, or *click-through rate*, a ratio calculated based on the number of viewers who click on a specific hyperlink in your message, is another way of gauging the success of your email campaigns.

Keeping your email blasts short and focused on one or two topics will increase your readership. And note that messages sent early in the week usually have the highest rate of readership. We have found that many of our customers read their email at work, so an email sent on Friday, Saturday or Sunday is less likely to be opened.

Don't overdo the use of your list so that consumers tire of hearing from you. Once or twice a month may be enough, except during your busiest season. Make sure that your store is listed as the sender, and avoid using words like "free" and "guaranteed" in your subject line as they may send your mailing into the recipient's spam folder. The Federal Trade Commission's *CAN-SPAM Act* states that your message must include a clear and conspicuous explanation of how the recipient can opt out of getting email from you in the future.

> Customers appreciate predictability, according to Yvette Jones, President/ Creative Director of designCraft Advertising. "Establishing a biweekly, monthly, or even quarterly schedule of e-newsletters can help convince them they won't be overwhelmed with emails and let them know when to expect the next update, Some retailers even end by mentioning when the next update will come out."

Permission-based email campaigns offer an ideal opportunity to communicate information about new products, events, and special offers. They are particularly effective when they include a limited-time call to action or coupon. (Keep in mind that these coupons can be shared with other people—Starbucks once had to cancel a particularly enticing email coupon offer when it got forwarded to millions of people.) You might also want to mention that the coupon does not need to be printed out in order to be valid, inviting customers to show the offer on their phone.

There are a number of web-based email marketing companies that offer do-it-yourself templates for newsletters. In addition to helping design the content, they help you avoid spam filters, manage your list and do the mailings. You can even segment your list so that customers with a special interest can be targeted with a newsletter specifically for them. These email marketing companies help you manage your list by handling bounces, unsubscribes, and additions to your list from your website. You will have access to your list online, so you can update addresses at any time. The services report back to you on how many customers open your emails, and how many click on links within the newsletters.

A good place to start in looking for a company to work with is to take pay attention to any email blasts you currently receive—at the bottom of the message the email marketing service is usually listed. You can ask other retailers and your web designer for recommendations, and look at sample newsletters by Constant Contact, iContact, and My Emma, as well as MailChimp, which offers a basic service for free. Whatever service you use, make sure that you select a look for your emails that is in keeping with your store's image. You want to create a coordinated brand presence across all platforms.

TEXTING YOUR CUSTOMERS

Despite the popularity of texting as a quick form of communication, it has not been easy to get customers to share their cell phone numbers with independent retail businesses. There are a number of coupon and loyalty programs on the market that use texts, or SMS messaging, and perhaps you'll have success with one of them. Invite customers to sign up on their phone, prompted by a sign in the store or an email with a tempting offer. You will usually pay the service a flat fee based on the number of text messages sent every month.

Digital Media: Marketing Your Brick & Mortar Store

> "Use social media as a relationship tool, and humanize your content. Independent retailers have an advantage over big box stores—real people. Show pictures of yourself, your staff and your customers. Include your name at the end of a comment when answering a customer's question, share your top picks, your favorite items, and behind-the-scenes stories." Crystal Vilkaitis, Crystal Media

Social Media Strategies

The proliferation of social media has been a great boon to independent retailers. It offers us an inexpensive way to build ongoing relationships with our customers, and to connect with them on a regular basis. But there is also a downside to social media, and that is that it takes a great deal of time to keep the store's information fresh and to post with any frequency. You may want to consider using a program such as Hootsuite that allows you to schedule batches of posts in advance, or SnapRetail, which handles email blasts and website creation as well as social media.

At the moment, Facebook, Instagram, and Pinterest seem to be the favorites for shopkeepers, and our store has a presence on all of them. Facebook is our most important platform, and we try to post the most often there. We should do better with Instagram, especially since it is currently the highest rated platform for those trying to appeal to a younger market—and we do want to attract that demographic. Pinterest crosses over age categories and has an 80% female following, so it is well in line with our existing customer base.

FACEBOOK PROMOTIONS

Facebook is a great platform for building an audience of people interested in what your store has to offer. Setting up a Facebook page for your shop is fairly easy, and there is even a special category for local businesses.

Once you've established the account you can designate additional people as administrators, which means they can also post to the page (although you should establish a consistent tone for your postings, no matter who on the staff is doing the writing). When setting up your page, pay attention to the details, use great photos, and don't forget to include a *Call to Action* (CTA) "Shop Now" button if you sell online.

You'll want to encourage customers to "like" your page so that they will see what you publish. A good way to start is to invite your own Facebook friends to like your shop's page, which is easy to do by clicking below the page's cover photo and selecting Invite Friends. We also encourage our customers in the store to follow our Facebook page, and provide the link in all our email blasts and on our website.

What makes for a good Facebook post? Visuals are key—photos, especially ones with people and perhaps pets, are usually popular and short videos are surefire winners (be sure to add the "Watch Video" CTA button). Facebook Live is also a good option if you are prepared to show viewers something worth watching. Don't forget to have something happening in the store from time to time so that you can include events on your page.

We do a monthly Sampling Saturday featuring some of our specialty foods in part so that we are certain to have at least 12 Facebook events a year. Another great idea is to offer double the preferred customer points on any purchases made by Facebook friends mentioning a post during a very limited time period.

Plan to spend some of your budget promoting or "boosting" events, ads, and status updates on Facebook. If you want to increase the chance that your post is seen by a larger number of your customers, or by potential new customers, this is a good option (although some types of posts are not eligible for boosting).

You can designate the demographics and interests of your audience—we use 30- to 60-year-old female sale shoppers in Madison, WI for our clearance sale, for example—and determine how much money you'd like to spend over a certain number of days. One of my favorite features of this program is that you can see the number of people potentially reached, allowing you to adjust the amount and time allocated or perhaps expand the parameters of your selected group.

A more expensive option is using Facebook News Feed ads, and these can include a more specific call to action instead of just the likes and shares of a boosted post. Unlike the ads on the right-hand side of the screen, these ads are integrated in the user's news feed.

It is tempting to run contests on Facebook, rewarding for example the 50th person to like a post or your page. We have learned from experience that it's hard to track who that might be, and because you don't have personal data on the people who like your page it may be hard to notify the winner. Other contests run the risk of violating Facebook's tight regulations of this activity, so be sure to check the rules before you try something.

INSTAGRAM MOBILE MARKETING

Instagram is a photo-sharing app and social network that was purchased by Facebook for $1 billion just two years after it was created in 2010. Although it can be viewed on a desktop, this social platform—which has over 700 million monthly users—is primarily a mobile app, and you can only post using a smartphone or tablet.

You can easily connect an Instagram account to your Facebook account. Make sure that yours is a "business profile" so that you will have access to analytics and insights. Instagram postings center on photos (traditionally square) and videos, accompanied by short captions that often include hashtag identifiers. The home page for Instagram is a continuous stream of posts from users that you follow (similar to "liking" on Facebook), sponsored posts, and any posts that you've created.

Hashtags (#) are used on both Instagram and Twitter to follow a conversation or thread. You can add as many hashtags as you like to your photos and videos. However, Yvette Jones of designCraft Advertising recommends no more than 5 to 6 hashtags on any one post on Instagram. They can also be effective when used occasionally for humorous effect. You want to choose ones that will gain new viewers to your posts when someone enters it in the search feature. We've encouraged the businesses on our street to all use #monroestreetmadison, for example, and we always include #orangetreeimports—but we might also add #lovethosebadgers when posting something of interest to University of Wisconsin fans. Opposite is an Instagram sign you can download at www.specialtyshopretailing.com to customize with your store's hashtag.

Because Instagram is a photo-sharing platform, you'll want to post content that is likely to be shared, or at least commented on, by your followers. Pictures of customers modeling your clothing or accessories, for example, are likely to attract attention. You'll also want to encourage customers to post photos of products they love. Pictures that evoke emotion, including humor, are also good. The important thing is to post often—daily, or every other day—to keep your followers interested. And be sure to respond to any comments on your photos right away.

Instagram allows the promoting of posts much in the same way as Facebook, which is not surprising since they are owned by the same company. And Instagram now offers also offers a Shop Now button for in-app impulse buying.

Pinning on Pinterest

I enjoy using Pinterest to relax rather than for business (which is why I have a board for Danish food—the subject of my last book—with almost 6,000 pins). So I was a bit surprised to learn from the group of University of Wisconsin School of Business students advising us on our wedding business that Pinterest would be a great way to appeal to young couples.

Instagram sign.

It turns out that 52% of millennials use Pinterest every month. So we now have several "boards" for our store, including Wedding Ideas, Hot Products, Seasonal Specialties, and Recipes by Photo.

Unlike "friending" someone on Facebook, the act of following a pinner, or a specific board, is anonymous. And you can repin pictures and videos from anywhere on the Pinterest site without permission, even changing the caption if you want. You can of course also upload photos, and you might want to add a visible watermark to yours showing the store's web address so that it is always credited to you. Craft, decorating, and recipe ideas are popular topics. The option of Promoted Pins allows you to pay to have your pins potentially seen by more people.

If you want the products you feature on your website to end up being reposted on Pinterest boards, add the red Pinterest "Save" button to each photo. Connecting your website with Pinterest means that your profile picture will show up on every new Pin that comes from your site.

Responding to Reviews

Yelp, Google (on your store's Google Business Page), and Facebook allow consumers to give instant feedback when they are pleased—or displeased—with a retail experience. Happily, we are not impacted as much as restaurants, which can flourish or perish based on online comments. But it is still important that we pay attention to what potential customers will be reading about our shops, and that we immediately "claim" our business pages with these services so that we can respond to reviews. Good reviews are a great way to get shoppers excited before they even set foot in the store. And the occasional bad review can really hurt.

We recently had a negative review on Facebook, and I immediately replied with an apology for what the writer perceived as a bad customer service experience. My staff remembers the situation differently, but that doesn't matter much when it's out there for the public to read about. I try to respond right away to all good or bad reviews to let customers know we are listening.

Yelp suggests that you keep these points in mind when responding to a negative review:

1. Your reviewers are your paying customers

2. Your reviewers are human beings with (sometimes unpredictable) feelings and sensitivities

3. Your reviewers are vocal and opinionated (otherwise they would not be writing reviews!)

Digital Media: Marketing Your Brick & Mortar Store

After posting my response to our negative Facebook comment, I waited a few days and then asked our employees to see if a friend or family member would be willing to write a positive review. This moved the negative one lower down, or off, our home page. You could also ask a customer who is a big fan of your store to write a review.

If a customer is unhappy about a specific situation, consider inviting the customer to contact you via email so that you can try to make amends. This shows that you are taking the complaint seriously, and also "takes the fight outside" instead of continuing the discussion where everyone can see it.

Online reviews are an extension of the word of mouth advertising that we all know is invaluable. Hopefully your business gets enough positive ones to outweigh those that are negative. And even though it hurts to read criticism, legitimate complaints do give us a chance to improve. We can trust that the public is savvy enough to know that a single negative comment surrounded by positive ones shows that this less than perfect experience is unusual.

Using the Internet to Reach Local Customers

You might want to consider using some online ads to promote your business within your market area. Most newspapers now also have a web version that includes pages with up-to-the-minute information that readers know they can't get from the print edition. You might negotiate an advertising package that includes some online display ads, often referred to as banner ads, in addition to traditional print. One advantage to these ads is that they are clickable, so they can take the viewer directly to the home page of your website or a specific landing page that is created to provide further information about the item being advertised.

When deciding how best to focus online advertising that will bring visitors to your store, consider the option of *geotargeting*. This is the practice of delivering content based on the user's geographic location, whether it is their home base, or an IP address or device ID that recognizes their current location by using GPS signals on a mobile device such as a smartphone. This can help you stretch your online advertising budget by specifically targeting customers near your store. You will be able to know who is searching for a specific item or even reading about one, and also to select the day of the week and the time that is best for your ad to run. Marketing of the future will include more of this type of very specific targeting, using technology called *geofencing* that creates a virtual geographic boundary in order to trigger a response when a mobile device enters or leaves it.

The Internet provides an opportunity to expand your customer base nationally and even internationally. But it can also be a way to serve your local customers better. Just as a catalog allows customers to pre-shop before coming into the store, a website can offer an opportunity to present in-depth information about the products you offer. A futon store, for example, might have the sizes and specifications for all their furniture on their website, allowing shoppers to have the measurements on hand in their home when considering what to buy. The final decision will be made in the store, but the information on the website is easy to access 24 hours a day.

CHAPTER 13
BRICKS & CLICKS:
MAXIMIZING ONLINE OPPORTUNITIES

The Internet provides an unparalleled opportunity for those who want to expand their market beyond the customers who walk through the door. But you need to be willing to set up a system to fulfill orders and ship them out, and to stay on top of the inventory you offer on your site. The biggest challenge in being a bricks-and-clicks (or clicks and mortar) retailer is that when it comes to attracting customers, your store is no longer just up against the big store down the street – you are competing with giants like Amazon.

Many retailers who start with a storefront location eventually face the question of whether or not to add a shopping cart, or *clickability*, to their website. How do you decide whether or not to sell online? There is the question of whether it's worth the time and money it will take to become an omnichannel retailer, and also whether it's the right move for you and your store.

I must confess that we don't sell much on our website (with the exception of autographed copies of this book!). One of the primary reasons we don't do more retailing on the Internet is that our greatest satisfaction comes from face-to-face contact with customers, and you just don't get that with an email, or even telephone, transaction. We don't really like packing merchandise to be shipped (especially since our goods come in all sizes and shapes), and are not set up to do so efficiently. We also don't carry many items unique enough that customers would find us when searching for them on the web. But if you offer a line of African dancewear, or peavey hooks for rolling logs—items that you're not likely to find in many shops, online or otherwise—you might well want to make your goods available to a wider market on the Internet.

You may also do well if you have sell products created exclusively for your store, or highly desirable collectibles (such as Beanie Babies in their prime) - or if you offer a discount on popular merchandise. Search engines keying into the main words describing these products will help bring customers to your site, and good customer service will help bring them back.

Well established stores, with a loyal customer base, have a head start on doing well on the Internet. Shoppers are often pleased to know that they have the option of buying the goods they know and like without always having to visit the store. Or perhaps they have moved away, or have other limitations that make coming into the store difficult. If this is the case the combination of real-store retailing and online e-tailing can be very successful, with each side of the business helping grow the other.

The buy local message should still resonate with those who prefer buying from independent stores, even when they can't do so in person. Be sure to include information about the location of your shop and the "About Us" story that makes it clear that you are a locally owned small business.

WHAT WORKS FOR YOU?

Give careful thought to how much of your inventory you want to sell online. You might want to feature just a few best-sellers from each of your product categories, or to invest the time and money in having most of your store's merchandise mix available to Internet shoppers. Just be realistic about the amount of effort that goes into doing this, and keeping it current. If you are going to pursue online selling with any regularity it is helpful to have a digital camera and a light box set up so that you can

take your own product photos, and then upload the product images and information.

Shops that have many more items available in the store than on their website can use the site to invite customers in to see the full selection and to experience the shop's excellent customer service. But if you have products online that you don't carry in stock, it is wise to let your customers know not to expect to see everything on the website in the shop.

Keep in mind that 15 to 30% of Internet purchases are returned, especially clothing or other apparel. Decide whether you want to deal with this, and also whether you only want to ship orders within your home country. The Internet brings your merchandise to the attention of customers worldwide, and shipping overseas can be a complicated

"Many years ago we thought about opening another store," recalls Arlene Placer of Hobbymasters in Red Bank, New Jersey. "We decided against it because it would stretch us too much employee-wise. But thanks to the Internet, our website has become a second store for us. Not only do locals see us online and come in, but we also have people from all over the globe ordering from us." Hobbymasters now bills itself as "The World's Largest International Hobby Store."

process. On the other hand, since the customer is usually paying the shipping charges, it may be worth doing.

Setting Up Your Virtual Shop

There are several options for selling on the Internet, ranging from equipping your own website with a shopping cart and secure credit card processing to selling just a few items through person-to-person auction sites such as eBay.

Your own online store gives you the most control over the entire process and is also the most expensive to set up. In addition to being able to offer secure credit card transactions, you'll want to have a search feature on your site so that customers can easily find the items they are looking for. You'll need a way of compiling and receiving orders, and a software system that allows you to complete each transaction and print out a shipping label without reentering a lot of data.

One of the best features of having your own website for online selling is the ability to track information about customer interests. You can do this by asking customers to register in order to access your site, although studies show that many visitors will not stay if asked to register. You can also compile data by tracking online orders and making suggestions based on what customers already purchased. Amazon has developed this feature, often called CRM (*customer relationship management*), into an art. But there is no reason why a small retailer can't use customer purchase history and data from like-minded shoppers to make customized, individual recommendations to their customers via email or phone.

eBAY, Amazon and Other Alternatives

There are several alternative selling platforms that allow you to sell online through their portals. One of the best known is eBay, which now has 1 billion live product listings at any one time. You can list individual items through eBay's auctions, with the option of showing your store name and web address in order to generate brand recognition with those interested in your type of product.

We've used eBay to sell odds and ends of collectible merchandise, since we know that reaching a wider audience is a good way to find a home for items our local customers don't want. If we wanted to, we could keep in touch with those who bought our items and offer them other merchandise they might like.

In addition to its regular auctions, eBay offers an opportunity for retailers to become eBay Store sellers. An eBay Store is an online storefront where sellers have a central shopping destination showcasing all of their eBay listings. A store must have a certain number of positive feedbacks from eBay buyers in order to achieve this status, and there is a monthly user fee in addition to a percentage taken from each sale. You can provide a promotional link on your website to the "About Me" page for your eBay Store, which can be personalized with a unique web address.

Many retailers use eBay for all their online selling, utilizing both its regular auctions and also the "buy it now" fixed price sales posted on their eBay Store's page. Check the eBay site for tips on how to use their site to your advantage to promote your business.

Amazon Marketplace offers a program similar to eBay's, but without the latter's auction option. At this time, listing on Amazon is free, but you pay a per-item fee, as well as a referral fee for the sale with this basic seller's account. You will need to make sure that your prices are competitive if you are going to go up against the other sellers on the Amazon site.

Etsy is an online platform for handmade and vintage goods, as well as craft supplies, that started in 2005. It now has over 1.8 million active sellers, many of whom are individuals. There is a listing fee per item and a commission on every sale made. Products listed on Etsy must meet their very specific criteria. Incidentally, Etsy has a wholesale marketplace that can be worth investigating if you carry handmade and vintage goods in your shop.

OPTIONS FOR YOUR SOLO SITE

Another alternative is participating in a program that seamlessly becomes a part of your own website. Instead of only using a dedicated site created entirely on your own, you integrate it with a platform that provides added content and sophisticated features. We use "Cooking Schools of America," for example, to handle our class listings and online registration.

Bridge is an innovative e-commerce platform that offers retailers the choice of using a customized Bridge store as their website, or adding a link to the Bridge store and products from an existing site. The company was founded in 2007 by New York-based web designer Jason Solarek, who saw the wisdom in asking vendors to input and maintain data about their products instead of having every retailer do this on their own.

Today, Bridge connects some 100 home goods manufacturers with the websites of nearly 300 specialty retailers. The company syncs 58,000 product photos and descriptions with its members' retail sites. When a store receives an order via the platform, the retailer fulfills the order or arranges for the item to be drop-shipped to the customer. This means that the retailer can offer a much wider range of products from each of their vendors on their website than they are able to feature in their store.

Shopping Cart Security

Taking credit cards online, either via an online shopping cart, via email, or by phone, exposes you to a higher level of credit card fraud than accepting credit cards in the store. In fact the protection you receive against loss from fraudulent credit card use in the store probably does not apply to transactions when the card is not present. While EMV chip technology is helping to protect stores from in-person credit card fraud, it is more difficult for online purchases.

If you receive credit card information via your computer, you need to protect your customers by limiting access to that information. Using passwords and information encryption are important when dealing with credit card numbers and other sensitive, personal data.

You should also take steps to protect your own data from being lost by a computer crash or virus. And if you are doing a thriving Internet business, give some thought to having a backup server in case you are unable to get online through your regular server. A gap of 12 or 24 hours could have serious business consequences, especially during the holidays.

Programs such as Shopify take care of providing a secure online shopping cart for your business, and will also help set up the product section of your website or even your Facebook page. Most e-commerce platforms like this one charge a low monthly fee and a fee per transaction, although stores using WordPress to create their web site often opt for the open source (i.e., free) plug-in WooCommerce to power their online store. Your shop still handles the shipping of the orders, unless you have an arrangement with a fulfillment service or your vendors drop ship.

Filling Internet Orders Efficiently

As a retail store owner, you have a clear advantage over a purely Internet outlet because you have the merchandise in stock and probably are already set up to send out packages via UPS or FedEx. However, it may work better for you to use an outside fulfillment house if you are planning on selling just a few items, but in large quantities. A fulfillment house provides warehouse space for your products and then fills and ships your orders. They have the technology and equipment to efficiently handle the paperwork and package the goods, though there is of course a charge for the service.

Another alternative is to link to a supplier who will ship to your customer directly from their warehouse. These items will be drop-shipped to the consumer with your business name on the label, however the margins in this type of arrangement are slim. You are unlikely to make a profit unless the items have a retail price of $50 or more.

Speedy shipping is a must because Internet shoppers are usually hoping for instant gratification. They also love to get free shipping, even if the cost of shipping is hidden in the retail price. The fact that it was often quicker and cheaper to get the goods by visiting an actual store made it seem unlikely that the Internet was ever going to replace brick-and-mortar retailing—until Amazon Prime made free next-day shipping commonplace. We have to work harder than ever for our share of the market thanks to this added competition.

The BOPIS Option

BOPIS, which stands for *Buy Online Pick-up In Store,* is a good way to make use of your online shopping cart to bring customers into the store. At first glance, it may seem hard to understand why a customer would want to make a purchase online and then visit the store to pick up the merchandise. I must admit that this is not something that I would be likely to do. However, I can see the appeal to a younger demographic that is more comfortable shopping online than in person.

Here are a few of the advantages of BOPIS:

- It avoids the frustration of going to a store and not finding what you are looking for
- It allows you to consider a wider range of goods than are usually available in the shop
- It saves time once you're in the store

This service works best for stores that have more than one branch, or a warehouse, so that orders for items not already in stock can be fulfilled. If your store doesn't have an online shopping cart, you can still offer to put merchandise featured on your website on hold for customers so that they can pick it up easily when they stop in—or you can offer to deliver it to them curbside. And unlike larger retailers, it is easy for a specialty shop to promise to have a gift beautifully wrapped and ready to go.

Attracting Customers to Your Website

"If you build it, they will come" may be true of baseball fields in Iowa, but with the myriad of sites on the web right now, you need to make a real effort to draw visitors. To bring local customers to your site, mention your web address in all your advertising, and include the link on social media sites. If you are underwriting public television, you will probably be allowed to mention it in your promotional spot. You could put it in the gusset of your shopping bags or cash register receipts or other inserts that go home with customer purchases.

Attracting national attention is more difficult. You will want to pay particular attention to your site's SEO, or *search engine optimization*. Google can assist you in finding specific *keywords*, the terms most relevant to the products and services you offer. You'll want to use the most accurate and descriptive words possible in the copy on your web pages. Search engine "crawlers" seek out this information to match it to the terms the consumer has entered. Give careful thought to what words you want to use, and what brands you want to list. Happily, Google now offers suggested corrections of common misspellings of keywords that customers may not get quite right.

The type of content on your page also influences how quickly it comes up on search engines. High-resolution images, original text, and answers to frequently asked questions are indicators of quality content. Sites with video are engaging and popular with customers, which may make them rank higher in search results.

If you are selling a product that you think shoppers might be searching for, you can place ads that appear when people search for terms relevant to your product. This way of advertising your site is called "pay-per-click," and you only pay when someone clicks through to your site after seeing the paid link on the search engine's list.

The placement of the ad on the search results page depends on several factors including the relevance of your landing page (usually the website home page) and ad content, and the price you are willing to pay for the ad. The price will vary based on the popularity of the terms—if you wanted to be one of the top three hits for Disney movies, for example, you would pay a lot more for each click than if your keywords were pickled peppers.

Google shopping campaigns can help promote your online and local inventory, as well as boost traffic to your website or store. This program is designed to help Google match your merchandise with what consumers are searching for. You start by sending Google your product data using your Merchant Center account, and then create a shopping campaign in AdWords. (You'll need to link your Merchant Center account to your AdWords account to get started.)

Google will use your product data to create ads on Google and around the web where potential customers can see what you're selling. These placements are called shopping ads, to use Google's terminology, because they're more than just plain text—they show a photo of the product, plus a title, price, the store name, and more. They give users a strong sense of the product before they click on the ad, which means that the lead has expressed a high level of interest. And you only pay when someone clicks through to your site.

Counting Clicks

The more ways that consumers can click through to your online store, the better. Include hyper-text links in everything you can, including blog posts and even your email signature.

Don't forget to ask your suppliers to include a link to your website on their site, especially if they provide consumers with a listing of retailers who carry their merchandise. Often a shopper will research a specific product and then want to buy it online (or in person) from a nearby retailer. If your website functions as both an online store and an advertising vehicle for your physical shop, it's doing double duty.

CHAPTER 14
PRODUCTIVE MARKETING:
CREATING PROMOTIONS & EVENTS

"Operating a business without proper promotion is like winking in the dark," according to retailing experts Don Taylor and Jeanne Smalling Archer in their cleverly titled book *Up Against the Wal-Marts*. "You know you're doing it, but no one else does." Imaginative promotions help specialty shop retailers distinguish themselves from their larger or less resourceful competitors, garnering free publicity and that most treasured form of advertising, customer word of mouth. Finding creative ways to attract shoppers and to entertain them once they enter the store is both challenging and enjoyable.

Promotion includes the many different ways retailers attempt to catch customers' attention: coupons, special events, sales, contests, and even celebrity appearances. Promotions often tie in naturally with publicity and public relations (PR), the free media coverage of the store and any of its activities that might be considered newsworthy. Paid advertising is part of the marketing packaging for many promotions, but some are created especially with free publicity in mind. Give special consideration to any promotion that you can use in your social media posts, or that might result in some mention in the news. Editorial coverage has more validity in the customer's eyes than any paid advertising—and it's free.

Productive Marketing: Creating Promotions and Events

Sale, Sale, Sale

Sales are the most overworked promotional concept in retailing today. Some stores hold sales every week, celebrating mythical founders' birthdays and holidays that the public has otherwise forgotten. This approach leads to customers' refusing to shop in a store unless there is a sale. Competing on price by discounting merchandise through frequent sales is a game you're not likely to win.

But most shops do need to hold a clearance sale occasionally to move out inventory that is reluctant to leave on its own at full price. We call our spring clearance "Orange's Lemon Sale" and kick off the event by giving out fresh lemons to the first one hundred customers. There is always a banner in the window announcing the Lemon Sale, prompting one of my fellow retailers to comment that he thought it was wonderful I was so willing to admit my mistakes in public. All sale merchandise is marked with a lemon-yellow tag and displayed on long tables. We have found that clearance shoppers (a special breed we sometimes jokingly refer to as "sale vultures") appreciate being able to look at all the discounted items in one place.

Our annual fall street festival, or sidewalk sale, allows us to clear out unwanted goods before the busy holiday season. We set up lots of tables outside and hope for good weather. We continue to lower prices as the day goes on, and much of the merchandise that is left by the end of the day goes to charity.

We used to have a permanent clearance area in the store, but found that the odds and ends of clearance merchandise never looked good. However, an attractive sale display can be made if you feature a large quantity of a single item or an entire line. Some retailers bring in special discounted merchandise to sell on sale. These discontinued or overstock items are offered by suppliers at a low wholesale price so they can be sold at full markup, but at a price the consumer finds attractive. If you are certain that these goods will sell, special purchases for a sale can generate a bit of extra income from customers attracted by the prospect of a good deal.

A storewide discount sale is useful if you have a sudden need to raise cash. Some stores also use this type of promotion to attract new customers or to bring existing customers back into the store. The drawback to holding a "20% Off Everything" sale is that no one wants to shop in the store immediately before or after the sale. If it is a regular event, customers will wait for it or feel bad if they miss it and have to pay full price.

Timing is crucial on a sale. If a sale runs too long, customers feel no sense of urgency and may put off coming in until they forget to do so. A limited number of days is preferable. We send out a mailing to the preferred customers on our list, offering a day or two head start and an extra discount before the sale is advertised to the general public.

REDUCED PRICE OFFERS

Promotional pricing on individual items or entire lines can be used to draw customers' attention to them. Often suppliers offer special pricing on their products, allowing retailers to promote the line on sale while maintaining full markup. You can mark items with a sale price or use a percentage off sign and take markdowns at the register. Most customers are not very quick at math, so unless you are offering something simple such as a 10% discount, you may wish to put the sale prices on the merchandise in addition to posting sale signs.

Before and after prices are an effective way to draw attention to an attractive price. We use a white tag to show the regular price and a red tag marked "special" for the promotional price.

Variations on price promotion include *buy one, get one free* (also known as *BOGO*), which is equivalent to a 50% discount off each item. When I was a child in Pennington, New Jersey, I loved the corner drugstore's Penny Sale. If you bought one notebook for full price, you could buy a second one for only a penny (which even then didn't usually buy much). I'm not sure that I would have been as intrigued by a "half off selected notebooks" sale, although that is really what was being offered; a second notebook for only a penny seemed to be a real bargain.

Gift with purchase (GWP) is another way to discount a specific item by selling it at full price but offering a second item with it for free. Perfume is often offered this way, with the value of the travel bag or other GWP sometimes exceeding that of the original item. These promotions usually originate with the supplier, but there is no reason that a nursery, for instance, can't offer free flower seeds with a special garden tool set. Customers love the idea of getting something for nothing.

PRICE PROMOTION IN ADS

The majority of all advertising for big stores and the Internet is centered around price, and few specialty stores can compete with them on price alone. Ads for individual products should sell the features and benefits of the item and perhaps also mention service, location, or other factors that might draw a customer to your store. Having said this, I hasten to add that you probably also need to mention price, and the price should be reasonably close to what a competitor would charge. The fact is that most customers want to get high value, quality service, *and* the lowest price. Not all items in your store need to be at the same low price as a big store's, but the items you advertise should be competitive.

Creative Ideas for Promotions

There are many ways other than holding a sale to bring new customers into the store and to encourage existing customers to return. To select the best approach for your shop, it is important to think about whom you are trying to reach in your promotion and what will motivate him or her to make a special trip to your store.

You may find that different promotions are necessary to reach various parts of your target market. As long as your efforts are in keeping with your store image and aren't all aimed at the same consumer, there is nothing wrong with running several promotions at the same time.

CUSTOMERS LOVE COUPONS

Coupon promotions are an excellent way to test the response to store advertising because they require customers to bring in physical proof that they have seen an ad. Coupons can be distributed in many ways: through direct mail, in print ads, in an email blast, as bag stuffers, or even door to door (as long as you don't use the mailbox, which postal regulations restrict to US mail). But coupons are not for every store. They are not upscale enough for very sophisticated shops and may be ineffective for stores depending mostly on transient tourist or walk-by traffic.

A number of services specialize in delivering coupons. In many areas there are magazines of coupons that are mailed to households that meet certain criteria. If your store is in a tourist area, you might suggest that merchants, restaurants, and motels put together a tourist packet of offers for visitors.

Coupons can also be sent out together with offers from other businesses in a *marriage mail packet*, so called because it combines the advertising from one firm with that of several other noncompetitive businesses, allowing everyone to share the cost of the mailing. Coupons are an effective way of bringing existing customers back into the store. At the time of purchase, give customers a "bounce-back" coupon to be used during their next visit, making sure to include a start and end date. You may be able to program your POS system to issue these coupons automatically on the cash register receipt.

To make a coupon work well, the offer must be attractive enough to motivate a customer to make the trip to the store and to bring it along. A

Productive Marketing: Creating Promotions and Events

10% or greater discount storewide, or on popular items, or a special free gift or service are all enticing coupon offers. The cost of any giveaway items should be considered part of the advertising budget. If coupons for a free sample bar of Crabtree & Evelyn soap cost $50.00 to print and distribute, and 200 bars wholesaling for $1.00 each are given away, the total cost for the promotion is $250. The cost per customer brought into the store is $1.25, which probably would compare favorably to the response to other forms of advertising at the same cost.

If you include a coupon in a printed newspaper or magazine ad, be sure to request special placement on an outside edge so that customers can tear it out easily. It is also important to proofread coupon copy carefully to be certain that customers will not misunderstand the offer. Coupons should always mention your store name and address and have an expiration date, including the year.

Keep all coupons turned in by customers, making a notation in the corner of the total amount of the customers purchase. When a customer shows a coupon on a smartphone, you'll need to write down these details to be compiled later. This information is essential for measuring the effectiveness of the promotion.

TARGETED DISCOUNTS

We offer a special discount to encourage restaurant chefs to shop with us, giving them 10% off on all items purchased for professional use. A hospital gift shop might offer a special discount to the hospital's employees. Other stores offer special discounts to companies buying corporate gifts. Special discount cards can be given to qualified individuals or businesses in the shop or used as part of a promotional mailing aimed at a special segment of the store's market.

Rewarding Customer Loyalty

Retail stores have discovered another way of keeping frequent shoppers coming back: programs that give customers special benefits to reward them for the amount they spend in the store. These customer loyalty programs, modeled after the airlines' frequent flyer programs, often require that the customer present a card to track of purchases. It is more customer friendly, but also more complicated, for the store to help keep records for each customer. The store might offer to help keep a copy of the frequent buyer card numbers on file in case a customer forgets to bring theirs in, or use a program that ties the card number to the customer's phone number.

What will you call your frequent buyer program? In an effort to sound chummy, J. C. Penney at one time had a "Bra and Panty Club." When I received my membership card, I asked the sales associate what sorts of things went on at the Bra and Panty Club meetings. She didn't seem at all amused.

Rewards for frequent purchases range from free pair of socks with the fourth pair of shoes at a shoe store to a 50% discount on any one jewelry item under $100 when purchases total a certain amount at a fine crafts gallery. Awards can also include items that promote the store, such as t-shirts, tote bags, mugs, and other items bearing the shop's name and logo.

PREFERRED CUSTOMER PROGRAMS

Even small shops now have the option of offering a more sophisticated loyalty program at a reasonable cost using an online program and customized plastic loyalty cards. These programs capture data that can be used both for tracking rewards and for compiling information about customers' buying habits. In our store, customers are offered a card when they spend $25 or more. Whenever a purchase is made, the card is run through a special card swipe unit that records the amount of the sale and credits the customer's account. If you use a POS system, you can undoubtedly tie a loyalty program into the data being recorded by the cash register system.

We have created a registration card for our rewards program that provides us with information about the customer's interests, mailing address, email contact information, and birthday month. We send out postcards offering our rewards customers a small birthday gift, which brings them into the store sometime close to their birth date. Other stores invite their best customers to come in on their birthday for a 20% discount that day.

A reminder about rewards programs: if a customer makes a return, be sure to deduct the corresponding number of points from their account in your program. Otherwise you will be rewarding customers for dollars that you did not get to keep.

ANNUAL MEMBERSHIP PROGRAMS

The cost of maintaining a current customer is considerably less than that required to obtain a new one, and many stores make their regular customers feel appreciated by offering them special benefits. Some bookstores, including national chains such as Barnes & Noble, sell an annual membership card to their regular customers for a nominal fee. The card provides a discount on all books purchased during the year, encouraging shoppers to make their investment in the card pay off by buying all their books from the same source.

Many grocery chains use valued customer cards called smart cards, or fidelity cards. When scanned at the register, the card provides the customer with coupon-like savings on advertised products, check cashing privileges, and in some cases points toward rewards. The merchant is able to compile a useful database on its customers from the smart card application form and from the data captured with each purchase, allowing the store to target special promotions and advertising at its best customers. There is no reason why other types of retailers that attract the same shoppers regularly could not adapt this system for their own use.

Special Events to Attract Shoppers

A special event is often an effective way to create a sense of excitement in your advertising and social media posts, encouraging customers to come in during the one day, or several days, that the event is being held. Special events are also fun for staff members, providing them with the opportunity to do something a little differently with displays and hospitality.

PRODUCT DEMONSTRATIONS AND SEMINARS

Retailing as entertainment can mean just that: live music in the store or a magician to entertain shoppers' children. It can also refer to myriad creative activities that bring customers into the store and enhance their shopping experience, from food sampling to makeup demonstrations. Even shoppers in a hurry enjoy stopping for taste samplings of specialty foods. And those who are shopping as a recreational activity are attracted to stores that offer something more than just sales and a display of products.

Product demonstrations can be held at random times when the store is likely to be busy or scheduled for specific times and promoted through advertising. Larger stores may be able to schedule several demonstrations at the same time, increasing their chances of good traffic. Ask your staff members to demonstrate products, or ask your vendors to recommend someone who specializes in working as a "brand ambassador." Sales reps often enjoy the opportunity to get feedback from the buying public by talking about the items they sell.

Having someone demonstrate an activity in your store window always attracts attention. Resort shops know how visitors, especially young ones, can be mesmerized by watching someone make taffy or fudge or create blown glass animals. Stores in other areas draw customers by featuring craftspeople—weavers, spinners, calligraphers, or painters—at work in their windows.

In addition to live demonstrations, consider making use of a small DVD unit to show informative videos about your merchandise. Ask vendors for promotional videos about their products in a format that loops continuously without your having to restart it. Keep the volume low so that those not interested in listening are not distracted as they shop.

GUEST APPEARANCES

Other special events in the store might include appearances by local or nationally known artists, craftspeople, or authors. The guest can answer customers' questions about their work, pose for pictures with their fans, and sign autographs. If you invite a celebrity to your store, be certain that you can attract enough interested customers to make the appearance worthwhile for the guest visitor.

Give some thought to providing a comfortable, attractive place for the celebrity to sit, and have a staff member on hand to fetch more product, a new pen, or a glass of water. Those who are on long publicity tours appreciate any thoughtful hospitable touches that make them feel especially welcome in your town and in your store, such as a home-cooked meal, a gift certificate to a local coffee shop, or a small fruit basket in their hotel room.

Suppliers or publishers sending artists and authors on tour to promote their products should provide you with publicity materials well in advance of the event. They also usually send an agreement spelling out your share of the expenses. If you decide to bring in a celebrity guest on your own, you will, of course, need to pay for transportation, hotel, meals, and perhaps an appearance fee. Check with retailers in nearby cities to see if any would like to have the same person in their store so that you can share the airfare costs. You might also be able to contact a celebrity scheduled to perform a concert or play in your area and arrange for the person to make an in-store appearance to promote a product or charity in which he or she has an interest.

COSTUMED CHARACTERS

Families with children love the photo opportunity that a costumed character offers. The classic pictures with Santa promotion is still a must for almost every large mall in America, as is having the Easter bunny in residence in the spring. A specialty shop can distinguish itself by offering something a little different, such as an appearance by a licensed or storybook character or a life-sized version of a stuffed animal. You might consider an appearance by a local sports team mascot. One of our favorites is Henry the Lion, the mascot of the nearby Henry Vilas Zoo.

Costume shops can provide full body costumes, such as a cow for June Dairy Month (a major event here in Wisconsin) or a nutcracker for a Christmas promotion. Wearing one of these costumes is not as easy as it looks. Our toy buyer, Nanci Bjorling, offered to lead a children's parade dressed as a troll during the heyday of troll collecting. The rubber headpiece turned out to be quite hot, and, of course, she couldn't take her head off in front of the children.

Remember that the person in the costume can't take a drink of water or usually even speak while in character. Limit appearance time, or build in breaks where the person can relax in private. It is also very important to have an assistant on hand to handle inquisitive children and to help the costumed character move around, especially if the costume limits vision.

Consider a frame or character cut-out that can be used as "selfie" opportunities in your store. Shops in tourist areas should consider whether there is an outdoor display relating to their area that visitors would enjoy photographing. Be sure to have a sign with your store name placed so that it will be included in the picture.

Productive Marketing: Creating Promotions and Events

CONDUCTING CONTESTS

The creativity of my customers never ceases to amaze me. We have held many contests over the years, and only once, when we held a rather vague "create a Christmas ornament" contest, have we been left without enough entries to make an interesting display. Other contests include one in which customers were invited to decorate small silver Christmas trees (purchased very inexpensively at the summer closeout sale of a competitor) and another that focused on creating holiday packages using gift wrap designed by Frank Lloyd Wright and donated by the licensed supplier of this wrap at the time. The results of both contests were spectacular.

We have held a gingerbread house contest several times, and although the entries in the last contest were few, they were magnificent. We have also sponsored wooden nutcracker, dollhouse Christmas tree, guess the jelly beans, and children's art contests. Our annual egg art contest, with a special category for the best Ukrainian egg, is going into its fortieth year.

The cost for running these competitions is extremely low. The contests are promoted through social media, email blasts, and flyers both posted in the store and mailed to past entrants, as well as one or two print ads. We send press releases to the local media, which usually result in at least one mention in the paper.

Entrants fill in a form when they bring in their creation and are given a receipt. Contest entries are all numbered so no one can see who made each one. They are then judged by a volunteer committee of staff members, sometimes assisted by one of our sales reps or another outside guest. We give out as many prizes as possible. We keep a supply of inexpensive prize ribbons, imprinted with the store name, on hand at all times for this purpose. Winners also get merchandise prizes and gift cards, with a $25.00 or $50.00 shopping spree often serving as the grand prize. All entries are displayed in the store or in the window. Shoppers

> At a seminar I gave at the Toronto Gift Fair, an attendee named Taylor shared an idea from an ice cream shop he had managed. Once a month the shop drew the name of the winner of a grand prize sundae for six. But during slower times in the year, they also called everyone who had entered to say that although they had not won the big prize, they were entitled to a small ice cream cone as a consolation prize. Since few people would come in alone for their cone, this built traffic during their off season at a very low cost.

love to see what other customers have created, and we have received a great deal of free newspaper and television coverage of our various contests.

Shops can also band together to hold competitions. Our shopping street was enlivened one Halloween by a window painting contest, and an art contest for local preschools provided dozens of pictures to display on various storefronts during a spring street fair. Shopping center stores can band together to hold events such as a celebrity look-alike contest or an Easter egg roll in the mall area.

Most states have strict regulations about raffles requiring the purchase of tickets but allow stores to conduct free drawings, or sweepstakes, for prizes. A prize drawing can be used to compile a special interest mailing list during an event such as a celebrity artist's appearance. Ask the supplier sponsoring the appearance to donate a door prize, or have the artist autograph an item from your stock to be given away. If businesspeople are an important part of your target market, have a drawing that customers enter by dropping their business card into a bowl. Add all the names from your trading area to your mailing list.

HOSTING BLOGGER EVENTS

There are an amazing number of blogs (and video vlogs) posted every day, often aimed at readers with a special interest that may correspond with your target market. A contest or event for local bloggers is a great way to gain free publicity for your store. We hosted a local food blogger evening at Orange Tree Imports with wine and a taste sampling, and while the writers were there we gave them a tour of the latest and greatest cooking items in our store. Before they left each one got a goodie bag of kitchen tools provided by three of our suppliers.

The contest we sponsored was based on the question "If I had $100 to spend at Orange Tree Imports, what would I buy?" Participants wrote carefully thought-out and well-illustrated blogs listing their favorite kitchen items, keeping within the $100 limit. They invited their readers to come into the store to enter a prize drawing for a $100 spending spree, and the blogger who had the most readers enter the drawing also won a $100 gift card. We promoted all the entries through our social media, as did the bloggers, so we know that they got wide readership. The total cost to us for this promotion, beside the gift cards, was the refreshments for the evening event. The resulting PR: priceless.

$100 orange tree imports shopping spree

SPECIALTY SHOP RETAILING

VARIATIONS ON A THEME

Bloomingdale's pioneered the idea of an all-store merchandising and marketing event lasting for several weeks. These promotions were an essential part of what was called the Bloomingdale's Blitz. A theme, such as products from China, was used to create displays and demonstrations throughout the store. New merchandise was brought in, or even custom-made, for the event. Music, food, art, and entertainment throughout the store tied in with the theme. The result was a unique and exciting retail event that fascinated and attracted curious visitors as well as serious shoppers.

A smaller specialty shop can't put on an event as grand as one of Bloomingdale's, but the concept of putting together a longer, multifaceted event based on a season, a merchandise category, or a country is a good one. Work with several vendors to select a product mix that ties in with the theme, and ask them to back you up with product samplings, special offers, and demonstrations throughout the event. Arrange for window displays, refreshments, and entertainment to fit the theme.

If your event focuses on merchandise from one nation, contact that country's trade consulate or embassy and ask for posters, brochures, and other promotional materials. We promoted Danish, Norwegian, and Swedish goods with a Scandinavian festival supported by the various embassies and tied in with a silent auction of items donated by our suppliers to benefit the Scandinavian Studies Department at my alma mater, the University of Wisconsin.

OPEN HOUSES

Inviting customers to an open house sounds both hospitable and homey. For many stores, the only thing actually happening during an open house is the serving of refreshments and perhaps a percentage off on a certain line, or item, in the store. To make an open house more memorable, include live music (we favor quiet instruments such as harp) and gifts or favors for everyone attending. Some stores have drawings for door prizes or offer a special item for sale that is available only during the event.

Guests can be treated to a crafts demonstration or have items signed by a visiting celebrity, or watch a video presentation about some of the shop's merchandise. Staff should dress up for the event, and you should use fresh flowers and other touches to dress up the shop as well. An open house should always feature light refreshments, such as punch and cookies or wine and cheese—but avoid sticky foods that might cause

Kathi Frelk is a cookie baking and decorating expert who signed copies of her cookbook, *Kathi's Cookie Chronicles*, during the holiday open house at the Cornerstone Shop & Gallery in Lake Geneva, Wisconsin. She is pictured here with store owner Karin Bennett. (Photo courtesy of Karin Bennett)

messy fingerprints on the merchandise. You'll also want to check local alcohol licensing regulations, and find out whether food can be served that is not prepared in a commercial kitchen.

Offering a percentage of sales to a charity is an excellent way to attract free publicity for your open house. Ask the charity for permission to use its name and ask that it use its own social media to spread the word about your event. Be sure to keep the charity's staff informed about your plans so they can answer any questions that come to them. Invite prominent citizens who are supporters of the charity, and encourage them to bring their friends and associates. Send out a press release about the event, and invite any members of the press who might like to attend.

There are many types of open houses: a men-only shopping night, a two-day event highlighting a certain product line, a private evening for members of a club, or a seasonal open house officially launching the Christmas holiday season.

Your Grand Opening

The debut of a new shop or a branch store is a joyous occasion. The celebration of a grand opening is an opportunity to announce the store's arrival and let the public know what type of promotion, hospitality, and service the shop plans to offer. It pays to do it right because you can only do it once.

Most people wait a few weeks before inviting guests to visit them in a new home. The same rule of thumb should apply to inviting the public to the store's grand opening, because there are always some glitches when a shop first opens. (These sometimes stressful initial few days are sometimes called a *soft opening*.) Wait until most of the merchandise has arrived, the staff has gained some experience, and the displays are set up the way you'd like them to look. When you feel you have things under control, then it is time to throw your store's first special event.

Productive Marketing: Creating Promotions and Events

A grand opening is often done in two parts: a private evening affair for friends, neighbors, fellow retailers, professional advisers, and suppliers, and a two-day or one-week event open to the public. You could also invite the members of the press, or influential city officials, to a special open house soon after your store has opened. Entertainment, refreshments, and special sales will help attract a crowd. Signage and advertising should be planned to promote the event, including invitations mailed or delivered to neighboring households.

Taking It On the Road: Events Outside the Store

Not every retailer has the imagination to look beyond the four walls of the shop for promotional opportunities, but those who do find new ways to reach customers and interest them in their products. Consumers are often eager to buy something to help them remember the event they are attending—bookstores often do very well selling in the back of the room at a lecture or seminar, for example. Food specialty shops offer tastings at international fairs. Interior design shops decorate rooms in charity designer showcase homes or lend props to other stores to display in their windows. Tabletop stores display their china and silver at wedding shows, and hardware stores set up booths at home improvement expos.

There are two types of out-of-store events: those that are strictly promotional, such as exhibits and displays, and those that seek to sell merchandise. For promotional events, insist on attractive signage to identify the merchandise from your shop. Send along a supply of your business cards, brochures, and store catalogs. For out-of-store events that involve selling goods, you will need a travel kit with the essentials of day-to-day retailing: a cash register or cash box, change, a SquarePay or other mobile credit card device, pens, signs, scissors, tape, and bags for the merchandise.

Bring along literature promoting your store, including a coupon or another incentive to bring the shoppers in to see your full selection.

Check in advance to see if you will need to bring your own tables, table coverings, carpeting, lights, and chairs. Take enough merchandise and props to create an attractive display that will represent your store well.

Over the years, we have set up temporary shops in a number of locations, including a cat show, a baby fair, a wine and food gala, an antique show, and an art fair. It's a lot of work to transport goods and set up the display, but it's also fun to isolate one segment of our merchandise, such as cat-related gifts, and present them to a closely targeted audience. Several of the events we've been involved in have had a charity tie-in, which is something we always look for in promotions.

Garnering Publicity and Positive PR

Paid advertising is often an integral part of marketing a special event in the store, along with promotion via social media, but one of the advantages of sponsoring a creative promotion is that there is a good chance that it will net some free publicity. There are two advantages to this type of press coverage: You don't have to pay for it, and it has greater credibility with the public than the advertising you do pay for.

The disadvantages are that you can't ever count on getting free press coverage, and you have little control over the content of the coverage you do get. Most newspapers and radio and television stations maintain a policy of keeping commercial advertising and editorial coverage separate, so spending a lot of money on ads is unlikely to have any effect on how much feature coverage you are able to generate. You should, however, try to coordinate your marketing and public relations campaigns so that one supports the other.

Because free publicity is a gift, it pays to be very nice to anyone from the press. Many years ago an article about our shopping area failed to mention one merchant, and she called the newspaper and read the poor reporter the riot act. I'm sure that the next time that newspaper wanted to do a feature on a specialty shop, hers was not the store they called.

Productive Marketing: Creating Promotions and Events

We are approached from time to time by reporters working on a seasonal shopping story or by a TV station needing a kitchen in which to film a segment on new trends in cooking, and we always do our best to cooperate, even if we don't end up being mentioned by name.

When you are contacted by the media, cooperate in every way, keeping their deadlines and other restrictions in mind. Do what you can to make it easy for them to get the information and footage or photographs that they need. As Jay Conrad Levinson, Rick Frishman, and Jill Lublin, the authors of *Guerrilla Publicity,* point out, "The media feeds on information. It devours massive amounts of content that must constantly be replenished."

Remember that some days, such as Sundays, are slow news days, so your chances of getting some television or radio coverage are much greater than on a busy weekday. Even if you haven't sent out an official press release in advance, you may be able to get a reporter and camera person to come on short notice to cover some interesting event at your store if the station is short of feature stories for that day's news.

If you are to be interviewed for television or radio, ask if you can get a general idea of the questions you'll be asked a few minutes before the interview begins. Tell the reporter how you would like the store's name pronounced and try to get him or her to mention the location as well as any other points that you feel are important. Speak clearly and briefly. Very little of what you say—just short sound bites—will be used, so choose your words carefully. Never say anything to a reporter that you don't want publicized, even if you are speaking off the record.

THE PRESS RELEASE

A press release announces an event, a unique new product line, important personnel appointments or promotions, an in-store visit by a celebrity, or other newsworthy information to the media. The more human interest there is in your story, the more likely it is to be used. Remember that a press release should not sound like ad copy.

Press releases should be sent to TV newsrooms, magazines, and all local newspapers, including the smaller papers in nearby towns. You can usually send them by email. Shorter press releases are appropriate for community calendars and other radio coverage. Be sure to send out press releases at least two weeks prior to an event and even earlier than that if you hope for coverage in a monthly magazine. All press releases have similar basic elements:

- ◆ To: The name of the publication or station and the name of the editor or other contact person

- ◆ From: The store name, address, telephone and email, and website; and the name and title of the store's contact person for the media

- ◆ The date of the press release: If the item can be printed right away, add, "For immediate release." If the news is not to be announced until a certain date, indicate "For release on _____."

- ◆ The facts about the product or event: Be sure to answer the questions: *who, what, when,* and *where.* State all key facts in the first sentence. Write as if you were writing an article. Limit your release to one page, and be sure to mention the most important information in the first paragraphs. If the story has to be shortened, the final paragraphs will usually be dropped.

- ◆ Attach good photographs: Send at least one photo with the press release as a high resolution JPEG. Be sure to list a caption and the photographer's credit line, and to mention that additional photos are available. Include a signed release for any individuals in the photo, especially if they are customers or other non-employees.

When you send out a press release, consider enclosing a general fact sheet about the store. This information probably won't be used by the press, but it can't hurt to supply it. It pays to know in advance the name of the best person to contact at each publication or station and to make sure the information goes directly to that person. For important press releases, follow up with a telephone call a few days later, asking if the release has arrived and if there are any questions you can answer. Most people don't do this, and the follow-up can make a real difference in the likelihood of the story being carried.

FINDING AN ANGLE

The key to getting in the news is to do something newsworthy. Shops that are frustrated by a lack of free publicity often don't have an angle to get the press interested. Brainstorm with your staff about special events, services, or products that set your store apart from others, and send out press releases until you are successful at garnering some coverage.

Don't forget that business reporters are often eager for stories about shops with an unusual approach to management or merchandising or for information about stores that have recently expanded or changed. There is also nothing wrong with sending out a press release to announce a significant charity donation you are making or a service project that your staff is involved in.

Human interest and humorous stories are often considered newsworthy. We once called a local columnist to tell him about the "nonsense file" we keep, with clippings about the silliest products offered to us over the past 40 years. Unfortunately, some of his readers misunderstood the story, and we received numerous telephone calls asking the prices of items we'd never carry, such as Styrofoam wind chimes ("if you love the look but hate the sound") and video aquariums. Add local newspaper and magazine editors to your store email list so they are always aware of what is happening at your shop. This is an easy way to be sure the press hears from you regularly, but it shouldn't take the place of formal press releases.

You can become known as an articulate spokesperson in your field by volunteering to speak to community groups on subjects relating to your merchandise. Bring along samples of what you sell, and don't forget to bring catalogs, product literature, and business cards. When we give talks, we usually also bring a little gift for everyone attending and a coupon offer to entice each person into the store. Invite a member of the press to attend your talk, or send an email to the media mentioning that you are an experienced speaker on a topic sure to be of interest to their audience.

POSITIVE PRESS RELATIONS

The press does you a favor by mentioning your shop, especially if the feature is complimentary. (Thankfully, specialty shops are not usually subject to the same type of reviews as restaurants. A few negative comments in the press can quickly kill a fledgling eatery.) Remember to express your gratitude to the reporter or publication, and mention that you'd be happy to talk with the person again at any time.

Post framed copies of any positive articles about your store, along with any popularity awards, such as Best Antique Store, you may have won. You should mention these awards in your ads, in your social media and on your website. The fact that the compliment comes from an unpaid outside source lends it greater authority, just as any article or news feature seems more trustworthy to the public than the advertising you pay for.

CHAPTER 15
RESPONSIBLE RETAILING:
DOING WELL BY DOING GOOD

The positive public relations generated by being a good corporate citizen often far outweigh any advertising that could be purchased for the same amount of money. Donating merchandise and gift cards, and sponsoring fundraising events are very visible ways of doing good, and those actions form a natural part of most specialty shops' public relations campaigns.

Retailing also offers the opportunity to make a positive contribution to the local and global community through wise buying choices, good environmental policies, and even thoughtful hiring practices. Generosity and good business ethics can greatly enhance your store's reputation as a business leader, and most customers are eager to patronize stores whose spirit and community involvement they admire.

Charitable Donations: What and Where to Give

On some of the slower days of winter, I think requests for donations sometimes outnumber the customers wanting to buy things. Retail stores are easy for nonprofit groups to approach and are undoubtedly asked to give more often than the average insurance office or electrical contractor. Fortunately, retailers are also more visible to the public, so we are in a position to gain more by supporting causes in which our customers are involved and by helping to sustain the community our business depends on.

When someone approaches us for a donation, we always start by asking a few questions:

- ♦ Who will benefit?
- ♦ How will the gift card or merchandise be used?
- ♦ When and where is the fundraiser?
- ♦ Is there any special benefit for donors, such as a free program ad?
- ♦ Have we donated before—and, if so, what did we give?

We have a policy of giving to most arts, environmental, and social service organizations. Because we're not personally big sports enthusiasts, we tend to say no to team sponsorships. We also don't usually give to individual churches or religious groups, although we always make an exception for any charity in which one of our employees is actively involved.

Gazelle Sports, featured in this Grand Rapids, Michigan Local First campaign, has earned the designation of being a certified B Corp. B Corp is short for benefit corporation, which identifies companies focused on environmental and social change in addition to monetary profits—the so-called triple bottom line. (Courtesy of Grand Rapids Local First)

Responsible Retailing: Doing Well by Doing Good

In a small town, it may be important that you donate to the major service clubs, local schools, churches, and the Little League. In a larger community, you may feel freer to choose to donate to environmental causes or to support the opera. The choice is yours; however, it helps to have a policy in place so that you can give a quick and polite response to those soliciting donations.

Every good cause is happy to receive cash, but this is rarely the best choice of donation for a retail store. If a performing arts group is soliciting funds, you can usually buy an ad in the program instead of making a monetary donation. Don't just hand over a business card to be reproduced; a program ad should be as attractive as the rest of your ad campaigns. These ads tend to be standard sizes, so it is practical to have a few predesigned that you can easily send via email when needed.

Other charities might be able to use your monetary donation to purchase uniforms or t-shirts, which could be printed with your name or logo. If you donate money toward a fundraising event, perhaps you can be listed on the invitation as an underwriter or host.

If you do make a cash donation, get a receipt from the charity, and post the amount to the donation account in your bookkeeping system. Most cash donations to nonprofit organizations are tax deductible. Merchandise donations, however, do not get deducted in the donation account because when you take your next physical inventory, the value of your inventory will have been lowered by the cost of the goods donated. It is still a good idea to ask for a receipt for merchandise given, especially if you are tracking the causes of inventory shrinkage.

One of the advantages of having a shop is that you can generously donate merchandise with a high retail value, and the cost to you is whatever you paid for it wholesale. For this reason alone, it is usually advantageous to give goods rather than cash if the charity has a way to convert the merchandise into money. Many nonprofit organizations hold raffles and silent auctions to raise funds.

When we are donating goods that will be bid on, we first try to ascertain if the merchandise will be displayed or just listed. A showy item representing our shop is the logical choice for auctions where bidders will see the goods, especially our local public television auction, which nets us free TV exposure. In most other instances, we give a gift card, which will bring the high bidder into our store to shop.

We also get many requests for door prizes, but I'm not wild about giving door prizes because they rarely have a direct effect on the financial success of a charity event. Still, we will give low-amount gift cards and small items as door prizes when we can. For example, we were able to provide almost 500 table favors for the YWCA's annual Women of Distinction luncheon several times, thanks to a few of our favorite suppliers. Each company donated small perfume, bath gel, or hand lotion samples for the event at no charge, and we added labels with the name of our store.

You may want to give your customers a chance to support a fundraising project by bringing donated clothing, shoes or other items into the store. Shoppers enjoy this opportunity for doing good and recycling, especially if they are given a discount on replacements.

"Making Nisswa, Minnesota and our surrounding communities a better place to live and visit is a core value at Zaiser's. Giving to those non-profit organizations that do so much for our neighbors is a win-win effort. We have found over the years that the more one gives the more requests one receives. We needed a tool to make sure our donations are used in a way that agrees our store's culture and does the most good, so we set up a form on our website that says, 'If you have a cause that is looking for support, please fill out the application below. Donations are awarded on a quarterly basis every calendar year.' We don't use it for every small request; however, for those big giving opportunities, it has worked very well." —Biff Ulm, Store Manager, Zaiser's

Responsible Retailing: Doing Well by Doing Good

Customers can also be asked to make a voluntary donation to a cause, for example by "rounding up" their purchase to the nearest dollar. Some stores also involve customers in the planning of charity events by allowing them to vote on which organization should be the recipient of the money raised.

Wholesale suppliers are often very generous when asked to donate an item to be used as a raffle prize or auction item. When asking for a donation, allow plenty of lead time, and be very specific about the nature of the cause and what you hope will be donated. If you work through a sales representative, you may find that the rep has out-of-date samples of products that he or she is willing to donate. Our reps know that we are happy to find a worthy home for any merchandise they want to dispose of, including the one-of-a-kind greeting card samples that my daughter's Girl Scout troop used to send to nursing home residents during the holidays. Follow up any donation with a written thank-you note to both the supplier and the sales rep.

NEW HOMES FOR UNWANTED GOODS

No matter how low you mark clearance goods, you will never get rid of the very last item. Yet even a pathetic-looking pile of picked-over sale items in most cases can be put to good use by someone. Resist the temptation to throw it all in the trash, and sort through the remainders looking for items that you can donate to charity.

Some stores are hesitant to donate merchandise with their name on it. I once stood in line behind volunteers from a local theater's garage sale who were humorously discussing some of the less desirable items our shop had given them. You can avoid this by removing all the tags or require the charity to do so.

Use your imagination when finding a home for leftover goods. Can some of the items be used by an after-school program as crafts supplies? Could a kindergarten class use them to play store? Would a nursing home find them useful as table decorations? Charities that sponsor flea markets, garage sales, or resale shops are often happy to receive odds and ends, but avoid the temptation to donate shopworn or unsalable merchandise to those asking for donations for auctions and raffles. If a cause is going to showcase your donation, give something you are proud of.

Hosting Fundraisers and Benefits

As a retailer, you are in a unique position to hold fundraisers of your own, either as an effort to help a charity in which you believe strongly or to give a boost to a store promotion such as a grand opening. When you decide to do something to help a charitable organization, be sure to contact its office or board of directors so that it can assist you. The organization will probably end up fielding telephone calls about the event, so keep its staff well informed.

One of the most popular ways of doing an in-store fundraiser is to pledge a percentage of all sales, or sales of a particular item, to the cause—perhaps for one day during regular store hours or at a special event held when you are normally closed. The hope is that shoppers will spend a bit more than they would have otherwise so that the 5 to 15% donated to the charity is offset by an increase in sales.

If you are doing a benefit for a charity, ask if the organization will send an email blast to its members and other supporters announcing the event. This is an excellent way to attract new customers. We also invite the group to have representatives in the store on the day of the benefit, thanking people for shopping and giving out information about their organization.

For a grand opening, you might choose to have an evening benefit in which you allow guests to shop with a percentage of sales going to a charity. If you don't want to have the cash registers in action during your elegant affair, you can either make a cash donation in honor of the occasion or have patrons buy admission tickets, with all the proceeds going to the cause.

Responsible Retailing: Doing Well by Doing Good

For several years, we sponsored a chocolate festival as a fundraiser for local arts organizations. The bountiful chocolate buffet featured culinary creations that had been entered in our two chocolate cooking contests. The entrants in the amateur competition were rewarded with numerous prizes donated by our suppliers. In the category for professional chefs, restaurants, and bakeries, the prizes were framed certificates to display in their place of business, and, of course, these certificates mentioned our shop as sponsor. At the chocolate gala, little girls dressed as chocolate kisses sold Hershey's Kisses with numbers under them that

Suraphong "A" Liengboonlertchai is the owner of Simplicity Decor and Simplicity ABC in Kirkland, Washington. He offers kids the opportunity to run a Lemonade Stand for a Cause in front of his shop, with proceeds going to the charity of their choice. In addition, the store donates 10% of the store's sales to the chosen charity during each shift at the lemonade stand. "Owning a business is not about making sales," Liengboonlertchai said. "It's all about working with the community, getting to know them, giving back to them and this is another opportunity for me to do so."
(Photo courtesy of A Liengbooklertchai)

could be redeemed for small prizes, such as chocolate bars, also donated by our suppliers.

When a Ronald McDonald House for the families of critically ill children was being built in Madison, we supported it by publishing *The Orange Tree Imports Cookbook*. The book includes recipes from our staff and our cooking school instructors, and the proceeds furnished one of the guest rooms at the house.

Selling Goods that Do Good

Many years ago, when we first started selling UNICEF cards at Christmas, 100% of the sales went to the United Nations Children's Fund. Obviously, we lost some sales of our regular boxed Christmas cards to those buying UNICEF cards, but we felt strongly about supporting this cause. We also sell calendars, note cards, and Christmas cards that are produced by local groups, usually at no markup as a way to support their work.

Because we are more aware of merchandise trends and marketing than most local nonprofits, we also offer to advise them on the items they are producing. Unless the production cost and artwork is all donated, local groups can easily end up losing, rather than making, money on the merchandise they produce.

Some of our most popular lines of Christmas cards and calendars are published by organizations such as the Sierra Club, the World Wildlife Fund, and the Audubon Society—and we earn full markup on the merchandise. This type of cause marketing is a painless way to support worthwhile charities and to allow our customers to feel good about their purchases. Many of our suppliers have selected a charity to work with and are pledging a percentage of sales on certain items to these organizations. The amount of money that ends up being donated is generally kept confidential, but some cases these corporate donations are in the millions.

Responsible Retailing: Doing Well by Doing Good

TAKING A STAND WITH WHAT YOU DON'T SELL

What you decide not to sell is also a reflection of what you and your business stand for. If you believe that war toys and play guns are harmful to children, then your toy shop should boycott that category. Selling cigarettes is a profitable business, but if you want to discourage smoking, your pharmacy or grocery store should not offer them.

Many other buying decisions are less clear. Should a bookstore offer works that it considers to be racist or offensive to women? The University Bookstore in Madison, Wisconsin once had a small press book on its shelves on how to shoplift. Where should the line on free speech be drawn? Should your shop buy products from manufacturers that may exploit their workers, knowing that if you don't, these workers will be unemployed? Should you boycott countries that have human rights policies you find objectionable, even though your dollars would help the innocent people who live there?

All of these decisions require careful consideration and some difficult deliberations. You might involve your staff members in discussing these issues and in establishing a policy that reflects your store's philosophy and image.

Museum and Hospital Shops: Retailers Who Serve

Among the most successful types of specialty shop are hospital shops, museum stores, and others that serve a single purpose: to raise funds for the institution that houses them. They often must appeal to a limited market of the supporters or visitors. There is an advantage, however, in having a captive market, and often shops do quite well by learning how to target the merchandise to their audience.

A nonprofit organization must be able to prove that the retail shop is a related business in order to have it be exempt from paying business income tax (payroll taxes must still be paid). The IRS has ruled, for

Even the Los Angeles County Coroner's office has a gift shop. Skeletons in the Closet, which has been in operation since 1993, sells t-shirts, mugs, beach towels, door mats, jewelry, caps, and other items emblazoned with designs like a victim's chalk outline or skeletons. The purpose of the store is to promote how fragile life is and create awareness and responsibility toward one's actions.

example, that a hospital may operate a gift shop to serve its patients, visitors, and employees and that a museum may create products to sell at wholesale or retail if they are related to its exhibitions.

Museums may also operate gift shops selling merchandise that contributes to the accomplishment of their exempt function, which is often education. If unrelated items are sold, there is a special assessment of Unrelated Business Income Tax (UBIT). There is usually some leeway in the enforcement of the IRS policy when it comes to small quantities of merchandise; however, you should check the IRS web site for the latest regulations on this issue so that you can stay within the letter of the law.

Environmentally Sound Retailing

When Earth Day and the environmental movement captured the imagination of the public in the 1980s and 1990s, the retail industry jumped on the bandwagon, creating thousands of t-shirt designs with rain forest slogans and entire stores dedicated to Mother Nature.

The irony, of course, is that Mother Nature would undoubtedly prefer to be left out of the retailing world. There are frankly very few products sold in the name of saving the environment that actually do any good, because consumption itself is usually a negative. Unless a store sells nothing but items such as bulk foods and natural fiber clothing, chances are that it is encouraging people to buy things they don't really

Responsible Retailing: Doing Well by Doing Good

need. But this does not mean that shopkeepers have no means of sharing in the responsibility for the future of our planet.

In *The Ecology of Commerce,* Paul Hawken challenges small businesses, including retailers, to conduct their businesses according to this economic golden rule: "Leave the world better than you found it, take no more than you need, try not to harm life or the environment, make amends if you do." While admitting that much of what consumers will buy is unnecessary, he argues that there is virtue to be found in marketing items "of clarity and simplicity, products that cut through the clutter of our lives and allow us to perform the daily acts of living in a more satisfying way." These items should be "objects of durability and long-term utility whose ultimate use or disposition will not be harmful to future generations."

The consumer, unfortunately, is not always willing (or able) to pay for lasting quality. Although it makes sense to offer a range of prices to satisfy all customers, I feel that a retailer should not knowingly carry items such as poorly made plastic toys with a short lifespan of play value and a long lifespan in a landfill.

Durability is not always a factor in buying decisions, of course. A clothing retailer, for instance, knows that no fashion will last forever. Most clothes are, however, easily reusable and eventually recyclable into scrap fiber. Some types of fabrics, such as natural, undyed cottons, do less harm to the environment in their manufacturing process than synthetic materials. Educating the consumer about these factors can lead to an environmentally informed decision, although the percentage of customers making choices based solely on these factors is unfortunately limited.

Many retail businesses are natural recyclers. Antique shops, vintage clothing stores, and even baseball card dealers keep products flowing back through the economy rather than creating new goods. But those that must purchase new goods to sell can still give consideration to the ultimate disposition of these products once the consumer tires of them.

WHERE WILL YOUR MERCHANDISE GO?

Countries such as Germany and Japan involve manufacturers in planning for the disposal of their product, or at least its packaging, when they manufacture it. In the United States, we have a long way to go. Inexpensive trash removal that carries the problem of discarded merchandise out of sight often alleviates any pangs of conscience we might have when buying a new product to replace an old one. But where do old appliances, computers, or broken pieces of furniture go when they die? Even if they can be incinerated, the fumes may contribute to air pollution. And we are kidding ourselves if we think that the manufacturing process involved in creating many of the new goods we sell does not contribute to the destruction of the environment, either here or abroad.

The environmentally conscientious buyer takes reuse, recyclability, easy disposal, and safe manufacturing procedures into consideration and selects products that do the least harm. Biodegradable plastics, for example, are better than other plastics because they will eventually disintegrate after being thrown away. But unfortunately these issues are rarely clear-cut; few standards have been set for what qualifies as biodegradable and recyclable. One manufacturer of plastic garbage bags, for instance, claimed that they were biodegradable, when in fact they just broke up into small but long-lasting particles. Evaluating these factors for every product used or sold in a store requires a commitment few people are willing to make.

As we move toward more international awareness of the importance of considering environmental factors, manufacturers will undoubtedly make it easier to compare the environmental impact of various products. Meanwhile, spending your buying dollars with companies that clearly express concern for the natural world will encourage others to imitate their environmentally sound practices.

Responsible Retailing: Doing Well by Doing Good

EDUCATING THE BUYING PUBLIC

Retailers have a unique opportunity to educate customers about the choices they can make regarding factors such as the durability and usefulness of the products they buy. A mission of Alfalfa's, a two-store organic food chain in Colorado is "to serve, educate, and inspire our customers through our tireless support of local, organic and innovative food, wellness products and culinary creations."

Product selection can also help customers make educated choices. When offered beautiful stationery products that happen to be made of recycled paper or paper that is chlorine-free, customers often select items that will have less of a negative impact on the environment than those usually offered by mass merchandisers. There is still some question as to whether customers are willing to pay more for environmentally friendly products, but for about the same price, they often appreciate this feature.

THE PRODUCT PACKAGING DILEMMA

Even shops selling goods that are consumable, such as foods and toiletries, have to face the dilemma of packaging these items. At the same time that we have become concerned with reducing packaging for the sake of the environment, additional packaging has been encouraged in the interest of safety and hygiene—and shoplifting prevention.

Unless you are a very large operation, you will have little control over how items come packaged to you. You can try to specify that you want an item not packaged, in case the supplier has the ability to provide the merchandise that way. But very few items are offered with optional packaging because manufacturers and importers prefer standardization.

They also like to package items to reduce breakage in shipping and to promote awareness of their own brand name. Many stores want to receive items packaged because the larger size is thought to discourage shoplifting. This was the rationale behind the shrink-wrapped cardboard "longbox" on CDs, which were eventually eliminated after musicians such as Canadian singer Raffi protested their wastefulness.

A package can also provide information about the product that will help sell it to the consumer and give directions for the item's use. It can allow an item to be hung, or pegged, for display. It can enhance the appearance of the merchandise and preserve the freshness of perishables. And yet in many cases we have to question the long-term effects of packaging that will outlive its contents by decades.

In evaluating whether to buy merchandise that comes packaged, take these factors into account:

♦ Is it necessary for this item to be packaged? If not, is the same item available elsewhere unpackaged?

♦ Is it overpackaged?

♦ Can the packaging be reused or recycled?

♦ Is the packaging biodegradable, or can it be incinerated?

♦ If an item doesn't come packaged, will customers ask the store to put it in a box when they buy it?

Do You Have a Box?

Customers often expect a gift item to be put into a box so that it can be wrapped, and certainly no one would want to struggle with gift wrapping a stuffed kangaroo without boxing it first. But many items come already boxed, and it is a waste of resources—environmental and financial—to take an item out of its box and put it in a gift box.

For items that don't come boxed, we provide gift boxes. Many packaging suppliers offer gift boxes made at least in part from recycled paper. These boxes are often attractive enough to require only a ribbon and bow, saving on the gift wrap paper that would have been used to overwrap it. Some stores use decorative gift bags made of recycled paper as their store wrapping.

Responsible Retailing: Doing Well by Doing Good

Almost all stores use bags for customers' merchandise. Most manufacturers offer bags made at least in part of recycled paper, and, of course, paper is easily disposed of. Paper bags do, however, take up considerably more storage space than plastic ones. Thin plastic merchandise bags are especially popular throughout Europe, but the environmental impact of plastic bags is a subject that is being hotly debated in the US. California led the country in banning single-use plastic bags at large retail stores, and other states and municipalities have followed.

The Danish grocery chain Irma had a wonderful solution to the proliferation of plastic carrier bags: it charged customers a small fee for each bag, encouraging their reuse, and used the money to support the work of artists whose creations were featured in full color on the sides of the bags. Customers are much more likely to reuse a bag that is a work of art—and a bag that is reused is better for the environment than either paper or plastic. At Orange Tree Imports, we reward customers who bring their own bag with a chocolate coin.

"And on this wall, I have my Irma grocery bag collection."

PACKAGING FOR SHIPPING

On a windy garbage day, one used to see swirls of Styrofoam peanuts being chased by broom-wielding shopkeepers in the alleys behind neighborhood shops. This wonderful, lightweight packing material was a shipper's dream: easy to use, clean, and a safe cushion for all the different kinds of merchandise being shipped in cardboard cartons.

But these peanuts have a tendency to escape from trash containers, and, more unfortunately, they have a tendency to last forever in landfills. Merchandise coming in our back door was almost always packed in peanuts, and merchandise going out the front door hardly ever was. The result was a buildup of packing materials that far surpassed our store's ability to reuse them in shipping gifts out for our customers. Happily, we were able to find a small ceramics manufacturer and a pack-and-ship operation that are only too happy to get our Styrofoam peanuts for free, so we now leave them stacked in clear bags for pickup by one of these companies.

Many of our suppliers now use packaging materials such as pellets that look like Styrofoam but dissolve in water. Others are using plastic bags inflated to make pillows to cushion the goods. It is easy to deflate these large bubbles so that the end material takes up little space in the landfill.

Sustainable Small Business Practices

REI, a national outfitter for outdoor sports, suggests that customers practice "minimal impact" camping and hiking. As a retailer, you can also try to minimize your impact on the environment by making intelligent choices about how your store is operated. In addition to exercising good judgment when buying merchandise, the environmentally aware shopkeeper makes informed decisions regarding such variables as energy usage, recycled paper products, and material recycling.

Responsible Retailing: Doing Well by Doing Good

A retail store usually requires an immense amount of lighting every hour that it is open. These lights generate a lot of heat, placing heavy demands on air-conditioning during hot weather. In cooler months, energy is needed to heat the store, with constant heat loss from customers opening the door to outside air. On the positive side, retail stores seldom have as many windows as a private home, so heat loss through glass is usually minimized.

See Chapter 4 for tips on energy efficient light bulbs for your store. You may also find that installing ceiling fans, setting back thermostats at night, and utilizing other energy-saving tips for home owners apply equally well to retail shops. Some stores in cold climates save heating energy by using a revolving door or a small entrance vestibule requiring customers to come through one door and close it before entering the second door. These entranceways keep blasts of icy air from coming into the store with each customer, but they are cumbersome for the disabled, parents with strollers, and customers carrying packages. You will need to provide an alternative entrance if you have a revolving door or automatic door openers on double-doored vestibules.

Turning things off and turning things down when not in use (electronic displays, computers, lights) should also help cut your utility bill. Be sure to perform routine maintenance on heating and cooling systems—changing filters, cleaning the condenser coils, and checking the airflow.

RECYCLING IN THE STORE

Recycling the aluminum soda cans from your staff lounge may have a very small impact on the environment, but recycling the mountain of cardboard and paper your shop generates can make a big difference. We are fortunate to have public recycling of cardboard, newspapers, and office paper in Madison, but we generate such a large quantity of recyclables that we supplement the city pickup with a private service.

A store that generates a lot of office paper might consider investing in a shredder to convert this trash into packing material for outgoing shipments. We reuse the cleanest cartons in which we receive merchandise to send out shipments of customers' purchases. They may not look as spiffy as brand-new boxes, but they are usually quite serviceable.

THINK GLOBALLY, ACT LOCALLY

To have a positive environmental impact on your own neighborhood, look for an opportunity to plant trees—or restore an older building to use as your store. Join together with your fellow business owners make sure your street events include recycling and composting of trash. Sponsor a park, or a school garden, or do whatever works to help maintain the environmental well-being of your local neighborhood.

Patron of the Arts

There are so many ways to contribute something to the community that sustains the store. For example, it is important to support the cultural life of your area—the arts are essential in creating a thriving local economy, and have been proven to help in attracting new residents to an area. They also drive tourist traffic, a key factor in competing with online retailers.

EARNING APPLAUSE

You can support the performing arts by serving as a ticket outlet for local groups, which brings customers into the store. We do this often enough that we have a special form for the organization to fill in listing the details of the event, ticket prices, how many tickets we've received, and who is authorized to pick up money or bring more tickets. If we receive a pair of complimentary tickets in thanks, we give them to our staff.

Many theatrical and musical groups ask retailers to advertise in their programs, a good way to get your shop name associated with excellence in the performing arts. Advertising in concert and theatrical programs provides support for nonprofit groups and at the same time creates a positive image for the store as a patron of the arts. It is always worthwhile to be associated with excellence.

SUPPORTING ARTISANS, MAKERS AND ARTISTS

Your support and advice can make the difference between success and failure for a craftsperson, maker or artist. Galleries have traditionally played an important role in the work of artists, promoting their work to collectors and handling business transactions so that the artist is free to create. Many well-known artists owe their rise to fame to an art dealer who truly believed in their work.

The role of patron is not limited to art galleries. Almost any shop can purchase some merchandise that is handmade by a craftsperson or artisan. Even if these purchases are made through an importer or wholesaler, the income eventually will reach the artists, making it possible for them to continue to ply their craft.

The income derived from handcrafts can have a significant impact on the life of a person living in poverty. By buying a product that someone has made, you may be helping that person support his or her family and community. The term *fair trade* is often used to describe this merchandise. This refers to a trading partnership in which the goal is improved conditions and sustainable development for excluded and disadvantaged producers. Shops such as Ten Thousand Villages carry only items made by artisans in third-world countries who need a dignified way to make a living. Many of the crafts they sell are traditional arts from the area, so their shops are helping to preserve cultures that might otherwise disappear.

One World Market in Durham, North Carolina, has taken to a new level the idea of using buying dollars to help people. In addition to purchasing handmade products, it gave a grant of $1,000 to Candlemakers of Hope, a crafts co-op made up of women trying to help themselves escape the grip of poverty. Thanks to One World, Brenda Johnson of Candlemakers of Hope could say, "A few months ago we were welfare mothers looking for a break. But now we are actually struggling businesswomen with viable contacts and inventory—and we are beginning to see the light at the end of the tunnel. That light is a candle, and it is burning bright."

If artwork and handmade crafts do not fit with your merchandise mix, consider helping artists by using their work as part of your store decor or displays.

Alternative Advertising

Public television underwriting can be an effective way to buy television advertising for your store. Surveys of our customers indicate that many of them are supporters of public television, so it makes good sense for us to be underwriters. We look for shows that have a relationship to what we sell, and there are customers who drive to our shop from adjoining states because they have seen our name as a sponsor of cooking programs. You may find that public radio promotions are effective in drawing customers to your shop, and in Madison we also support WORT, a community-sponsored radio station.

Advertising dollars can do good when you place small ads in church bulletins, neighborhood newsletters, school yearbooks, and other publications that benefit your community. Some stores consider these ads to be charity donations rather than advertising, but they do generate goodwill toward the store—and that is really the goal of any advertising you choose to do.

Not every piece of advertising needs to be commercial in nature. As a store owner, you are in a unique position to run an ad that promotes a cause you believe in or makes people think. As long as ads align your store with what you strongly believe to be important and just and do not offend important segments of your customer base, there is no reason that your advertising cannot be used as a force for good. Benetton and The

Responsible Retailing: Doing Well by Doing Good

Body Shop, for example, often lobby for humanitarian and ecological causes in their ads, winning the goodwill of customers who are of a like mind—though they do risk the ill will of those who don't agree with their views.

Partnering with Schools

The students of today are the employees and customers of tomorrow. There are several ways your specialty shop can play a positive role in your community's schools. You can offer to speak to classes about retailing or about some of the merchandise you carry. You can invite groups to tour your store, including a behind-the-scenes look at what is involved in running a business. Every year we host a group of elementary school students studying English as a Second Language (ESL). I particularly enjoy trying to show each student some merchandise from his or her home country, and I ask them questions about the items to give them some practice in speaking English. One year, I showed them some black pasta and asked them to guess what is used to make it that color. Squid ink is the correct answer (which is why I've never eaten any, I must admit), but this question really had them puzzled. They knew Americans had strange eating habits, but they couldn't quite think what we would eat that was black. Finally one little boy raised his hand and shyly asked, "Ants?"

Many high schools have work-study programs in which students are placed in local businesses to gain real-world experience. If your operation could offer some challenging work to high school students, call your nearest high school for details about this program. Work-study students sometimes continue in their jobs after graduating, so this could be a source of future employees. There may also be a program in retailing at the high school, running the school store, or the concessions at sports events that could use your help as an outside adviser. Consider sponsoring an entrepreneur club after school, encouraging students to learn about small business and free enterprise. Their math and reading skills, as well as their self-confidence, will benefit from starting and running their own business projects.

High schools and middle schools are always looking for incentives to motivate students to come to school, stay in school, and do well academically. In Spring, Texas, merchants offered discounts to students who achieved good attendance, completed their assignments, and did well in class. You might provide merchandise or gift cards as incentives for student achievement programs in the middle and high schools in your area or reward students with good grades with a discount on toys or games.

Be a Community Leader

You may not have the influence of a celebrity spokesperson like Robert Redford, but by virtue of being a retailer, you have more status in your community than many less visible businesspeople. You can choose to use that position to help the entire community, whether it is by raising money or awareness.

Your store can serve as a focal point for a special interest group such as writers, feminists, runners, or even model train buffs. You can provide these groups with leadership, materials, lecturers, and a place to meet. In exchange, they are likely to become loyal customers. There is more than one example of a troubled store being saved, or at least

---

The Brooklyn Superhero Supply Company was created to support 826NYC, a writing center for 6- to 18-year-old students. The retail store not only generates some income for the center, but also students and volunteers enter the tutoring center through a revolving bookshelf in the shop. And what does the Brooklyn Superhero Supply Company sell? Capes, masks and inspiration, of course.

helped, through donations from its supporters to a crowdsourcing effort such as Kickstarter.

Mentoring other businesspeople can be a way to help your community. Many years ago, we helped organize the first merchants' association in our area. In addition to stretching our advertising dollar by doing joint promotions, we encourage and support each other, to our mutual benefit. As an experienced retailer, I am happy to be able to meet with individuals, especially other women, who are thinking of starting a retail or a wholesale business and offer them some guidance.

Hiring that Helps

The Americans with Disabilities Act mandates that businesses make jobs available for those with physical disabilities. In many situations, this is no sacrifice on the part of the employer because staff members who need some assistance are usually just as valuable as those who don't. We often assume, however, that most jobs in retailing are too physical for someone in a wheelchair or require more communication than a person who is blind or deaf can easily handle. But I have been waited on by a deaf employee at Walmart and have seen someone stocking merchandise from a wheelchair there. Perhaps the rest of the retail world will learn a lesson from this discount giant and give physically disabled employees more opportunities.

There are also individuals who need meaningful work in their lives who cannot perform the same jobs as others. If you need someone to do routine clerical tasks, stocking, or housekeeping duties, consider contacting an agency that places mentally, emotionally, and physically challenged individuals in businesses. The agency often provides customized training and a job coach to help the client succeed at work. This will also help make the rest of the staff comfortable with the employee.

Tasks that arise from time to time, such as stuffing envelopes with sales literature or attaching labels to hundreds of table favors for a fundraising event, can be performed in a sheltered workshop. Check to see if there is a facility in your community looking for projects for its clients. There are many ways your payroll dollars can be used to help those in need.

Diversity in the workplace is also a way to improve your community. When you get to know people of different social, ethnic, or racial backgrounds as co-workers, it helps build harmony and understanding. And this type of hiring has a direct benefit to the store as you try to reach out to the diverse market that represents the consumers of the future.

Volunteering Your Time

If your shop decides to support a particular cause, your staff may want to be involved. The best way to ensure their participation is to have staff members help select the charity to support, but involvement beyond duties directly related to the shop should always be optional. Employees may already have projects of their own—or may not share your enthusiasm for the one you select.

Adopting a cause can be a good way to build team spirit among staff members. One year we bought gifts for a large family in the rural south through the Box Project, a nonprofit organization that assigns donors to a specific family in need. Many staff members brought in wrapped gifts to supplement those purchased by the store. Other shops sponsor a staff team to participate in a fundraising run or bike-a-thon, or they get together a group to answer telephones during the public television station's pledge drive.

If there are times when staff members are not usually busy, you could loan interested employees to a good cause while paying their salary. The US Environmental Protection Agency suggests volunteering to pick up unspoiled food to deliver it to food pantries, and perhaps your store could sponsor a once-a-week route. If your local United Way sponsors a community-wide Day of Caring event, consider paying your staff members their regular hourly salaries to join the many other volunteers improving the lives of those in need. You could also sponsor an employee interested in volunteering at a local school to tutor or at a nearby meal program to help serve lunch to the hungry.

The Rewards of Giving

Good deeds do not usually go unnoticed. Chances are that you will receive some public recognition for your efforts, and there is no harm in seeking this recognition by sending out press releases or mentioning your work in social media or in-store signage. Your efforts may well inspire other retailers and individuals to get more involved in supporting good causes. As Tracy Mullin, past president of the National Retail Federation, said, "Participating in charitable causes is one way to remind customers that we are all dedicated to making this world a better place." If you make your customers feel that they are part of something worthwhile when they shop at your store, they will reward your generosity with their loyal patronage.

CHAPTER 16

COPING SKILLS:
SURVIVING TOUGH TIMES

O
n a good day, retailing is more fun than work. When you arrive in the morning, a few customers are already waiting outside, eager to buy, your staff is cheerful and ready to help them, your store window displays are eye-catching and attractive, and you know the merchandise your customers want is all in stock. In reality, some days are like that. And some are not.

The retail business is made up of people, buildings, money, and merchandise, and something can go wrong with all of them. Employees may steal, quit, or neglect their duties. The government may decide to audit you. Your roof may leak, or the front door may fall off (this actually happened to us the week before Christmas some years ago). Customers may shoplift or switch their alliance to the new discount store on the edge of town. Your main supplier may go out of business. Your boxes and bags may arrive late. The money may run out. Your store may catch on fire. Chances are not all of these will happen to you, or at least not all at once, but it is wise to plan for when things do go wrong—because eventually something will.

Insuring against Crime, Disasters, and Other Crises

No business can afford to be without some form of insurance, and your insurance agent should be a member of your advisory team from the start. If you can't trust the agent not to sell you more insurance than you need, perhaps you should find a new person to deal with. Ask the other businesses in your area to recommend an insurance agency experienced in the retail field.

Basic business insurance includes liability coverage protecting the individuals who come in contact with your store: staff, customers, and other visitors. It also protects against loss in the event of fire, with extended coverage available against storms, explosions, riots, and other disasters. Policies often have separate coverage for window breakage, signage, and company-owned vehicles.

In choosing coverage and deciding on the amount of the deductible, determine how much you are comfortable covering yourself in the event that something happens. If you can absorb a $500 replacement cost on a broken window, for instance, then it makes sense to get window coverage with a $500 deductible. This will be cheaper than insurance with a lower deductible. If your signs are not worth much money, skip the added cost of signage insurance.

The lease on your store will probably specify how much liability insurance you are required to carry. It will also specify who will pay for fire insurance for the building and whether you need additional special fire liability insurance in case a fire starting in your part of the building damages other premises. Be sure to check which parts of the store you are responsible for insuring. In some strip malls, for example, you may need insurance coverage for the windows but not the door.

Stores located in areas prone to flooding, hurricanes, or earthquakes may find it difficult to get insurance to cover these natural disasters. Check to see if there is a government-sponsored program in which you can participate, or try to get a policy with a high deductible and put aside the amount of the deductible as self-insurance.

Insurance written to cover the replacement value of your store's inventory and fixtures in case of fire actually insures only part of your loss. You will also lose money by not being able to be open for business.

This is the reason for business interruption insurance, or business income insurance, which compensates you for the temporary loss of income due to fire or other natural disaster. This gives you time to get your business back on its feet and allows you to pay your employees during the time you are closed. There are different types of business interruption insurance, and some pay benefits based on your past net profit—which can be a problem if your business is not very profitable. Ask your agent for details about what policies are available to you and which one would best suit your needs.

If customers routinely leave items with you for repair or resale, be sure to look into property damage liability insurance. Customers will appreciate knowing that their diamond ring or antique table is insured in the event that something happens while it is in your store.

Company-owned vehicles must be insured; if staff members use their own cars to run business errands or make deliveries, check to see what coverage is available for them. Even if they have their own auto insurance, you may be liable in the event of an accident. Investigate the driving record of anyone who will be entrusted with a store-owned vehicle, and insist on courteous and safe driving by those representing your business.

Will insurance cover you in case of theft? If your store is broken into while it is closed, damage to the building and stolen merchandise should be covered by theft insurance. Robbery, in which force or the threat of force is used, can also be covered. But shoplifting, that all-too-common form of shrinkage that takes place during open hours through theft by customers or pilferage by staff, is unlikely to be paid for by insurance. Your only insurance against this type of theft is prevention.

Coping Skills: Surviving Tough Times

Curtailing Shoplifting and Employee Theft

Major retail chains spend millions of dollars to prevent theft. For most small shops, the best solution is a simple one: attentive customer service. Greet every customer entering the store, and make the person feel welcome. A certain percentage of shoplifting occurs because the thief feels angry at the store, sometimes because of the lack of personal attention. Don't make it easy for a shoplifter to steal something by leaving areas of the store unattended. Check back periodically with shoppers who are browsing so they know you are aware they are still in the store.

It is much better to deter a shoplifter than to try to catch one. Confronting someone and accusing him or her of taking something is always awkward, and in many cases, the law prevents you from stopping someone unless he or she has clearly attempted to leave the store with merchandise not paid for. Consult with your local police about what you legally can and cannot do when you catch someone stealing, and pass this information along to your staff.

Teenage (and preteen) shoplifting is a serious problem, and word gets around quickly if your store is considered an easy mark. Stores carrying products appealing to teens need to take special precautions and to make it clear that anyone caught shoplifting will be dealt with seriously. As with potential shoplifters of any age, the best solution is prevention. Don't treat all teenagers as potential thieves—because most are not—but don't tempt teens to steal by putting desirable items in a blind area or by ignoring young customers. Greet everyone entering the store, and offer attentive but not suspiciously overbearing service.

From time to time, we call the parents of a young child who we have seen pocket something, or a parent will bring in a child who has taken something from our store. I usually ask the adult and child to come with me to an area where we can talk in private, and then I explain to the child that shoplifting is stealing. If the parent agrees with my suggestion, I ask the child to give back the item and to pay for it—the opposite of getting something for free by taking it. We also ask that for one year, the child not come in the store without an adult. This policy seems fair and is kinder than calling the police, yet we almost always lose the family as customers because the parents are embarrassed to return.

One young shoplifter actually suggested that we get convex mirrors to deter theft from some of the less visible parts of the store, and we reluctantly took him up on the idea. Other stores may find that surveillance cameras are an effective deterrent, and these cameras are available in an inexpensive dummy form that may fool some amateurs.

Professional shoplifters are much harder to deter, and they often work in pairs or teams to distract the sales staff so they can steal. There is little you can do to combat this type of crime except to call the police as quickly as possible. Be certain to warn neighboring businesses if you think professional shoplifters are at work in the area.

Large-ticket items and goods such as jewelry, leather goods, and electronics that can easily be resold by shoplifters may require special shoplifting-prevention devices. A number of electronic article surveillance (EAS) systems are available that require a magnetic encoded tag or ink-filled device to be removed when the item is purchased. If someone leaves the store without having the tag removed, an alarm sounds, and when an ink-filled tag is removed at home, the garment is ruined. Unfortunately, employees occasionally neglect to remove or deactivate the sound-alarm tags, embarrassing legitimate customers who set off the alarm when leaving the store. When the alarm sounds, approach the customer calmly and first offer to correct the situation, rather than assuming the hapless individual is a thief.

Small, very expensive items should be kept in locked, or at least closed, cases. Keep in mind, however, that items in cases do not tend to sell as well as those that customers can handle. A shop with all of its merchandise behind glass does not appear inviting to customers who want to browse.

Discuss shoplifting with your staff members so they can be alert to suspicious behavior. If a customer appears to be looking around nervously, a sales associate should ask if he or she needs help, and then stay near the customer, dusting shelves or straightening displays. Watch for individuals with oversize coats, especially in warm weather, and large shopping bags or backpacks. If you are concerned about shoplifting, you could require that bags and backpacks be checked while shoppers are browsing.

CRIME FROM WITHIN

No one wants to believe that someone on staff would steal, but national statistics point to employee theft as a major problem for retailers. Although there are unscrupulous individuals who will steal given any opportunity, most people will not try to harm a business they love. It is important that employees feel involved in the business and that they feel appreciated. As with shoplifting, retail theft by an employee can be a way of expressing anger.

If you are concerned about employee theft, take a look at your loading areas and back exits. By flattening cartons before putting them out for pickup and limiting staff access to this area, you may be able to curtail some theft. Large quantities of merchandise can be taken very quickly by someone backing a truck up to the loading dock and filling it with goods. You might also require that staff purchases be rung up by a manager, and do spot checks of staff parcels and backpacks when employees are leaving work. Take a periodic physical inventory of any area you suspect may be subject to theft rather than waiting for the annual inventory. Employees are often in a position to know what merchandise wouldn't be missed until inventory time.

Controlling the number of people who have access to the building after hours is also a good idea if you are concerned about theft. Some security alarm systems can provide a record of who left the store last and of anyone who enters after hours. Each employee is provided with a personal code to disarm and arm the system.

It is important to realize that the store's merchandise is often very tempting to employees. A generous store discount will encourage staff to acquire the items they want without resorting to dishonesty. We offer our staff all merchandise at 10% above wholesale, and we also have a free box with merchandise they can help themselves to. These items are usually slightly flawed products for which we've received credit from suppliers or display items that are no longer in perfect condition.

Retail businesses are also in danger of losing large amounts of money from embezzlement or theft from the till. Have a background check done before you hire bookkeepers or managers who will have access to the store's checking account. Review the shop's bank statements and other financial information regularly, and be alert to irregularities. Match credit card invoices to the business expense receipts turned in by employees who hold cards.

Watch for suspiciously low sales or high refunds when certain employees are working the sales floor or frequent redemptions of credit slips and gift certificates, which may mean someone is pocketing the money. Insist that customers always get a cash register receipt so that no one can ring up a lower amount than the actual sale or no sale at all, and keep the proceeds.

Cash registers were, in fact, originally called the "Incorruptible Cashier" because every time the drawer was opened, a bell rang. According to author Bill Bryson in *Made in America*, his informal history of the English language in the United States, this is the original reason for using odd amount prices such as 99¢. The need to give some change on all purchases meant the register's bell would sound during every single transaction.

Coping Skills: Surviving Tough Times

Cautionary procedures may help catch the occasional dishonest employee, but the best deterrent to theft from within is to make all staff members feel that they are a valued part of the business. Let your employees see that you always deal honestly with suppliers and customers, setting a high moral standard for your store. Unfortunately, circumstances beyond your control may sometimes lead an employee to steal. When this happens, you must cope with both the loss and the bitter feeling of having been betrayed by someone you trusted.

Preventing Burglaries and Holdups

Some loss from shoplifting is a fact of life for most retailers, but we all fervently hope to avoid more invasive crimes such as burglaries and holdups. Most police departments will offer advice on crime prevention that is specific to your store location and layout. They will probably advise you to have a burglar alarm to deter break-ins, and they may have other suggestions regarding outdoor lighting and closing procedures.

We have invited the detective who specializes in this field to address our staff on security issues. Although it is frightening to discuss all the possible ways one can become the victim of a crime, we were able to use what we learned to make the store a safer place. Here are some of the safety pointers:

- ◆ Try to have more than one person working on the sales floor at all times.

- ◆ If someone demands money or threatens you, always give the person what he or she wants and try to get him or her to leave. As a Madison police officer told us, "Give them the money—the government prints more of it every day. But people are irreplaceable."

- ◆ Avoid being taken along as a hostage if at all possible.

- After the thief has left, lock the door before calling 911. This will keep him from coming back in if he sees police or witnesses outside.

- Do not keep excessive amounts of cash on hand. Consider a safe if you need a place to store money before depositing it.

- Vary the time that deposits are taken to the bank and the route that the person making the deposit takes to get there.

- Trust your instincts. Call the police if someone seems suspicious.

- Do not go into a basement or storeroom alone after closing in case someone is hiding there. You could restrict access to these areas by having a locked door or one that buzzes when it is opened.

- Empty your display window of valuables at night if you sell high-end merchandise.

- Leave the cash register drawers open and empty when you are closed.

- If possible, arrange your window displays and entranceway so that at least some of the store's interior can be seen from outside.

- Leave a few lights on at night so that suspicious activity will be visible from the street.

- Have a safe place for employees to keep their purses while they work.

- Consider installing an alarm system.

- Be sure your doors, windows, and locks are secure and cannot be jimmied easily.

Coping Skills: Surviving Tough Times

> Movin Kids, a children's shoe store, was the victim of an unusual type of retail theft. A large shipment of expensive boots was stolen from right in front of their eyes when a trucking company that did not require drivers to carry deliveries inside unloaded several cartons on the sidewalk in front of the store. After it was signed for, a car (which may have been following the truck) drove up, loaded all the cartons in the back, and sped away.

ENSURING PERSONAL SAFETY

Providing a safe environment for your customers and staff is the best way to prevent as many accidents as possible. Look around your store for safety hazards in your displays, such as unsteady racks or sharp hooks at eye level. Be sure your entrance is well lit and kept clear of ice and snow in the winter. If your staff leaves by a back exit, make sure that it is also well lit and free of trash and other hazards.

We sometimes pay for taxi rides home for those who work late, for example helping with a Cooking School class. In some cities, this may be the only way to get employees to work after dark. Consider setting up a contract with a taxi company, ridesharing company or car service if your staff will be making regular use of this benefit.

Fires, Storms, and Natural Catastrophes

Several times a year the fire department inspects our store for compliance with fire codes. Although we may grouse at the time, we do appreciate the fact that the firefighters want to be sure we have safely marked exits, doors that can be opened easily in an emergency, and stairways and aisles that are clear of merchandise. They also require that we have fire extinguishers on hand that are in good working order; in fact, each extinguisher must be inspected and certified annually. Be sure your fire extinguishers are well marked and that your staff know how to use them.

Smoke alarms are a good idea for stores located in a neighborhood where someone would hear the alarms if they went off at night. Smoke detection systems can be set up as part of your alarm system, connected to a central monitoring office. Sprinkler systems are costly but effective in halting the spread of a fire. Check with your insurance company about rate reductions on fire insurance if your store has a sprinkler system installed—and mention other alarm equipment that might lower your rates.

Your store's computer equipment should have surge protectors to prevent it from being damaged by an electrical power surge or lightning strike. Backup copies of all important computer files, including sales records, customer mailing lists and tax records, should be made daily to an external hard drive and stored "in the cloud" through one of the many companies that host data. Copies of deeds and important financial documents should be kept in a safe deposit box. Take photographs of your store and any major fixtures or expensive inventory items in case you ever need to place an insurance claim. Store these pictures and copies of other important papers somewhere other than the shop in case of fire.

Every part of the country has its weather-related hazards: hurricanes, flash floods, mudslides, dust storms, earthquakes, and so forth. In Wisconsin, ours are blizzards and tornadoes, so we have established procedures for closing the store and taking shelter in the event of a tornado warning. Customers are invited to take shelter in the basement with us, a behind-the-scenes glimpse that they often find quite interesting. We keep a battery-operated radio and flashlights in the waiting area, so we will know when it is safe to go upstairs. If members of your staff are likely to have to take action in the face of a sudden natural disaster, make sure they know what to do.

Coping Skills: Surviving Tough Times

The headline in *The New York Times* read "Fire Races Through Stretch of Shops in Heart of Mystic." Peppergrass and Tulip owner Mary Ellen Grills arrived home from Florida the night of the fire to find several notes on her door saying if you need any help, please let me know. "I had no idea what the notes even meant until I went inside and listened to my phone messages. Then I knew that my store had been one of those destroyed." But Peppergrass and Tulip not only survived the Mystic, Connecticut Great Fire of 2000, it flourished. After the trauma of the fire, the shop opened in a new location that allowed more room for merchandise, including home decor pieces and new lines of clothing, and has recently celebrated its 32nd anniversary. (Photo courtesy of Mary Ellen Grills)

All stores should have emergency telephone numbers posted by the telephones and a well-stocked first aid kit on hand. In the event of a minor injury to a customer, a little first aid and a lot of concern, including a follow-up telephone call, can prevent the episode from escalating into a lawsuit. Managers should know the basics of first aid, and everyone should know where the first aid kit is located. We offer our full-time staff the opportunity to take CPR training on store time, although we hope this is a skill they'll never need to use.

What to do When Disaster Strikes

It is every retailer's nightmare to hear fire sirens during the night and realize that they are headed toward their shop. If your store is ever subjected to a catastrophe such as a fire or explosion, your first concern, after making sure employees and customers are safe, should be to secure the premises, blocking off any hazardous areas, and getting broken windows and doorways boarded up.

Once you have taken care of these safety issues, and after the dust has settled, you must decide if you want to stay in business. If you do, it is essential that you get the store up and running as soon as possible. Assure the public through the media that you will be back in business soon. Set up temporary office space so that you can communicate with suppliers. Keep staff on the payroll as much as possible, working to get new merchandise and fixtures ready.

When You Lose Your Lease

A change of location is sometimes forced upon a store by circumstances beyond its control. If the landlord decides to sell the building or raises the rent excessively, you may have to relocate your business. Or you might decide to move because of changes in the tenant mix or neighborhood. Take advantage of this opportunity to do a *strengths, weaknesses, opportunities, and threats (SWOT)* analysis (see page 378) to decide if you want to make any changes when you move. Look at your sales statistics so that you can dedicate the most space in your new location to your best-selling categories.

It is important to transfer the loyalty of your customers to the new location. Hold a moving sale before relocating to bring customers into the store to hear about your plans for the new location, and give them a coupon good for a discount when you reopen. You might even ask for their input as you design your new store. Don't forget to make good use of your mailing and email list to keep in touch with your customers during the transition. Post a sign for as long as possible on the old storefront listing the address of the new shop so that anyone looking for your business can find it.

Customers Can Be Trouble

The customer is not always right. Individuals experiencing unhappiness in some other aspect of their lives sometimes take it out on easy targets, such as the sales staff of a store. Others may try to appear powerful and controlling by dominating the retail transaction, insisting on special pricing and services. Returns seem to bring out the worst in people, and customers with returns often enter the store with a combative attitude as if expecting a battle.

Whenever possible, the best way to disarm problem customers is by listening to what they say, empathizing with their complaint, and asking, "What can we do to make this right for you?" A cheerful refund for a return, for instance, gives the customer braced for an argument little to complain about. But there are people who seem to need to complain or who appear to enjoy making others unhappy.

The fact is that some of these customers are not worth keeping. They take their toll on staff morale and upset other customers. From time to time we have had to send a letter to individuals like this refunding their

When you feel that your customers are being unreasonable, compare them to Jeremy Dorosin. He was so unhappy with two espresso machines that he purchased from the Starbucks coffeehouse in Berkeley, California, that he spent $10,000 of his own money on newspaper ads demanding an apology. The chain had already offered to replace the $469 worth of machines with more expensive models. Despite a subsequent offer of a refund and the replacement machines, Dorosin wanted Starbucks to spend $247,182 for an ad apologizing to him in the *Wall Street Journal*.

money (it seems that things always come to a head over one item) and suggesting that because we don't seem to be meeting their needs, they try the Internet sites and other local shops we list for them.

The majority of problem customers don't fall into this category. Most people respond well to a sincere effort to solve their problem, the frequent use of the word "sorry," and a generous dose of empathy. When someone called to complain about another customer getting waited on before her, I could honestly say that I would have been irritated, too. I tried to find out the details of when it happened and who was involved and asked her what action she wanted me to take to be sure it didn't happen again. I also thanked her for calling the problem to my attention. A customer who complains gives you the opportunity to make things right, but customers who are angry and don't call probably tell their friends about it.

Coping with Vandalism and Graffiti

Parents constantly worry about their toddlers breaking something in the store, but most of the damage to merchandise and displays is done by adults. The era of the "You break it, you bought it" rule has passed in most retailing environments, but customers are still afraid to admit that they have accidentally broken something. We usually find broken items hidden in our displays rather than being brought to us by the customers who broke them.

If an item is accidentally broken by anyone, adult or child, we absorb the loss. Items that are very valuable or fragile are kept in a closed case. We very rarely put a sign by fragile items requesting that customers ask for assistance if they would like to look at them more closely. Merchandise that can freely handled always sells better.

There is a big difference between accidental breakage and vandalism. A customer once informed me that a teenager was stomping on bath oil beads in our cutlery department, and this clearly was no accident. When I insisted that the girl clean up the mess, she informed me that she was only responsible for squishing some of them. Her friends had apparently made a quick escape.

Graffiti can be a headache for retailers, especially in urban settings. Prompt removal of graffiti is thought to be the best deterrent to future damage. There are surface treatments that can be applied that will make graffiti removal easier. Most police departments can give retailers advice about dealing with this potentially expensive and destructive problem.

Surviving Personnel Problems

Someday I will accept the fact that all of my staff can't be happy all of the time, but nothing upsets me more than personnel problems. Sometimes one individual is grumpy and sets the tone for the rest of the staff. Sometimes the entire group is unhappy about a work-related issue, such as salaries or work schedules. And sometimes it is necessary to confront an employee about his or her inadequate performance or behavior, which is never easy to do.

Staff morale is vital to the health of a retail operation, and nothing upsets a customer more quickly than an unpleasant encounter with a crabby salesperson. I prize enthusiasm and a strong spirit of cooperation above almost all other virtues in an employee and have been known to encourage whiners to look for work elsewhere because they have a negative impact on the rest of the team.

Creating job satisfaction is a continuing challenge. Studies have shown that employees are not just looking for money when they work; they also want a feeling of doing something meaningful and being appreciated. Many retailers find it difficult, or even embarrassing, to praise their staff constantly. One reason may be that they don't feel appreciated themselves.

When Bob Greene, author of *1001 Ways to Reward Your Employees*, spoke to store owners and managers at the American Booksellers Association convention, his audience made it clear that few of his listeners felt anyone had expressed appreciation for them recently. If you own your business, you need to look to your own need for self-esteem. If you employ one or more managers, be sure they often hear from you that you think they are doing a good job.

"Just put the store logo somewhere between 'Mom' and the bald eagle."

Coping Skills: Surviving Tough Times

Encouragement can take many forms. Recognition plaques, trips, gift cards, and even the use of a car, such as Mary Kay's famous pink Cadillacs, are ways to keep your staff fired up and content. My personal favorite is Bob Greene's suggested reward of a tattoo of the store's logo, although no one on my staff has taken me up on it yet.

When problems do come up, take them seriously. Be available to meet immediately with any staff members who have a concern. The issue may not seem urgent to you, but if it is important to them, they will appreciate that you make it a priority. Listen carefully, and if necessary repeat back what you understand them to be saying. Ask for suggestions for solutions, and promise to do what you can. If appropriate, make a note about the conversation and any follow-up in the employee's personnel file.

Communication is a great antidote to festering discontent. Allow staff an outlet for their frustration at regular staff meetings or smaller conferences. Have a suggestion box if you feel there are complaints that employees would be hesitant to bring up in public. Encourage everyone to propose constructive solutions when a problem is brought up. Never belittle anyone's concerns or discuss an issue involving only one or two individuals in front of the group.

If there are employees on your staff who don't get along, try to schedule them so they are not working side by side. Take into account that employees experiencing personal problems may require some leeway in their job duties. It may be difficult to accept the fact that all staff members are unique, complex individuals, with distinct personalities and problems. Try to treat everyone with respect and understanding.

When You're in Financial Trouble

Once you've gotten past the turbulent and exciting first years of owning a shop and have started showing a profit, you might expect that retailing will settle into a comfortable pattern of growth. This is often the case, with some fluctuations, but sometimes factors beyond your control send sales or profits into a downward spin. Suddenly you may find it hard to meet your payroll or to pay your suppliers. Merchandise that used to sell quickly begins to languish, tying up capital unproductively. Perhaps you see sales declining, or expenses increasing, or the demographics of your neighborhood changing. When you feel that things are not going well, it's time to analyze your options by stepping outside your usual routine. As the saying goes, "You can't read the label when you're inside the bottle."

The SWOT Analysis

One way to examine your store's position in its market area is to take time periodically to do an exercise called a SWOT analysis, which stands for the following:

- Strengths
- Weaknesses
- Opportunities
- Threats

This can be a useful exercise even for stores that are not experiencing a crisis. Retailers can't keep doing what they've been doing and continue to grow or even stay in business. Many stores languish because they fail to change as the world around them changes.

Write the preceding four words on large sheets of paper, and invite your staff to help you come up with as many responses as possible. You may find that there are opportunities for your store that you hadn't thought of or changes in shopping patterns that present new threats. Getting input from your staff will help you see the big picture more clearly and give you all the opportunity to brainstorm about the future.

Coping Skills: Surviving Tough Times

You might want to compare your current SWOT with the assumptions you made when you first wrote your business plan. As the many factors that affect your store change, you can update the business plan to a strategic plan stating your short-term and long-term goals for your shop and how you plan to achieve them.

WHAT ARE YOUR OPTIONS?

If the results of your SWOT analysis are not hopeful for future success, it is time to consider your options. Try to take time away from the store to give some thought to the following ideas:

- Closing or selling the store

- Becoming part of a franchise

- Moving to a new location

- Refocusing your merchandise selection

- Adding new customer services

- Giving your storefront or fixtures a facelift

Be sure that your display techniques are up to date, your staff well trained, and your customer policies competitive. Consider diversifying your product mix or adding a related side business. You might want to reread Chapter 2 and do a new market study to see what products might sell better than those you are currently carrying.

To augment her lines of lifestyle products, Pod owner Julie Baine expanded into clothing. "I resisted the move at first," she comments. "But customers kept asking us for apparel items. Since a few of my existing housewares vendors had diversified themselves and were offering clothing collections, I was able to try it without sinking a lot of money into the first round of buying. Two years after the leap, clothing was our fastest growing and most lucrative category of products. I set aside a small budget for the experiment, and it worked."

SURVIVING A CASH CRUNCH

If your business is short of money, you have two options: 1) increase your debt by seeking additional loans and investments or 2) raise cash by quickly selling some of your inventory and assets. Banks don't generally like to be approached for loans in a time of crisis, but if you have a preapproved line of credit with your bank, you can draw on it when you need to. You might also be able to bring in a new partner or investor, or try a crowdsourcing campaign.

Consider asking your vendors to lend you money by extending the due date on their invoices. If you do take advantage of delayed dating terms, be sure you are doing so with the express approval of your vendor. "Leaning on the trade" without prior agreement is unfair and transfers your cash flow problem onto someone else's shoulders. Wholesalers, too, have payrolls to meet and rent to pay.

If you are unable to pay your vendors on time, be sure to notify them of the delay, and tell them when payment can be expected. Keep in regular touch with those you owe money so that your staff won't be on the receiving end of angry telephone calls from your creditors. If at all possible, come up with funds to make regular partial payments on the amounts you owe.

You may find that you have some sources of personal funds you hadn't considered using. A second mortgage on your home may generate funds if the house is not part of the collateral you pledged to get your original funding. You might be able to borrow against a life insurance policy. In a pinch, retailers have been known to use credit cards to pay for inventory and even expenses. The interest rates on some credit cards are much higher than others, so shop around and consolidate your purchases onto one card that is guaranteed to remain at a low rate. Consider a card that will give you a discount or points toward a frequent flyer program. Be sure to pay the credit card debt off as soon as possible.

Coping Skills: Surviving Tough Times

An inventory reduction sale can raise funds in just a few days. Offer a flat discount, such as 20% off on everything in the store or an attractive reduction on expensive items. As long as you are making some profit on the merchandise sold, you can raise the cash you need and then later replace the inventory with fresh goods. Excess merchandise is often a source of cash flow problems, so it would be wise to review your buying policies if you are often short of cash.

Is there some other way your store could raise funds? You might have some office space that you can lease out. You could also lease space on your selling floor to an independent vendor, for example, a florist. Department stores have done this for years, with areas such as the shoe department being run by a separate business.

Cutting overhead can help solve a cash flow problem—perhaps you could reduce the hours you are open or cut back on buying trips. If payroll is your major expense, you may have to make the painful move of laying off some of your staff. Be honest with your employees if you think layoffs may have to happen. Reassure those who are laid off that the decision is not a reflection on their performance, and if you will not be rehiring them, help them look for new work. Let your employees know about any unemployment benefits they may be entitled to. And if you hope that the layoff is only temporary, keep in touch with those who are not working so that they know how things are going for the store.

When times are bad, resist the temptation to eliminate essentials such as advertising. You want your old customers to know that your business is still alive and well, and you need to continue to attract new customers. Project an image of success and confidence, no matter how tough things are.

Responding to Bad Publicity

One book on retailing suggests that as a cute marketing gimmick, you hire people to picket your store with signs that say something like "Prices Too Low." Most of us, especially in politically correct cities such as Madison, would rather avoid even the appearance of controversy. Negative publicity, which is often unfair, can do a great deal to damage the reputation of a store.

When confronted with any situation in which you need to work with the media, do your best to be upbeat and cooperative. Keep in mind that reporters are working under a deadline and need your timely response. When replying to their questions, avoid "no comment," which to the public means you are hiding something. Be honest, and after consultation with your lawyer, admit blame if it is appropriate. If someone has been injured, show compassion for the victim even if you are not at fault.

Thriftway Market in San Francisco was faced with picketing from a grocery clerks' union that wanted to organize the small shop's employees. In order to make sure that the public knew its side of the story, the store used window signs including enlargements of letters of support from fellow merchants and even copies of its payroll records. The signs mentioned that more information was available inside, where well-written flyers were available telling the store's side of the controversy.

Once you are certain that the public is also aware of your side of the story, patience is the best remedy for negative publicity. Eventually the public's attention always turns elsewhere.

Facing New Competition

If you have been fortunate to start your business before a major big-box store or online retailer such as Amazon came into your market, the arrival of these challengers may feel very threatening. And to be truthful, many long-term locally owned businesses have been put out of business by these giant competitors. Those who say that you can easily survive these challenges often oversimplify the situation or assume that you have enough capital on hand to make the changes necessary to compete. However, it is also not true that every local business is done in by the arrival of a new competitor. Here are a few of the steps you can take:

♦ Don't roll over and play dead

♦ Get to know your competition

♦ Analyze your strengths and weaknesses (see above)

♦ Remodel your store

♦ Extend your hours

♦ Add staff training

♦ Offer additional services

♦ Team up with other retailers and your community

♦ Be a trendsetter

♦ Diversify; go more upscale

♦ Get free PR by discussing the situation in the press

♦ Advertise and promote your business

♦ Cultivate your current customers

Keeping an Upbeat Attitude

We all have bad days, and while customers may want to talk to you about theirs, they don't want to hear about yours. It is important to maintain an upbeat and polite attitude even when you are feeling low. Customers want to associate with success. No matter how poorly things are going, resist the temptation to complain.

That doesn't mean that you should keep the stress of dealing with problems to yourself. Rather, be selective about when and where you discuss what is going wrong. One of our young employees once asked if we had any other "boss friends" we could talk to. Luckily we do. It often helps to trade stories with other small business owners and managers. Not only do we get to complain without worrying about upsetting our customers or staff, but we sometimes find that other retailers have solutions to the problems that are bothering us.

I strongly encourage you to cultivate a spirit of camaraderie rather than competition among your fellow merchants. You can also look to community organizations for businesspeople, such as the chamber of commerce, a women-in-business group, or service clubs such as Rotary, for opportunities to meet others dealing with the challenges of running a business. Seminars such as those offered by the Small Business Development Center can be wonderful places to meet other owners and managers.

Stress is a factor in everyone's life, but when you are in charge, it is important that you have ways of coping with it that will not harm your business or your staff's morale. Eat regular meals, get some exercise, and get enough rest. Probably the best antidote to the stress of retailing is to get away from the store. Go on real vacations, not just buying trips. These breaks from running your shop, even if only for a long weekend, can give you a fresh perspective on your life and your business.

It is important to develop other interests and friends outside the shop's four walls. Do some volunteer work, and pursue a hobby. The late Stanley Marcus, founder of the famed Neiman Marcus chain, said in his memoir *Minding the Store*, "Despite my great love and devotion to the specialty store retailing field, I don't regard it as the most important activity of mankind, and I don't mind saying so. I take my business seriously and work extremely hard at it, as I would at any other endeavor which attracted my interest, but I can still take a good philosophical look at it and its relative importance in the world scene."

Coping Skills: Surviving Tough Times

Try not to carry your worries home to your spouse all the time, and be sure to make time for your family and friends. After all, business is only one small aspect of your life. If you make it the only focus of your existence, it will be hard to keep a healthy perspective when things do occasionally go wrong.

CHAPTER 17

STRATEGIES FOR SUCCESS:
IMPROVING PROFITABILITY

A lthough it would be nice to say that retailing gets easier the longer you are in business, seasoned shopkeepers tell me that there are always new challenges to face, some of them quite daunting. The national and global economies are continuously in a state of flux, the competition facing specialty shops changes and multiplies, and there can be a decline in the consumer market for your products or in the viability of your location. But every day brings a new opportunity for a retail store to do better by increasing sales and profitability.

As I've mentioned earlier, it is important to have profitability as one of your goals for several reasons. A profit can mean increased income for you and your employees and higher contributions to worthy causes in your community. It can help fuel an increase in inventory and fund remodeling costs to keep the store growing and changing. It makes your business more attractive to bankers and investors when you need to borrow money. And if you ever decide to sell the store, it will have a major impact on the value of the business.

There are really only three factors that impact a store's bottom line: sales volume, markup, and expenses. If you bring in more income and have the same level of expenditures, your profits will go up. If you bring in the same income but make more markup on the merchandise you sell, your profits will go up. If you spend less and have the same level of sales, your profits will go up. Continuous efforts on all sides of this equation are necessary for the business to have a healthy future.

Strategies for Success: Improving Profitability

Even if your store is doing well, you still can't sit back and continue to do things the way you always have. To paraphrase poet Percy Bysshe Shelley, "You can't rest on your laurels. Nothing wilts faster than a laurel rested upon." Retailing is a dynamic and ever-changing field. If you don't keep up with your competition, you will fall behind.

Increasing Your Sales

After a certain number of years, a store's sales often even out. Although this can be a good thing, if you are profitable at that level, it eventually can lead to a decline if the public tires of your product mix or if new competition comes into the marketplace. You must constantly be experimenting with new merchandise and displays, watching your sales by category to see what is selling best and putting more inventory dollars and floor space into that area. You might also choose to experiment with new outlets for selling the merchandise you already carry, for example, home parties or Internet sales.

How long has it been since you changed your advertising formula? If you've always used newspaper and other print media, maybe it's time to try radio or an expanded use of your email list.

Customer service is also something that needs to be examined from time to time. Are there products your staff needs to know more about? Is there something you can do to make your checkout procedures more efficient? Visiting other stores for ideas of how they do things may be useful in fine-tuning your own store's service.

The Buy Local Boost

The Buy Local movement has had a significant impact on the success of independent retailers. This international effort draws upon the interests of environmentalists, economists, farmers, politicians, and retailers. It has resulted in a groundswell of support for locally owned business that has been a real boon to independent shopkeepers trying to compete with chain stores and the Internet.

The buy local trend is based on a number of different factors, the most important of which is probably the desire to build and support community. Locally owned businesses help define our town or city and can emphasize regional products in a way that other stores cannot. They also provide opportunities to promote diversity in our society by encouraging minority entrepreneurs. There is a strong buy local agricultural movement supporting regional farming and the use of local foods in restaurants. Independent retailers have much to be gained by aligning themselves with these efforts.

Economics also support the concept that locally owned business gives more back to the community than chain stores. A recent economic impact study in Salt Lake City, Utah found that the local retailers return a total of 52% of their revenue to the local economy, compared to just 14% for the national chain retailers. This makes good sense—after all, the independent hires a local lawyer, advertising agency, and accountant and keeps any profits in the community rather than sending them off to shareholders in some other city.

STARTING A BUY LOCAL CAMPAIGN

If your community doesn't already have a shop local campaign, it's the perfect time to rally your business neighbors to get involved. Your customers may not realize the importance of where they spend their dollars, and a buy local campaign can help build awareness about the economic and environmental impact of locally owned businesses. Rather than coming out as "antichain," these public relations efforts encourage thoughtful decision making in each buying choice, recognizing that there are some products that are only available from big retailers or online.

We are part of the Dane Buy Local, which works to educate consumers through a website, a printed guide and newspaper advertising

Strategies for Success: Improving Profitability

about which businesses are locally owned. They also sponsor networking gatherings for members and several community events such as Independents Week close to Independence Day.

Many of the buy local campaigns are aligned with the Business Alliance for Living Local Economies (BALLE, www.bealocalist.org) movement or the American Independent Business Alliance (AMIBA, www.amiba.net). These national organizations are a great place to start if you need ideas for starting a buy local organization.

Band Together for Community Promotions

We do a number of events every year with our fellow Monroe Street businesses, including the Monroe Street Festival in the fall. Right now we are gearing up to help everyone survive a major roadwork project next year. To receive matching funds available from the city of Madison for this purpose, we recently organized our group as a 501(c)6. After 40 years as the de facto head of the Monroe Street Merchants Association,

Amy Ruis is the owner of Art of the Table, a Grand Rapids, Michigan, tabletop and gourmet shop that has the good fortune to be located on Wealthy Street. She has been active in the Local First organization there for years. "Our Local First has a Street Party, a true close-down-the-block event held annually on a side street downtown to celebrate local business," Amy reports.

"As a member of Local First, you can get a booth to exhibit and sell your food and other merchandise. There are food trucks and a beverage tent with only local beer and wine to purchase, and local bands playing throughout the day and evening. It's open to all ages with crafts and art activities for kids of all ages. We get a ton of free media coverage, so the event pulls in a lot of interested people - hundreds in our first year to over 16,000 in our 13th year!"

it's nice to have a board of directors and lots of new energy from the various businesses in our area.

One of our new projects is designing a set of gift cards that will be valid at our shops, restaurants and service businesses during the time that the street will be under reconstruction next year. We plan to sell them in a zippered tote with an "I Love Monroe Street" logo on it this December. For more ideas of how the Monroe Street businesses support each other, please take a look at our website, www.monroestreetmadison.com.

Benefitting from Small Business Saturday

Thanks to American Express, the concept of Small Business Saturday on Thanksgiving weekend is now as well known as Black Friday. Statistics show that an estimated 112 million consumers spent $15.4 billion dollars at independent retailers and restaurants on this day in 2016. And although one of the underlying goals of Small Business Saturday is to encourage consumers to use American Express cards—and to have more small businesses accept them—this promotion of the virtues of "shopping small" has clearly been a huge boon to independent stores.

ESTIMATED
$15.4 BILLION
SPENT AT SMALL INDEPENDENT
BUSINESSES ON THE DAY

Strategies for Success: Improving Profitability

> "Many of the businesses in little New London, Minnesota get together monthly for a New London Area Merchants Group meeting," according to Anita Stulen of Mill Pond Mercantile. "We take turns meeting at our various locations so we can get to know what each of us offers. We pool our yearly membership dollars to use for marketing that includes radio, billboard, print ads, coupon flyers, group visitor goodie bags and much more.
>
> We also host several events each year: a spring event (this year with a biking theme); our annual Water Days with a customer appreciation free breakfast, crazy days sidewalk sales, a parade, and fireworks; a fall Harvest Festival and a Ladies Night Out. In November we have our biggest event, a Christmas open house called Home for the Holidays. Also in December we take part in the town's Santa Train event and Dickens Christmas. Considering that downtown New London is only two blocks long, I think we keep pretty busy!"

American Express provides marketing materials and national advertising at no cost to retailers. You can access these materials on the Shop Small Studio site. Our business association registers every year as a "Neighborhood Champion" group, so we receive supplies to distribute to everyone who is interested. We will also use the logos and suggested posts in our social media, encouraging shoppers to come to our area.

Even if you aren't part of a group, you can promote Small Business Saturday, and shopping at your store, on Facebook and Twitter (and don't forget to share postings from the Small Business Saturday Facebook page for the event). Use the hashtags #shopsmall and #smallbizsaturday to be part of the larger conversation. This is a great opportunity to share some of the statistics about why shopping small is good for our communities.

The event guide from American Express has lots of ideas for individual shops to consider, and of course, you can also research what has worked for other retailers. Here are a few favorites:

- Create a party atmosphere by decorating your storefront with SBS signs, balloons and the doormats.

- Set up a scavenger hunt involving the other small businesses in your area.

- Offer refreshments, entertainment and other "open house" hospitality.

- Highlight merchandise made by local artisans, or small manufacturers.

- Ask your vendors if they have any special deals and discounts you can promote, which may include some intended for "Black Friday."

- Partner with other shops to offer a discount or gift for those who visit multiple stores.

- Get together with a local restaurant to offer shoppers a treat with a store receipt.

Growing Sales through Relationship Marketing

Offering a high level of personalized customer service has helped many specialty retailers improve their sales, because focusing on the customer as an individual is something that a larger store or Internet business can't do as well. And we all know that cultivating existing customers is much less expensive than investing advertising dollars to attract new ones. You can do this by consistently providing top-notch customer service and by paying special attention to the key customers who spend the most dollars in your store.

Strategies for Success: Improving Profitability

Walmart may be known for having official door greeters, but independent retailers have always known that making a customer feel welcome is important. If at all possible, greet your regulars by name. Try to get to know your customers' likes and dislikes as well as something about their lives outside your store. This will help you tailor your service to fit each individual's shopping preferences. The needs of a woman executive with three children at home are different from those of a retired male accountant, and even if they are looking for the same merchandise, they may not want the same type of shopping experience. You want to cater to each individual as much as possible in order to meet and exceed their expectations of your store.

A sure way to motivate your staff to provide individual service at a very personal level is to pay your employees a commission on each sale, in addition to a base salary. As mentioned in Chapter 10, this only works well if you are selling fairly expensive items. But this arrangement encourages staff members to develop a professional relationship with a list of clients, contacting them regularly regarding new merchandise and promotions. This encourages frequent visits to the store, which is a surefire way to increase sales.

It is important to learn who your top customers are so that you can target them with your buying and advertising. Technology such as a POS system and customer loyalty program can help you compile data on your most frequent shoppers if you make a diligent effort to acquire and record important details such as birthdays, purchase history, and preferences. We sometimes send out a present or gift card to the customers that we know are in our top 50, and we know from their thank-you notes how much they appreciate this special attention.

Here are a few ideas for surprising your best customers and making them feel appreciated:

- ♦ Give them a free add-on item occasionally.
- ♦ Send a personal thank-you note.

- Remember their pets' and children's names.
- Offer services such as wrapping or delivery for free.
- Give them a coupon or gift card for their next visit.
- Arrange for a free cappuccino at your local coffee shop.
- Follow up on a major purchase to see if they are satisfied.

You may wish to set up a system for acknowledging customers who refer their friends or relatives to your store. Send a personal note and, perhaps, a small gift to thank the customer for the referral and for the confidence they've shown in your business by recommending it.

Targeting New Markets

You might be able to expand your sales by appealing to markets that are sometimes underserved, for example male shoppers, teens, or the Latinx market. It is important to start this process with some consumer research. Talk to individuals or a focus group to determine where these customers are shopping now, what their buying habits are, and what kind of merchandise they are potentially interested in.

APPEALING TO LUXURY SHOPPERS

You can increase your sales, despite challenges from competition, by targeting customers with more disposable income who can afford to make larger purchases. These shoppers are eager for an enjoyable, pleasant shopping experience. They spend more time shopping and looking at products online, so they are generally quite knowledgeable about the goods they might want to buy. Keep in mind, though, that even the wealthiest shoppers love a bargain, and so perceived value is always important.

Strategies for Success: Improving Profitability

Consumers with a higher-than-average level of income are said to be placing more importance on quality experiences than on goods (which is also true of many other potential customers today). This is one reason that disposable income is often spent on travel rather than on objects. However, a good independent retailer can provide a memorable shopping experience in addition to unique items that speak to the customer's desire to express his or her individuality.

These shoppers are also looking for products that enhance their quality of life, such as tools that make their work easier, systems that help them get organized, and decorative accessories that make their home environment more comfortable and pleasing. They also enjoy products that pamper and help them reduce the stress in their lives.

The desire for pampering, and items that might be considered a luxury, is not limited to the wealthy. As author Pam Danziger, president of Unity Marketing, says in *Shops that Pop! Seven Steps to Extraordinary Retail Success*, "Satisfying shoppers' desires, not their needs, is where the serious money is to be made. It is tapping into the emotion behind all consumer purchases, from the most mundane to the most extraordinary, and appealing to shoppers' emotional desires, not the normal, physical, everyday needs. While nobody needs luxury, everybody wants it!"

GOING AFTER THE CORPORATE MARKET

The corporate gift business may be an untapped market worth pursuing. Companies that support the buy local movement might enjoy giving their employees or clients a gift card, either to your shop or to your shopping district. Often employee gifts are given as motivational rewards, and the opportunity to select an item from a local shop has a lot more appeal than something branded with a corporate logo.

Gifts with a local theme also help a business express its support of the community. We find that for an office gift, food items that can be shared are popular. It is fun to put together an assortment of our specialty products in an attractive manner that will make the donor proud.

A shop that decides to pursue the corporate market aggressively will need to develop a plan, supported by samples, materials, and sales work in the field or by phone. Once a relationship is established with a large business, repeat orders may come easily. A bank, for instance, will probably call the same gift basket business or florist every time it needs a baby gift.

Some shops have been successful in hosting holiday parties for companies such as realtors and pharmaceutical firms. The shop provides an elegant setting in exchange for the purchase of gift cards or favors to give out, and the company takes care of issuing the invitations and arranging for catering and music.

There is ample opportunity for the specialty shop that decides to offer its products to business clients, although the competition is strong. Start by researching the types of purchases local businesses are making and the sources they are using. Membership in a business organization or service club would be a good source for leads on corporate accounts. Even if you choose not to pursue corporate sales actively, you may want to give businesses a quantity discount if they come to you for a large number of items.

Markup can Make Up Your Margins

Margins can make a big difference to your store's bottom line. Simple math shows that an item purchased for $1.00 and sold for $3.00 yields a higher gross income than a $1.00 item sold for $2.00. The higher your average markup, the lower the percentage of the retail price that will go toward the cost of goods sold. To increase profitability, it is important to take at least as much markup as you feel your market will bear. Watch for opportunities to buy goods at a reduced price or to get a discount for paying invoices early so that you can make a higher margin without adding to the retail price.

The cost of goods sold also usually includes shipping costs, and the amount of money to be saved by looking for free freight offers or by consolidating smaller shipments into larger ones can be significant. Specify that you want all shipments to be sent using the cheapest and best method rather than always using small parcel services. When feasible, avoid shipping altogether by buying at a cash-and-carry show or from a local resource.

Expenses Down = Profits Up

To keep expenditures under control, you need to look at your profit and loss statements each month to see how your money is being spent. There are two general categories to consider: merchandise purchases and the expenses of running the business, which include utilities, rent, payroll, and even the salary you draw from the business.

WATCH YOUR BUDGET

There are some categories of expenses that are fixed, such as rent and other fees associated with leasing a space. Most others are somewhat within your control: payroll, advertising, utilities, and insurance, for example. It pays to periodically review each category that you can influence. Retail stores operate on such a slim margin of profit that a small change in just a few of these categories can have an important impact on the bottom line.

Ideally, you should create a budget that shows what you plan to spend in each category over the next 12 months, and make decisions accordingly. This will help you plan your advertising and hiring, for example. You can accompany this with a cash flow prediction indicating how the money coming in from sales (or loans) will cover the expenditures for each month. However, there are many factors outside your control that can impact even the best-laid plans, so you need to use these budgets as guidelines and goals.

WHAT'S NEGOTIABLE?

It is important that every dollar spent on operating expenses be productive, especially if you are paying interest on the money you used to pay for them. Small changes can add up to a big change in the bottom line, as illustrated in the table that follows. Here are a few of the areas you should review periodically to make sure you are getting the best deal possible:

- ◆ Credit card fees: If you are doing a large volume, these can add up to considerable expense. Competition in credit card processing and banking make it possible to negotiate a better rate.

- ◆ Bank processing charges: There may be hidden costs here that you aren't aware of; check with your banker about ways to reduce them

- ◆ Insurance costs: Check periodically to see whether your business and health insurance dollars are being spent optimally.

- ◆ Utility costs: Make sure that you are using all the energy-saving techniques available to you (see Chapter 15).

- ◆ Advertising: Can you negotiate better rates for print advertising by signing a contract for more frequency or save money by doing joint promotions with other businesses?

- ◆ Personnel: Are there ways to make more efficient use of your payroll dollars? Changes in scheduling and duties are a potential source of savings.

- ◆ Supplies: Look around at the supplies you use regularly, and see if there are any less expensive options—or something you could do without.

Strategies for Success: Improving Profitability

SAMPLE FINANCIAL ADJUSTMENT

This table shows the result of decreasing variable expenses (not rent) by
10% and increasing markup so the Costs of Good Sold goes down by 2%.

	Year 1	Year 2
Gross Sales	$ 500,000	$500,000
Cost of Goods Sold*	-280,000	-270,000
Gross Income	$ 220,000	$ 230,000
Expenses		
Rent	60,000	60,000
Utilities	10,000	9,000
Payroll & Salary	100,000	90,000
Advertising	25,000	22,500
Bank & Credit Card Fees	8,000	7,200
Interest	5,000	4,500
Supplies	10,000	9,000
Insurance	5,000	4,500
Other Expenses	10,000	9,000
Total Expenses	$ 233,000	$ 215,700
Net income (profit)	- $13,000	+ $ 14,300

♦ Refinance your debt: If you are paying interest on a credit
card for merchandise, look for a lower rate. If you have bank
loans, consider paying off some of the principal, or meet
with your banker to see if they can be restructured so that
you pay less interest.

The Dangers of Too Much Inventory

The more inventory you have on hand, the more selection you can offer
your customers. However, being over-inventoried, or carrying too
much stock, can be fatal to a retail store. Why? Because of the cost of the
debt service on borrowed money necessary to pay for the inventory.
Most retailers do not have unlimited personal funds, so there is a bank or

other lender involved in financing at least some of the merchandise purchases. Every month the interest must be paid on these loans, and this can be a considerable expense item.

Even if you haven't borrowed the money, there are still three hidden costs: 1) the expense of storing the merchandise, 2) the lost opportunity to use the funds to buy newer merchandise or to pay other expenses, and 3) the amount of interest you would be earning if you had put the money into a more traditional investment. In other words, if you have $2,000 tied up for five years in some pieces of jewelry that do not sell, at the end of that time the items may be a bit shopworn and out of fashion and worth only $1,000. If you'd put the money in a savings account that paid 5% per year, it would have grown to over $2,500.

In his blog, popular author and marketer Seth Godin in his blog uses a wonderful parable to describe the dangers of holding onto merchandise too long. "On the first day, all the fish at the fish stall are fresh. Some sell, some don't. The second day, the sold fish are replaced by newer, fresher fish. The unsold fish remains, even though it isn't so attractive. The third day, of course, the unsold fish are noticeably unfresh, and it doesn't take much effort to avoid them. At this point, part of the fishmonger's stock is demonstrably unappealing, bringing down the quality of the entire counter. Pretty soon, of course, the drop-off in business means that the owner can't afford to buy the freshest fish, even to replace his sold inventory, and the end is near. The alternative? On day two, discard the unsold fish. Obvious, but difficult. So difficult that we rarely do it. We'd rather lower the average and see if we can get away with it instead."

Keeping your merchandise at just the right level can be tricky. You want to move slow sellers out and keep the items customers expect you to always have on hand in stock. This requires constant vigilance and a willingness to mark down merchandise that you love but your customers don't. As the saying goes, "Don't let your inventory become family."

Strategies for Success: Improving Profitability

Plugging the Holes

We all know that shoplifting costs money, especially your money. If you suspect that you are the victim of frequent shoplifting or employee theft, you can increase your profitability by working to curtail these drains on your inventory. Consult with a security company and your local police to take steps that will let everyone know that you are taking a serious stance against crime.

If you always seem to be mysteriously short of cash, there is also the possibility that you are the victim of embezzlement. It is essential that you review your financial reports and bank statements periodically, especially if you suspect that someone may be stealing from you.

Staying Alert to Change

Maintaining good margins requires constant vigilance because so many factors that affect your store's profitability can change from day to day. You should be receiving monthly financial statements from your bookkeeper. Review these regularly, comparing them with past statements and with your budgets. If you aren't sure how to interpret the financial information, meet with your CPA to review the forms. You want to be sure that your store stays as healthy as possible financially so that you can concentrate on the fun aspects of retailing such as buying the latest merchandise and helping your valued customers without having to worry about money.

CHAPTER 18
WHAT'S NEXT:
LOOKING TO THE FUTURE

When our shop was about seven years old, we had to decide if we wanted branch stores or children. It was a tough choice because we loved retailing and found our lives very full with the day-to-day challenges of running our shop. I can assure Erik and Katrina that we have never regretted giving the nod to babies instead of branches. However, we do realize that the future of Orange Tree Imports would have been very different had we opted for additional stores.

There are many crossroads in the lifetime of a specialty shop. When you first open, you are not concerned with whether the store will outlive you or whether you will eventually have 5—or 50—branch stores. If things do not go well at first, you need to decide whether to stay in business at all and, if you are going to stay in business, what to change to improve sales. If everything does go well, you need to decide whether you will stay the same size, expand, change your product mix, move, or open branch stores. Retail stores need to change constantly in one way or another in order to stay alive. A store that doesn't change at all may eventually be referred to by that most dreaded of all retailing real estate terms: an occupied vacancy.

What's Next: Looking to the Future

Riding the Wave of Success

Success can be as hard on a business as failure. When a store experiences runaway sales increases, management and buyers may have difficulty keeping up. Cash reserves and staff energy can be strained. It is better to plan for gradual growth than to wish for runaway success, which can result in an excess of debt and poorly planned expansion.

If a store achieves stellar success due to a passing fad, such as Beanie Babies, scrapbooking or any other product craze, the public may lose interest very suddenly – or find the product available at a discount elsewhere. One of my employees once asked why I didn't stop buying an item when it was at the peak of its popularity and about to die. The answer, of course, is that you can see the peaks only in hindsight.

The key to handling a fast rise in sales is caution. Don't invest too heavily in inventory if you think a trend may pass. Reorder often, or place future dated orders that you can cancel. Make sure you are taking extra markup to protect your bottom line from disaster if the fad passes.

Many, and maybe most, specialty stores are based on trends that may not remain at the same level of popularity forever. Supply will eventually outweigh demand as retail concepts live out their natural life cycle, leaving shops with a choice of diversifying or closing. Other businesses changes may happen because running a store no longer fits in with your lifestyle as you age, or your family situation changes. The decision to close a store should not be viewed as a failure. In order to be successful, a store does not have to survive forever. It is enough to have taken a good idea, created an exciting shop, and enjoyed however many years of success it could sustain.

Small Can Be Beautiful

A shop that is very successful from the start may be tempted to add branch stores early in its development, a move that is sometimes fatal.

To take a concept that seems to work well in one place and open more shops may appear to be a logical next step. After all, the joint buying power of several stores allows for better pricing and more efficient use of the buyers' time. But other expenses increase with each branch added: the initial cost of more fixtures and inventory, plus the monthly expenses for rent, utilities, insurance, and payroll.

A branch store usually requires a manager, and the manager's salary will be higher than that of most other retail employees. The financial strain of each branch, plus the added demands on the owner's time, can be detrimental to the health of the original store. If a branch is located too close to the original store, it sometimes is said to cannibalize the sales of the original store by drawing on the very same customers.

Confining yourself to one store does not mean restricting growth entirely. We have tripled in size at our single location and achieved an annual sales volume of over $1 million. Even with just one store, we are large enough to provide a number of different jobs for our 25 employees and to employ 8 of these staff members full time.

When considering additional branch stores, the first question you should ask yourself is, why do it? If you are interested in an increase in profitability, you may be disappointed. If you are looking for new challenges for yourself or opportunities for advancement for your staff, consider whether there are options for growth within your current location. It is sometimes better to run one store passionately than to have your attention diverted to several locations.

If You Decide to Grow Your Business

The reasons that compelled you to get into retailing to begin with may influence your decision to open a second, third, or fourth branch: an ambition to create a new and exciting store, a desire to fill an additional need in the marketplace, an eagerness to promote merchandise you have

What's Next: Looking to the Future

a passion for, and an interest in creating new jobs. It is also true that the more stores you have, the more money you can make if they are all profitable.

One particularly compelling reason for branching out is to provide opportunities for advancement for staff members. Although we have been fortunate to have staff members stay with us for more than 30 years, the fact of the matter is that working for a single-location store does not offer much of a career track, especially if it is a family business that will most likely be passed on to the sons or daughters of the owners. If you decide to open a branch store to provide a new management position for a loyal employee or a family member, consider offering a financial stake in the success of the branch to encourage the person to make a long-term commitment.

Managing multiple stores requires special skills and systems. Some functions, such as bookkeeping, adapt well to being centralized at a main office or in the mother store. Others, such as personnel management and day-to-day operations, need to be entrusted to a manager or management team in each location. Good communication with the individual store managers and, on some occasions, the entire staff of each branch is essential to the success of a multiple store operation.

A computer network is essential to convey sales data from each branch store to the home office or main store for order placing, but buying decisions function best when there is some autonomy at each location because the customer base will vary from one area to another. Shipments from vendors can be sent to a central warehouse and then allocated to the individual stores as needed or shipped directly to each branch (in which case, separate *bill to* and *ship to* addresses need to be specified on the purchase order). Freight, payroll, and storage costs are all factors in deciding how best to divide up merchandise shipments.

SPECIALTY SHOP RETAILING

FINANCING YOUR GROWTH

Anita Roddick, the founder of The Body Shop, saw her business grow to include 2,000 shops in 50 countries. Within six months of opening her first store, she was eager to branch out—so eager, in fact, that she pledged 50% of her company to a man who willing to lend her the money she needed. In 2006, Ian McGlinn's £3,000 investment was turned into £137 million when Dame Anita and her husband Gordon sold The Body Shop to L'Oreal for £652 million. "Giving away half the business is considered by many as the biggest mistake I have ever made," she commented, "but I don't resent it. I needed the money, I needed it quickly, and Ian was the only one then who would give it to me."

For every success story like The Body Shop, there are many stores that don't survive rapid growth. If you have decided to open a branch store, it is time to write a new business plan and to examine the sources of funding available to finance the new store while keeping the original store running. Not many people remember that Orange Tree Imports actually started out as a branch of Bord & Stol, a Scandinavian furniture store. After six months, the cash flow problems were acute, and Bord & Stol was having trouble paying the bills for the branch store. I'm sure it was a relief to the owners when Dean and I offered to buy the business.

If your business is incorporated, you could finance your growth by selling shares to employees, family, or other investors. Large retail operations might even consider going public, offering stock on the stock exchange. Investors who buy a certain number of shares can be offered an investor card good for a discount on merchandise.

Some states allow small corporations to raise up to $1 million in funds by selling stock through a *small corporate offering registration (SCOR)*. You could bring in new partners, giving these investors partial ownership of one or more of the branch stores. Crowdsourcing platforms such as Kickstarter may be effective, especially if you are already known and respected in your community.

What's Next: Looking to the Future

A crowdsourcing campaign, which requires a lot of sharing on social media to be successful, can be a great way to build buzz about your business. These donors won't expect partial ownership, but they will want a reward of some kind based on how much they contribute—gift cards of various amounts, an invitation to an exclusive event, or merchandise such t-shirts or mugs with the store logo.

FRANCHISING YOUR STORE

An additional option available for financing new stores is franchising. If you have a strong retail operation, you could consider franchising your idea to others, who would then own their own stores but pay you an ongoing franchise fee. Franchise owners provide the capital for their own store, freeing you from the need to find the funding. There is one caveat, however: You would not have the same degree of control that you have over a store you own yourself.

How do you know if your store concept is right for franchising? In an article for Entrepreneur.com, Kyle Zagrodzky suggests that you ask the following questions:

- ♦ Can you clearly articulate what your brand is?

- ♦ Can my business be replicated?

- ♦ Am I willing to team up with multiple experts? A franchisor has to delegate.

- ♦ What's the true cost of franchising?

- ♦ Is my vision for expansion realistic?

What will you be offering a franchise holder? You will already have made all the initial decisions about the store name, image, design, and merchandise. You will share what you have learned from your mistakes, providing a store concept that has already been time tested. Perhaps you have products that are manufactured or imported exclusively for your shop, giving the franchise holders the advantage of obtaining merchandise not otherwise available to them. Volume purchasing will allow you to offer store supplies, fixtures, and goods at a lower price than a single store could obtain. In exchange for these advantages, the franchise holder will pay you an initial fee, plus whatever percentage of sales or other periodic payment you negotiate.

In exchange for the benefits of franchising, you shoulder a responsibility to protect the investment made by your franchise holders. State and federal regulations governing franchising help to protect the interest of those investors. Check all the pertinent regulations and work with a lawyer experienced in franchises before making an offering to the public.

OTHER WAYS TO EXPAND

Branch stores are not the only way to grow your business. You might consider adding a sister store, carrying a different product line, in the same area. This second shop could just be a kiosk or pop-up, allowing you to experiment with a new merchandising concept that might work in your original store. You could also set up a second store on a seasonal basis, especially if there is a vacancy in your area.

Or you might take your show on the road, like Ann Foley-Collins of Glee Gift Boutique. Ann Foley-Collins is in her third season behind the wheel of Glee Gifts Boutique on Wheels. Having operated a traditional retail boutique for over ten years, Foley-Collins decided to trade in her brick and mortar business for a fashion/gift truck. She converted a 2006 Ford Utilitymaster truck that once carried potato chips into a hip and trendy traveling store that features women's clothing, accessories, jewelry and gifts. She "pops up" at events like festivals, farmers markets, food truck rodeos, and everything in between. "This isn't an easy business model, with Mother Nature and Uncle Sam as my business partners, but it's a lot of fun and interesting. Given the current retail climate, it's a model folks will begin to better understand and embrace—I am paving the road for others to follow!"

You may also want to explore selling your products, or one or two best sellers, through a different channel. As an experiment in large-scale mail order marketing, we once ordered 5,000 of Arabia's enameled serving bowls from Finland and ran a national ad in *Bon Appetit* magazine. This venture into selling by mail taught us that it can be quite boring to sell thousands of the same item to customers you never see. We broke even and decided to stay with traditional retailing. But for many stores, selling online (see Chapter 13) offers a natural opportunity for expanding your market without opening another store.

As more manufacturers get into retailing their own goods online, it may be time to turn the tables and have more retailers get into manufacturing. Constant contact with customers gives you the advantage of knowing what the public wants. If you see a need, explore whether you

Glee Gift Boutique on Wheels open for business. (Photo courtesy of Ann Foley-Collins)

> Direct-import items that sell well in your shop could also be a way to enter the wholesale market. The Ukrainian Gift Shop began in founder Marie Sokol's living room in Minneapolis in 1947. The company began supplementing the shop's walk-in trade by wholesaling imported gifts and Ukrainian egg decorating supplies, and now sells to shops around the country.

can have the product made for you at a reasonable cost. If this custom merchandise is successful at retail, consider selling it wholesale. Ask the sales reps who sell to you for advice on selling to other stores, and consult your accountant about whether the wholesale operation should be considered a separate business.

We recently took advantage of the popularity of coloring books for adults to produce a Madison and a Wisconsin coloring packet. We found our artists through word of mouth and Craigslist, and had a local printing company produce the items in time for holiday selling. One of our sales reps offered them at wholesale to retailers across the state so that we could benefit from the price break generated by printing a larger quantity.

Moving On: Selling or Closing Your Store

The high rate of retail failures does not reflect the fact that sometimes a shopkeeper decides to close the store for reasons other than lack of business success. Many shops do close because of financial reasons, of course, especially if they were started without adequate market research or enough capital to keep the doors open for the first year or two, or are in the wrong location. But you may find that your store concept is going out of fashion, that you want more free time, or that the local economy is taking a downward spin. You don't have to be open for decades to have been a successful retailer. It is a major accomplishment to have brought your dream to reality.

What's Next: Looking to the Future

LOOKING FOR A NEW OWNER

If you decide to leave retailing, you can either sell your shop as a going business or close the store. Allow enough time to explore both these options, especially if you want to try to sell the store as a going business if possible, but will close if you don't find a buyer. Both these options can take many months. Remember that either move will have a major impact on your staff, so it is important that they be kept informed of your plans. No one deserves to go to work one morning and find an "Out of Business" sign on the door. Incredibly, this does happen.

When you sell a successful shop as a going business, your goal is to arrange for such a seamless transition that it will be almost unnoticed by customers. In addition, if the store has been faltering, the announcement of new owners can bring with it the promise of a fresh start and a new direction.

To find a buyer for a retail business, start with those who know the business best: your employees and family members. If one individual can't come up with the financing to buy the business, perhaps two or three could join together to do so. You may have a loyal customer who is so devoted to the shop that he or she would like to consider owning it. A neighboring business owner may be looking for a new opportunity. In 1986 we expanded our store by buying the shop next door when the owner retired and connecting our two businesses. Perhaps one of your competitors, even one located in another community, would like to own your store.

You may wish to sell your business and stay on as a buyer or manager. Your new role relieves you of the worries of owning the shop and is one way to solve a severe cash flow crisis. The new owner, whether a corporation or an individual, will bring new ideas, new funds, and new energy into the business. If you find you are burned out on management duties or stretched to the limit of your financial resources, selling may be a way to keep the shop you love open and take on a different role. Allow yourself a retirement option, however, if you find you don't work well with the new owners.

To sell your business, you will need to have all your financial records in order. The buyer will want to know how profitable your shop has been, which is a good reason to keep accurate, honest records. In addition to paying for the furniture, the fixtures, and the wholesale value of the merchandise, the buyer may be willing to pay a premium called *goodwill* for the positive reputation of the store. The more profitable the shop is, the more you can ask for in goodwill.

If your store has done a good job in building customer loyalty, there is also value in these relationships, so the goodwill payment would cover passing along an active mailing or email list to the new owner. Be sure to

"And remember, Mrs. Smithers likes all her packages in the paisley gift wrap."

compile a list of awards you have won, and to present examples of your press coverage that shows the value of your store's reputation.

You can also request a payment for promising not to open a new store that will compete with the one you are selling. This **non-compete agreement** is usually valid for a certain number of years and a specific geographic area.

There are brokers who sell businesses, much the way a realtor sells buildings. These specialists will know of any individuals looking to buy a retail business, especially out-of-towners wanting to relocate to your community, and can also help you place a value on your shop.

As part of the sale of the store, discuss which staff members may be kept on by the new owner. Encourage the new owner to benefit from the experience of your employees by retaining as many of them as possible. You may also offer your services as a consultant or buyer for a certain number of months, or even years, after the sale.

GOING OUT OF BUSINESS: MAKING A GRACIOUS EXIT

Although it is gratifying to see the store carry on without you, the fact is that you may walk away with more money if you go out of business than if you sell to a new owner. This is especially true if you have not shown a profit, and there is no goodwill to be paid. Unless you are selling your building with the business, there is little to be gained by a buyer in obtaining a shop full of merchandise that has not been selling well enough to be profitable. And without the premium of goodwill, there is little advantage to you to selling all the goods at wholesale or below.

A going-out-of-business sale will in fact often start by offering the goods at close to full retail. The first weeks, or even months, the storewide discount may be just 15 or 20% off. A wider public will be drawn to the store closing by the promise of bargains, and a considerable amount of merchandise can be moved at this greater-than-wholesale value. As the sale progresses, the discount will need to be deeper, but very little will probably remain by the time the markdown is 50% or more. You might want to set up an email list of those who come in for the sale, and promise to send out messages to them when you go to the next level of discounts. The same customers will undoubtedly come back for another look as the prices go down.

Be sure to put signs on your fixtures indicating that they will be available for sale when you close. There are always new retailers looking for an inexpensive way to outfit their store. Leftover fixtures could be offered to resale shops or other charities, along with any merchandise left the day you close.

When you decide to close your business, you will need to talk to your landlord. Your lease may contain a holdover clause stating that you must give written notice of your intent to vacate. You may be responsible for an additional month's or year's rental agreement if you fail to give proper notice. If you have time remaining on your lease, find out whether you can sublet the space. If you are at the end of a lease period, you might want to negotiate a month-to-month extension in order to hold your final sale at the most advantageous time of year.

Signage is important in promoting your going-out-of-business sale, and you may find that your municipality has regulations regarding the type of banners and signs that are allowed. Make up the signs in advance that you'll need as you increase the percentage of discount to save some stress as the sale progresses.

There are companies that specialize in assisting businesses in closing, and we occasionally get mailings from them in discreetly unmarked envelopes. Some of these companies make their profits by bringing in their own closeout merchandise to supplement your stock. They have marketing gimmicks and games that they use to promote the sale, which may be a relief if you don't have the energy to run the sale yourself. But when one of our neighboring businesses brought in a company to close their store, their regular customers found it unsettling to be dealing with these outsiders, with their complex and potentially misleading promotional schemes.

If you decide to go out of business, you may be tempted to walk away from some of the bills not yet paid, especially if you are closing because the store is losing money. Suppliers complain that they suffer huge lossses each year from stores that close. The practice of leaving wholesale bills unpaid is no different than a customer paying for merchandise in the store with a worthless check. If you have ordered and received merchandise, you are required to pay for it, even if it takes a long time to do so.

Remember that the sales representatives who wrote orders with you will not get any commissions on goods not paid for and that other retailers (and ultimately the consumer) have to pay higher prices for merchandise to make up for any amount not paid by a store going out of business.

A store closing is a time of loss for those who loved the store, especially for those who worked there. Be sure to offer assistance to your staff in finding new positions, and a "staying on" bonus while you close up shop. Don't be surprised if they take job offers before you have finished

Sonia Mott learned a lot from closing Motif, her award-winning home decor store in Pewaukee, Wisconsin. "In order to maximize your income when you close your business, plan ahead and bring in off-price merchandise that you can price at two or three times your usual markup. We bought closeouts, showroom samples and even inventory from other shops that were closing, but we didn't say that the goods were for a going -out-of-business sale—we didn't want our customers to know until we sent them a personal email inviting them to a VIP preview. After that we put up big banners and signs announcing to the public that we were offering amazing bargains. We sold most of the goods at 20% to 40% off the retail price, netting us a nice profit."

your going-out-of-business sale. It can be distressing for them to see the store empty out and start to look shabby, which happens as the merchandise selection is reduced. Staff members need to protect their own future and take whatever opportunity comes their way. You may need to contact a temp agency for salespeople for the last weeks of the sale.

Life Planning Issues for Shopkeepers

The future of a store is often linked with the life plans of its owners. When the owner decides to retire or relocate, or if someone key to the business dies, major changes will usually occur in the store's operations. Planning for the transition brought on by the retirement or loss of the owners can help ease this transition for everyone involved.

THE IMPORTANCE OF HAVING A WILL

Do you and your business partners have wills? Few people would intentionally throw the business they love into utter chaos, but, in fact, the sudden death of an owner can have just that effect. Without the guidance provided by a will, there is no way to know who is going to own and run the store and pay the business's creditors, or what is to become of the employees and the shop full of merchandise. We are all mortal and need to face the fact that death could occur at any time. If your business is thriving, you will want to plan for it to be able to carry on without you some day.

When a spouse, family members, or other partners are involved in the day-to-day store operations, it is usually easy to decide who to list in your will as the successor. Check with your lawyer about ways to avoid heavy estate taxes after you have established who you would like to have inherit the shop.

Without a likely family member or partner, you may find that there is no one you would like to have inherit the business. In this case, you will need to ask your lawyer, or the executor of your estate, to arrange to sell the shop as a going concern or to liquidate the merchandise and assets.

Provisions can be made in your will to authorize the person of your choice to keep the shop running until the estate can be settled. Keeping the store's staff and customer base intact for a possible new owner will make the transition much smoother. Key-person life insurance, with the store as the beneficiary, can be a great help in paying off debts that are due or covering the salary of a manager to handle day-to-day store operations.

When we wrote our first wills, we did not have children. We decided that if we both were to die, we'd want our employees to have the first opportunity to bid on the business, followed by family members, and then the general public. Now that Erik and Katrina are adults, we would want them to have the opportunity to keep the business going if they so choose.

PLANNING FOR RETIREMENT

Corporate and government employers often offer their employees retirement benefits and pension plans that are the envy of those of us with small businesses. As an independent retailer, you need to save for your own retirement, and the earlier you begin planning for retirement, the better things will look when you finally decide to hang up your price gun.

The retirement plans available to you depend on whether you are a sole proprietorship, partnership, or corporation—and whether you offer a plan that covers all of your employees. Your accountant and lawyer can advise you of your options, which may include setting up a 401(k) or other pension plan for your staff or contributing to your own personal individual retirement account (IRA) each year. See Chapter 10 for more information about retirement plan options.

The equity you build up in your business will also be part of your retirement savings, but unless you plan to sell or close the business when you retire, you may find this asset to be less liquid than other savings. If the business can afford it, you could draw out some of your money or arrange to stay on the payroll as a part-time consultant after you retire. Check to see what course of action will be most advantageous from a tax standpoint, especially after you begin to take social security benefits and draw from your IRA.

FAMILY BUSINESS SUCCESSION

For family-owned businesses, part of the process of planning for the future may include deciding which family members will take charge of the store when the owner retires. This planning process needs to begin several years before retirement in order to ensure a smooth transition that is fair to all involved, including employees who are not relatives. Don't give these employees reason to resent family members who come into the business.

Keep family and business relationships separate, insisting on the same high standards of training and performance for all staff. Consider asking to be called by your name, rather than Mom or Uncle Joe, when in a business setting. Make it clear to other employees that there will be no favoritism in assigning schedules and responsibilities.

It was once said that if you hope your children will take over your business, watch what you say at the dinner table. If children hear only complaints about your customers, suppliers, and staff, they may not be interested in getting involved. Even if children do like the idea of running a shop, I think they should be encouraged to follow their own interests first. After they have gotten an education and experienced the outside working world, they will be better able to decide whether the family business is right for them.

There are many difficult decisions to be made when it comes time to pass the leadership of your store on to a successor. If you have more than one child, you will want to be fair to them all. If none of your children wants to be actively involved in the business, you will need to find someone else to run it or own it. And keep in mind the serious tax issues involved in having someone inherit your business. Depending on your business structure and other factors, the taxes may be so high that the store will need to be sold to pay them. Consult with your lawyer far in advance of retiring to facilitate a successful transition.

Running the Mature Business

When you first go into business, you are undoubtedly fascinated by visiting other stores, reading trade magazines, and studying books on retailing. As the years go by, it continues to be important that you keep up this search for new ideas and remain open to suggestions for change.

I once visited a large family-owned gift and stationery shop in Northern California that looked as if it had been frozen in time in 1965. Although the merchandise was new, the dated fixtures relied heavily on old-fashioned pegboard. The light fixtures and even the color scheme were vintage sixties. Tradition and loyalty were keeping the business alive, but it seems doubtful that this store would survive facing any significant new competition.

One way to keep your attitude toward retailing fresh is constantly to set challenging goals, such as finding more local sources of merchandise or creating as many new jobs as possible, that will keep you striving. Invite staff to help write a new mission statement for your store, such as the ones in the second chapter, reflecting goals you all can work toward.

You should always be asking yourself how you can do things better. There is no aspect of your shop, from your cash register procedures to your gift wrap selection, that can't be improved or changed. Continue to read and to study what other retailers are doing. Listen to motivational podcasts and go to seminars. Try to avoid the twin evils of burnout and boredom by having outside interests and by getting away from your shop regularly. If you make the store the sole focus of your energy, you won't be able to sustain that level of involvement for the long haul. Remember why you went into retailing, and do what you can to hold onto that vision and passion over the years.

The Future of Retailing

Change has been the one constant in retailing over the past decades, although the rumors that first catalogs and then Internet shopping would make stores obsolete seem to have been premature. Certainly, specialty shops have continued to evolve over the years (a book on small store retailing from the mid-1960s voted the corset shop "most likely to succeed"), but the basic premise of offering shoppers a variety of goods, attractively presented and available to be purchased on the spot, has not.

Customers enjoy the opportunity to see and touch the merchandise they are considering purchasing. Shopping can also be as pleasing a sensual experience as visiting an art museum and as entertaining as going to a movie. It is up to the creative retailer to make sure that the customer experiences an enjoyable social interaction and a presentation of merchandise that is a visual delight.

Instead of viewing online shopping as a threat, today's retailers use the Internet as a tool for promoting their shop and their goods. But it's worth noting that just as listening to a symphony on the radio is not the same experience as sitting in a concert hall hearing the orchestra perform, shopping via a smartphone or computer screen will always lack something. Going shopping allows customers to surround themselves with merchandise they may never have seen before and to consider buying items they didn't know they wanted. Shopping is an activity many families and friends enjoy doing together. A good specialty shop is also a place where customers can learn more about a special interest, and meet others who share that passion.

What's Next: Looking to the Future

As a retailer you have a unique opportunity to share your excitement about the merchandise you carry with everyone you come in contact with. You can have an important influence on the lives of your customers, provide meaningful work to your employees, and have a positive impact on the world around you. Your specialty shop should be more than just a means of making a living; it should be a creation you are proud of, and one that you continue to perfect.

RESOURCE GUIDE

BUSINESS PLANNING

The ABCs of Writing Winning Business Plans: How to Prepare a Business Plan that Others Will Want to Read and Invest In. Garrett Sutton and Robert T. Kiyosaki. New York: Business Plus, 2005.

The Business of Bliss: How to Profit from Doing What You Love. Janet Allon. New York: Hearst Books, 2004.

Creating a Business Plan for Dummies. Veeche Curtis. Hoboken, NJ: For Dummies, 2014.

Business Plans Kit for Dummies. Steven D. Peterson, Peter E. Jaret, and Barbara Findlay Schenck. 5th ed. Hoboken, NJ: For Dummies, 2016.

The Complete Book of Business Plans: Secrets of Writing Powerful Business Plans. Joseph Covello and Brian Hazelgren. 2nd ed. Naperville, IL: Sourcebooks, 2006.

The Complete Idiot's Guide to Business Plans. Gwen Moran and Sue Johnson. New York: Alpha Books, 2011.

How to Write a Business Plan. Mike P. McKeever. 13th ed. Berkeley, CA: Nolo Press, 2016.

How to Write a Business Plan: Create Your Strategy; Forecast Your Finances; Produce a Persuasive Plan. Sunday Times Creating Success Series. Brian Finch. 5th ed. New York: Kogan Page, 2016.

Inc. Yourself: How to Profit by Setting Up Your Own Corporation. Judith H. McQuown. 11th ed. Franklin Lakes, NJ: Career Press, 2014.

The Secrets to Writing a Successful Business Plan: A Pro Shares a Step-by-Step Guide to Creating a Plan That Gets Results. Hal Shelton. 2nd ed. Rockville, MD: Summit Valley Press, 2017.

Starting a Business All-In-One For Dummies. By Consumer Dummies. Hoboken, NJ: For Dummies, 2015

Successful Business Plan: Secrets & Strategies. Rhonda Abrams. 6th ed. Palo Alto, CA: Planning Shop, 2014.

Writing a Convincing Business Plan. Arthur R. DeThomas and Lin Grensing-Pophal. 4th ed. New York: Barron's Educational Series, 2015.

FRANCHISES AND BUYING A BUSINESS

The Complete Guide to Buying a Business. Fred S. Steingold, Attorney. 4th ed. Berkeley, CA: Nolo Press, 2015.

The Educated Franchisee: Find the Right Franchise for You. Rick Bisio. 3rd ed. Tasora Books, 2017.

E-Myth Revisited: Why Most Small Businesses Don't Work and What to Do About It. Michael E. Gerber. Revised ed. New York: HarperCollins Publishers, 2004.

Franchise Bible: How to Buy a Franchise or Franchise Your Own. 7th ed. Erwin J. Keup. Irvine, CA: Entrepreneur Press, 2012.

Franchise Your Business: The Guide to Employing the Greatest Growth Strategy Ever. Mark Siebert. Irvine, CA: Entrepreneur Press, 2016.

How to Buy a Business Without Being Had: Successfully Negotiating the Purchase of a Small Business. Jack Gibson. Bloomington, IN: Trafford Publishing, 2010.

HBR Guide to Buying A Small Business: Think big, Buy small, Own your own company. Richard S. Ruback and Royce Yudkoff. Brighton, MA: Harvard Business Review Press, 2017.

Street Smart Franchising. Joe Mathews, Don DeBolt and Deb Percival. 2nd ed. Irvine, CA: Entrepreneur Press, 2011.

Resource Guide

BOOKKEEPING

Accounting for Small Business Owners. Berkely, CA: Tycho Press, 2015.

Accounting for the Numberaphobic: A Survival Guide for Small Business Owners. Dawn Fotopulos. New York: AMACOM, 2014.

The Accounting Game: Basic Accounting Fresh from the Lemonade Stand. Darrell Mullis and Judit Orloff. Revised ed. Naperville, IL: Sourcebooks, 2008.

Bookkeeping All-in-One for Dummies. Consumer Dummies. Hoboken, NJ: For Dummies, 2015.

E-Z Bookkeeping. Barron's E-Z Series. Kathleen Fitzpatrick and Wallace W. Kravitz. 4th ed. Hauppauge, NY. Barron's Educational Series, 2010.

Finance for Non-Financial Managers. Gene Siciliano. 2nd ed. Brief Case Books. Chicago, IL: McGraw-Hill Education, 2014.

Keeping the Books: Basic Recordkeeping and Accounting for Successful Small Business. Linda Pinson. 7th ed. Chicago: Kaplan Business, 2007.

The McGraw-Hill 36-Hour Course in Finance for Nonfinancial Managers. Robert A. Cooke, H. George Shoffner, Susan Shelly. 3rd ed. New York: McGraw-Hill, 2010.

Simple Numbers, Straight Talk, Big Profits: 4 Keys to Unlock Your Business Potential. Greg Crabtree. Austin, TX: Greenleaf Book Group Press, 2011.

STORE AND WINDOW DESIGN

Contemporary Visual Merchandising. Jay Diamond. 5th ed. Carmel, IN: Pearson, 2010.

Inspired Retail Space: Attract Customers, Build Branding, Increase Volume. Corinna Dean. Gloucester, MA: Rockport Publishers, 2005.

New Retail. Raul A. Barreneche. New York: Phaidon Press, 2008.

New Trends in Visual Merchandising: Retail Display Ideas that Encourage Buying. Judy Shepard. South Salem, NY: RSD Publishing, 2012.

Reengineering Retail: The Future of Selling in a Post-Digital World. Doug Stephens. Vancouver, B.C.: Figure 1 Publishing, 2017. See also *The Retail Revival*.

The Retail Revival: Reimagining Business for the New Age of Consumerism. Doug Stephens. Hoboken, NJ: Wiley & Sons, 2013.

Retail Spaces: Small Stores No. 2. Judy Shepard, Retail Design Institute. South Salem, NY: RSD Publishing, 2013.

Signs Sell: Harnessing the Power of Your Interior Advertising. Rick Segel and Matthew Hudson, in cooperation with FASTSIGNS International. Kissimmee, FL: Specific House Publishing, 2014.

Silent Selling: Best Practices and Effective Strategies in Visual Merchandising. Judith Bell and Kate Turnus. 5th ed. New York: Fairchild Publications, 2017.

Store Design: A Complete Guide to Designing Successful Retail Stores. William Green. Roselle, IL: Zippy Books, 2011.

Store Design and Visual Merchandising: Creating Store Space that Encourages Buying. Claus Ebster and Marion Garaus. New York: Business Expert Press, 2011.

Stores of the Year (bi-annual). Judy Shepard. New York: Visual Profile Books, 2016 (etc.).

Visual Merchandising: Windows and in-store displays for retail. Tony Morgan. 3rd ed. London: Laurence King Publishing, 2016.

Visual Merchandising and Display. Martin M. Pegler. 6th ed. New York: Fairchild Books, 2011. Note: 7th ed. with co-author Anne Kong, coming in 2018.

Stores and Retail Spaces 12. The Institute of Store Planners and the editors of *Visual Merchandising and Store Designers* magazine. Cincinnati, OH: ST Media Group International, 2011.

Resource Guide

Ultimate Shop Design. Llorenc Bonet Delgado. New York: teNeues Publishing Group, 2006.

EMPLOYEE RELATIONS

1001 Ways to Energize Employees. Bob Nelson. New York: Workman Publishing, 1997. Note: *1,001 Ways to Engage Employees* coming in May, 2018 from Career Press, Wayne, NJ.

1501 Ways to Reward Employees. Bob Nelson. Reprint ed. New York: Workman Publishing Company, 2012.

The First-Time Manager. Loren B. Belker, Jim McCormick and Gary S. Topchik. 6th ed. New York: AMACOM, 2012.

Hiring Your First Employee: A Step-by-Step Guide. Fred S. Steingold. Berkeley, CA: Nolo Press, 2008

Managing for Dummies. Bob Nelson and Peter Economy. 3rd ed. Hoboken, NJ: For Dummies, 2010.

Nickel and Dimed: On (Not) Getting By in America. Barbara Ehrenreich. 10th anniversary ed. New York: Picador, 2011.

Not My Circus, Not My Monkeys: Why the Path to Transformational Customer Experience Runs Through Employee Experience. Lance Gibbs. Austin, TX: Lioncrest Publishing, 2017.

The Power of Positive Leadership: How and Why Positive Leaders Transform Teams and Organizations and Change the World. Jon Gordon. Hoboken, NJ: Wiley & Sons, 2017.

CUSTOMER SERVICE

The Customer Rules: The 39 Essential Rules for Delivering Sensational Service. Lee Cockerell. New York:Crown Business, 2013.

Customer Service Training 101: Quick and Easy Techniques That Get Great Results. Renee Evenson. 3rd ed. New York: AMACOM, 2017.

SPECIALTY SHOP RETAILING

Customers for Life: How to Turn that One-Time Buyer into a Lifetime Customer. Carl Sewell and Paul B. Brown. Rev. ed. New York: Currency, 2002.

Delight Your Customers: 7 Simple Ways to Raise Your Customer Service from Ordinary to Extraordinary. Steve Curtin. New York: AMACOM, 2013.

Delivering Knock Your Socks Off Service. Performance Research Associates. 5th ed. New York: AMACOM, 2011.

How to Wow: 68 Effortless Ways to Make Every Customer Experience Amazing. Adrian Swinscoe. Carmel, IN: Pearson, 2016.

Hug Your Customers: The Proven Way to Personalize Sales and Achieve Astounding Results. Jack Mitchell. New York: Hyperion, 2003.

No, Thanks, I'm Just Looking: Sales Techniques for Turning Shoppers into Buyers. Harry J. Friedman. Hoboken, NJ: Wiley & Sons, 2012.

Smile: Sell More with Amazing Customer Service. Kirt Manecke. Milford, MI: Solid Press, 2012. Also *The Training Guide for Smile,* 2015.

Super Service: Seven Keys to Delivering Great Customer Service. Jeff Gee and Val Gee. 2nd ed. New York: McGraw-Hill, 2009.

Zingerman's Guide to Giving Great Service. Ari Weinzweig. New York: Hyperion, 2004.

ADVERTISING AND MARKETING

1001 Ideas to Create Retail Excitement. Edgar A. Falk. Rev. ed. Upper Saddle River, NJ: Prentice Hall, 2003.

The Big Moo: Stop Trying to Be Perfect and Start Being Remarkable. The Group of 33. Edited by Seth Godin. New York: Portfolio, 2005.

Do It! Marketing: 77 Instant-Action Ideas to Boost Sales, Maximize Profits, and Crush Your Competition. David Newman. New York: AMACOM, 2013

Resource Guide

Engagement Marketing: How Small Business Wins in a Socially Connected World. Gail F. Goodman. New York: Wiley & Sons, 2012.

Guerrilla Marketing in 30 Days. Jay Conrad Levinson and Al Lautenslager. 3rd ed. Irvine, CA: Entrepreneur Press, 2014.

Guerrilla Social Media Marketing: 100+ Weapons to Grow Your Online Influence, Attract Customers, and Drive Profits. Jay Conrad Levinson. Irvine, CA: Entrepreneur Press, 2011.

How to Write a Marketing Plan. John Westwood. Philadelphia, PA: Kogan Page, 2016.

Jab, Jab, Jab, Right Hook: How to Tell Your Story in a Noisy Social World. Gary Vaynerchuk. New York: HarperBusiness, 2013.

Marketing to Millennials: Reach the Largest and Most Influential Generation of Consumers Ever. Jeff Fromm and Christie Garton. New York: AMACOM, 2013.

Purple Cow: Transform Your Business by Being Remarkable. Seth Godin. 2nd ed. New York: Portfolio, 2009.

Small Business Marketing Strategies. All-in-One for Dummies. By Consumer Dummies. Hoboken, NJ: For Dummies, 2016.

The Tipping Point: How Little Things Can Make a Big Difference. Malcolm Gladwell. Boston: Back Bay Books, 2002.

What Women Want: The Science of Female Shopping. Paco Underhill. Reprint ed. New York: Simon & Schuster, 2011.

ONLINE RETAILING

101 Ways to Promote Your Web Site. Susan Sweeney. 8th ed. Gulf Breeze, FL: Maximum Press, 2010.

Don't Make Me Think, Revisited: A Common Sense Approach to Web Usability. Steve Krug. 3rd ed. San Francisco: New Riders, 2014.

SPECIALTY SHOP RETAILING

Facebook Marketing All-in-One For Dummies. Andrea Vahl, John Haydon and Jan Zimmerman. 3rd ed. Hoboken, NJ: For Dummies, 2014.

Marketing Your Retail Store in the Internet Age. Bob Negen and Susan Negen. Hoboken, NJ: Wiley & Sons, 2006.

Starting an Online Business All-in-One for Dummies. Shannon Belew and Joel Elad. 4th ed. Hoboken, NJ: For Dummies, 2014.

Success Secrets of the Online Marketing Superstars. Mitch Meyerson. Irvine, CA: Entrepreneur Press, 2015.

ALTERNATIVE MANAGEMENT STYLES

Ben & Jerry's Double-Dip: How to Run a Values-Led Business and Make Money Too. Ben Cohen, Jerry Greenfield, and Meredith Maran. New York: Simon & Schuster, 1998.

The Business of Good: Social Entrepreneurship and the New Bottom Line. Jason Haber. Irvine, CA: Entrepreneur Press, 2016.

The Ecology of Commerce: A Declaration of Sustainability. Paul Hawken. Reprint ed. New York: HarperBusiness, 1994.

Humanizing the Economy: Co-operatives in the Age of Capital. John Restakis. New Society Publishers, 2010.

Leadership is an Art. Max DePree. Reprint ed. New York: Currency, 2004.

The Magnetic Leader: How Irresistible Leaders Attract Employees, Customers, and Profits. Roberta Chinsky Matuson. New York: Routledge, 2017.

The Soul of a Business: Managing for Profit and the Common Good. Tom Chappell. New York: Bantam Books, 1996.

A Stake in the Outcome: Building a Culture of Ownership for the Success of Your Business. Jack Stack and Bo Burlingame. New York: Currency, 2003.

Resource Guide

BUY LOCAL MOVEMENT

Big Box Swindle: The True Cost of Mega-Retailers and the Fight for America's Independent Businesses. Stacy Mitchell. Boston: Beacon Press, 2007.

Local Dollars, Local Sense: How to Shift Your Money from Wall Street to Main Street and Achieve Real Prosperity. Michael Shuman. Corvallis, OR: Community Resilience Guides, 2012

The Local Economy Solution: How Innovative, Self-Financing "Pollinator" Enterprises Can Grow Jobs and Prosperity. Michael Shuman. White River Junction, VT: Chelsea Green Publishing, 2015

Locavesting: The Revolution in Local Investing and How to Profit From It. Amy Cortese. Hoboken, NJ: Wiley & Sons, 2011.

RETAIL PROFILES

The 10 Rules of Sam Walton: Success Secrets for Remarkable Results. Michael Bergdahl and Rob Walton. Hoboken, NJ: Wiley & Sons, 2006.

The Bear Necessities of Business: Building a Company with Heart. Maxine Clark and Amy Joyner. Hoboken, NJ: Wiley & Sons, 2006.

Business as Unusual: My Entrepreneurial Journey, Profits with Principles. New ed. Anita Roddick. West Sussex, England: Anita Roddick Press, 2005.

Delivering Happiness: A Path to Profits, Passion, and Purpose. Tony Hsieh, CEO of Zappos. Reprint ed. New York: Grand Central Publishing, 2013.

The Everything Store: Jeff Bezos and the Age of Amazon. Brad Stone. Boston: Back Bay Books, 2014.

A Lapsed Anarchist's Approach to Building a Great Business (Zingerman's Guide to Good Leading). Ari Weinzweig. Ann Arbor, MI: Zingerman's Press, 2010.

SPECIALTY SHOP RETAILING

Minding the Store: A Memoir. Stanley Marcus. Denton, TX: University of North Texas Press, 2001.

The Nordstrom Way to Customer Service Excellence. Robert Spector. Hoboken, NJ: Wiley & Sons, 2005.

The Wal-Mart Effect: How the World's Most Powerful Company Really Works— and How It's Transforming the American Economy. Charles Fishman. New York: Penguin Books, 2006.

RETAILING IN GENERAL

BUYOLOGY: Truth and Lies About Why We Buy. Martin Lindstrom. New York: Crown Business, 2010.

Call of the Mall: How We Shop. Paco Underhill. New York: Simon & Schuster, 2004.

The Complete Idiot's Guide to Starting and Running a Retail Store. James E. Dion. New York: Alpha Books, 2008.

Guerrilla Retailing. Jay Conrad Levinson, Elly Valas, and Orvel Ray Wilson. Boulder, CO: The Guerilla Group Press, 2005.

Minding My Business: The Complete, No-Nonsense, Start-to-Finish Guide to Owning and Running Your Own Store. Adeena Mignogna. New York: Skyhorse Publishing, 2013.

The New Rules of Retail: Competing in the World's Toughest Marketplace. Robin Lewis and Michael Dart. 2nd ed. New York: St. Martin's Press, 2014. (See also *Retail's Seismic Shift*)

The Profitable Retailer: 56 surprisingly simple and effective lessons to boost your sales and profits. Doug Fleener. Boston, MA: Acanthus Publishing, 2005.

Retail 101: The Guide to Managing and Marketing Your Retail Business. Nicole Reyhle and Jason Prescott. New York: McGraw-Hill Education, 2014.

Resource Guide

Retail Business Kit for Dummies. Rick Segel. 2nd ed. Hoboken, NJ: For Dummies, 2009.

The Retail Doctor's Guide to Growing Your Business: A Step-By-Step Approach to Quickly Diagnose, Treat, and Cure. Bob Phibbs. Hoboken, NJ: Wiley & Sons, 2010.

Retail in Detail: How to Start and Manage a Small Retail Business. Ronald L. Bond. 3rd ed. Irvine, CA: Entrepreneur Press, 2005.

The Retail Sales Bible: The GREAT Book of G.R.E.A.T. Selling. Rick Segel and Matthew Hudson. Kissimmee, FL: Specific House, 2011.

Retail's Seismic Shift: How to Shift Faster, Respond Better, and Win Customer Loyalty. Michael Dart with Robin Lewis. New York: St. Martin's Press, 2017.

Shops that POP!: 7 Steps to Extraordinary Retail Success. Pam Danzinger and Jennifer Lorenzetti. Ithaca, NY: Paramount Market Publishing, 2016.

Small-Time Operator: How to Start Your Own Business. Bernard B. Kamoroft. 13th ed. Willits, CA: Bells Springs Publishing, 2013.

Start and Run a Gift Shop: What you need to do to turn your idea into reality. Val Clark. 2nd ed. Oxford, England: How to Books Ltd., 2009.

Start and Run a Retail Business. James E. Dion and Ted Topping. 3rd ed. North Vancouver, Canada: Self-Counsel Press, 2008.

Start Your Own Retail Business and More. The Staff of Entrepreneur Media and Ciree Linsenmann. Irvine, CA: Entrepreneur Press Startup Series, 2015.

Up Against the Wal-Marts: How Your Business Can Prosper in the Shadow of the Retail Giants. Don Taylor and Jeanne Smalling Archer. 2nd ed. New York: AMACOM, 2005.

What No One Ever Tells You About Starting Your Own Business: Real Life Start-up Advice from 101 Successful Entrepreneurs. Jan Norman. 2nd ed. Chicago: Kaplan Business, 2004.

Why We Buy: The Science of Shopping. Paco Underhill. Revised ed. New York: Simon & Schuster, 2008.

WEBSITES FOR RETAILERS

U.S. GOVERNMENT WEBSITES

www.commerce.gov An access point for locating government and business information, sponsored by the U.S. Department of Commerce.

www.irs.gov The official website of the Internal Revenue Service.

www.osha.gov The website of the Occupational Safety and Health Administration (OSHA) of the U.S. Department of Labor.

www.sba.gov The entry point into the U.S. Small Business Administration site, with information about starting and financing a business. For the Small Business Development Centers, go to www.sba.gov/sbdc.

www.uscis.gov The website of the U.S Citizenship and Immigration Services (USCIS) division of the Department of Homeland Security. Formerly the U.S. Immigration and Naturalization Service.

SMALL BUSINESS WEBSITES

www.amiba.net Extensive buy local information from the organization the American Independent Business Alliance.

www.americanexpress.com/us/small-business/shop-small Sponsored by American Express, this site has a variety of tools for independent businesses as well as information about Small Business Saturday.

https://bealocalist.org The website of BALLE, the Business Alliance for Local Living Economies, with information about joining the buy local movement.

www.bizmove.com A commercial site with many articles about small business.

Resource Guide

www.bplans.com A website with sample business plans and how-to advice.

http.businessbookpress.com Articles on buying or selling a business.

www.businessownersideacafe.com "A fun approach to serious business," with articles, message forums and a newsletter

www.entrepreneur.com Includes *Entrepreneur* magazine's lists of today's top franchises.

www.franchise.org The website of the International Franchise Association, a member organization for franchisors and franchisees.

www.Inc.com The website of the magazine *Inc.*, with articles on starting and growing a business.

www.kioskexpert.com Information for cart and kiosk vendors from *Specialty Retail* magazine.

www.mainstreet.org The Main Street program is a national movement aimed at improving all aspects of the downtown or central business districts in older U.S. towns and cities.

www.nrf.com National Retail Federation, the world's largest trade organization.

www.RetailOwner.com Articles and software relating to inventory control and cash flow from The Retail Owners Institute.

www.SCORE.org Online counseling and information about local SCORE chapters from the Service Corps of Retired Executives.

www.SmallBusinessSchool.org is an online library of educational videos based on the PBS series hosted by Hattie Bryant, including interviews with Carol Schroeder at Orange Tree Imports.

www.StartupJournal.com The *Wall Street Journal*'s landing page for business information.

ACKNOWLEDGMENTS

I have learned so much from my fellow shopkeepers, and from readers of the first three editions of Specialty Shop Retailing, so I'd like to start by thanking them for sharing the ups and downs of their retail experiences. I am also very grateful to the past and present members of the Orange Tree Imports staff. They have contributed in countless ways to the success of our shop, and their creative ideas are reflected in many of the examples I share in this book.

My sales reps are used to me asking their advice about more than just what to order, and I want to acknowledge the suggestions they've given me about what they think retailers need to know. I hope they'll be pleased with the sections on being nice to reps and developing positive vendor relations! Special thanks to Vikki Brandt, Sheryl Hanke, Steve Johnson, Jenna Kelly, Tana Kopydlowski, Kathy Landgraf, Beth Luedkte, Dick Roethe, PJ Schroeder, Kathleen Szuslik, David Tallaksen, Jean Whitmore, Susan Denk Zuehlke, and the others who make up the loyal cadre of sales reps who have called on us for years.

A number of store owners and managers from around the country kindly agreed to give me feedback on the 3rd edition, and their insights have been invaluable in making this new edition beneficial for today's retailers. I am very grateful for the input from Cathy Karl, Heart & Homestead, Manitowoc, WI; Linda O'Boyle, Metro Home Style, Syracuse, NY; Lisa Briggs, Bruce Company, Middleton, WI; Karen Tibbitts, Soaps & Scents, Wauwatosa, WI; Joanne Heuss, Puttin' on the Glitz, Perrysburg, OH; Lisa Gustafson, Periwinkle, Glendora, CA; and Julie Baine, Pod, Cambridge, MA.

SPECIALTY SHOP RETAILING

I very much appreciate the assistance of the specialists who provided professional advice on specific sections of this edition: Barbara Conley, Attorney; Randy Grobe, CPA; Lyn Falk of Retailworks, Inc.; Bill Harvey, lighting specialist; Jason Solarek of The Bridge and Karla Hofbauer of Wind River Financial. I also want to acknowledge the help I received from two women with great connections in the gift industry, Caroline "Keb" Kennedy and Julia Garreaud, in reaching out to some of today's most innovative shopkeepers.

Thank you to the retailers, vendors and individuals who generously shared their expertise through the quotes and photographs featured in this new edition. I'm pleased to include Mari Stein's whimsical cartoons, which are as delightful as when she created them for *Specialty Shop Retailing* twenty years ago.

Kira Henschel of HenschelHAUS Publishing worked tirelessly on this project, and I owe her a debt of thanks for making it possible for this new edition of *Specialty Shop Retailing* to be available to today's retailers. I was fortunate to have proofreading help from my friend Eve Galanter, and editorial assistance and encouragement from my daughter Katrina Schroeder Smith. Thanks also to Claire Splan for the fine index.

And finally, special thanks to my husband and business partner, Dean, who is truly 50% of Orange Tree Imports' success. Working together over so many years is one of the great joys of owning our own shop.

ABOUT THE AUTHOR

C arol "Orange" Schroeder and her husband Dean have been co-owners of Orange Tree Imports in Madison, WI since 1975. The store was recently selected as one of four finalists as Retailer of the Century by Gifts and Decorative Accessories magazine, and has received many local honors including over thirty Best of Madison awards and a Local Biz Award from Dane Buy Local.

The first edition of *Specialty Shop Retailing: Everything You Need to Know to Run Your Own Store* was published in 1997, and was translated into Russian the following year. Carol writes bimonthly column for retailers in *Gifts and Decorative Accessories* magazine and the weekly blog Specialty Shop Retailing (www.specialtyshopretailing.com).

She has spoken at gift shows across the U.S. and Canada, including New York, Chicago, Las Vegas, San Francisco, Los Angeles, Minneapolis and Alberta. Carol has also been a featured speaker at the North American Farmers Direct Marketing Association national conference and at an international Corn Maze Symposium, and was a charter member of the Retail Advisory Board of the national Gift and Home Trade Association.

In addition to running Orange Tree Imports, Carol does freelance writing, translating and consulting. She is an active volunteer in the community, chairing the Monroe Street Merchants Association for 40 years and serving on numerous non-profit boards including United Way of Dane County, Madison CitiArts, Forward Theater, the Monroe Street Library League, Madison Youth Choirs, Komen for the Cure and the Friends of Wisconsin Public Television.

INDEX

Index

Index

Index

Index

Index